CHIOS®
Energy Healing

CHIOS®
Energy Healing

Powerful New Techniques for
Healing the Human Energy Field

Stephen H. Barrett

Illustrations by Matt Hromalik

Copyright

Disclaimer

This book contains information and instructions for performing techniques in energy healing, but for informational and educational purposes only. The author is not engaged in providing medical, health or professional advice or services, nor making any claim of effectiveness of any technique herein for treatment of any medical condition, nor representing the information and techniques herein as being any substitute for care by licensed health care providers. Author makes no warranty or claim of effectiveness— expressed or implied—for the information and techniques discussed in this book and shall not be liable or responsible for any loss or damage arising out of their use. If you or someone you know has a health care concern, you should refer it to a licensed physician or other licensed health care provider.

Publication Data

Barrett, Stephen H.
    Chios Energy Healing: Powerful New Techniques for Healing the Human Energy Field
ISBN-13: 978-0615729350 (New Time Press)
ISBN-10: 0615729355
1. Energy Medicine   2. Energy Healing   3. Spiritual Healing
I. Title.

This book is dedicated to:

You the Healer, as you learn
and practice Chios®

and to:

All true teachers and healers
of the earth, as they work toward
a better day for humanity.

Contents

Major Exercises and Techniques

Illustrations

Preface

You the Healer

Welcome! This book is your definitive guide and resource for learning Chios®
(pronounced chee' ohss)[1], a relatively new yet very comprehensive system of energy
healing. Energy healing is based upon the premise that illnesses or afflictions of the body,
emotions, mind and spirit have as their ultimate cause defects in the higher-dimensional
energy field surrounding the body. This energy field is "higher-dimensional" because it exists
and operates upon higher vibratory levels of energy beyond the level we usually perceive in
the physical world. It is composed of the seven chakras and the seven layers of aura, which
have been known and discussed in many spiritual systems since ancient times. The energy
field is the higher "energy pattern" that mirrors conditions in the body, emotions, mind and
spirit of each individual and that must itself be healed in order for true physical, emotional,
psychological and spiritual healing to take place.

Chios® Energy Healing is based upon a series of powerful energy, color and light
channeling techniques that specifically and powerfully heal true, root energetic defects in the
chakra system and aura—techniques that have not previously been available in any spiritual
or energy healing system. These simple yet very powerful and effective healing techniques,
nearly all of which are unique to Chios®, are the product of spiritual guidance and twenty
years of careful experimentation and refinement (see Appendix #3-The Development of
Chios®). The Chios® Master Techniques, Chakra Charging, Chakra System Rebalancing,
Radiatory Healing, Seventh-Layer Focal Healing and Frisson Healing, are some of the most
powerful energy healing techniques available. Chios® healing treatments employing these
techniques provide healing that might otherwise be unavailable from other energy healing
modalities. They may also provide generally enhanced health to body, mind and spirit, and
facilitate spiritual growth for both healer and patient. The nature of the energetic defects,
and the simple mechanism of action of the Chios® techniques, are fully described in this

book with the hope of making a fundamental contribution to the art and science of energy healing and its future development.

Also included in Chios® is an integral meditation method especially designed for the energy healer (Chios® Meditation) that assists the healer in acquiring the state of expanded awareness necessary for healing work, plus a series of simple personal growth exercises (The Self-Knowledge of the Healer) that further facilitate the spiritual abilities and experiences that are beneficial to the energy healer (or anyone). New energy treatment procedures for complementary care of serious illnesses are also included and complete this integrated system of energy healing.

This Book Focuses on Empowering You the Healer, and Not On Complex Belief Systems—Old or New, Spiritual or Scientific

Energy healing originated in ancient times, yet within the last several decades has enjoyed a resurgent wave of popularity. A survey of the healing systems available today will quickly show that many incorporate complex belief systems, old or new, spiritual or scientific.

Many use concepts from modern science, for example, to attempt to explain the mechanism of energy healing or interpret the phenomena we experience in this work. There is no question that some intriguing areas in modern science are *beginning* to point the way towards a future understanding of the human energy field. It is also true that we are making a start towards applying a basic understanding of the operations of its lowest levels—the success of acupuncture and other meridian-based body energy therapies is a good example. Chios, however, is a "higher-dimensional" energy healing art—it works intensively with all seven "vibratory" levels of energy, above physical matter, and I would suggest the probability that the ultimate "substance" of the entire energy field, these higher ("subtle") energies and the higher (yet still unknown) laws of nature that must ultimately be involved in energy healing work are beyond our present scientific understanding. Because we really do not yet have the kind of firm scientific foundation for this work that would benefit the energy healer, in actual practice, such scientific interpretations and descriptions are not included in this book. I do not mean to denigrate science in any way or seek to minimize its remarkable achievements. I have had a deep abiding interest in science since early childhood, have great respect for the power of the scientific method and have a degree from one of the top science universities in the United States. I suggest, however, that if we enclose our understanding of energy healing "in the box" of present-day scientific knowledge, seeing energy healing through its lens and jumping on a conceptual bandwagon, we do so with the assumption that our present scientific concepts—based upon our empirical study of physical matter—are necessary and even sufficient to explain the remarkable phenomena comprising energy healing work. This assumption places a serious limitation on our knowledge and delays the scientific revolution I believe is imminent, in this field. There will most certainly be a scientific understanding of energy healing, in the future, on that extraordinary day when an appropriate theoretical formulation is brought to light that goes beyond the operation of physical matter and really explains the higher energies and higher laws behind energy healing and the many other spiritual phenomena experienced by so many people today.

Many energy healing systems today are also based upon spiritual belief systems, ancient and modern, that include highly detailed descriptions and explanations of the aura, chakra system and the phenomena in them. Many specify complex interpretations of the "meaning" of colors in the aura, for example, or in-depth descriptions of the "nature" of each chakra, highly-detailed descriptions of the structure of the energy field and its separate "systems," the "properties" certain colors possess and which colors which should be used to treat certain diseases, or the "structure" of metaphysical reality and how *we* should use *it* to heal (and yet, interestingly, often disagree in all these complex details). Like many people, I do respect the point of view of these healing systems, but these types of preordained conceptual interpretations and fixed systems of healing rules are not included in this book either. One reason for not including these belief systems is that, as with present-day science, we do not yet really know exactly how this healing works—there is presently no firm foundation that justifies limiting ourselves to such interpretations (especially where there remains such uncertainty and inconsistency). There is an additional practical consideration as well: energy healing, to be practiced at its greatest level of effectiveness, requires that the healer work from a state of *expanded, unbiased awareness*. When energy healing work is performed with an attachment to *any* complex belief system, the healer contracts his or her awareness into a realm of limited perception and action which the discrete premises of the belief system define: *perception*, because our very awareness can become colored with deep-seated assumptions and beliefs ("believing is seeing") and *action*, because we base our healing work, and act from, that state of biased, qualified awareness that we create in ourselves. To learn energy healing work, based upon the perceptions of others, and the specific descriptions offered in complex belief systems, colors our interpretation of reality from the start. It limits and potentially diverts the healer from his or her own true experience of reality and the extraordinary phenomena often experienced in this work.

And so, if we deemphasize belief systems—old or new, spiritual or scientific—what is left us? We are not left with nothing, far from it. We are left with the potentially unlimited awareness and consciousness within each of us. This book holds, as its most fundamental premise, that you already possess inside yourself consciousness, knowledge and power that goes far beyond anything you could possibly acquire from any belief system—scientific or spiritual, old or new. You already possess a thousand times the knowledge and power, inside yourself, that you could ever acquire from any of these, or even from this particular book. *You are already a healer*, and your true challenge is to discover this knowledge and power that already exists inside yourself. You will find this fact discussed in many places in this book, and (more important) you will find that the many simple exercises and techniques that you will learn are designed not to impose a belief system on you but to assist you in discovering this knowledge and power you already have inside you, and in gaining your own unbiased perceptions of the aura, the chakras and the healing energies we use, and to do your healing work on that basis.

This book's goal is to enable you to go far beyond any mere mental belief system or explanation and into the realm of being where you will experience the reality of this work for yourself, and become an extraordinary energy healer. It contains a great deal of information, but this is to give you the basic tools of the energy healer and help you practice them with maximum effectiveness. You will then be able to acquire your own perceptions and create your own understanding of this work, deep in your being. You will become your own healer/researcher on the leading edge of energy healing. Mental belief systems and the descriptions and concepts of others are, after all, are merely external tools of understanding and cannot take the place of our own conscious experience, borne of unbiased connection to the root of our being (where all genuine awareness and power reside). The genuine knowledge and power we use in energy healing (and every aspect of life) *always* springs from this essence of being inside us, and from nowhere else.

Learn Energy Healing by Doing It,
Step-by-Step and in a Spirit of Openness

Because real energy healing is always ultimately based upon your own perceptions and discovering your own inner knowledge and inner power, learning it can be a profound, fun and life-changing experience! There are, however, some practical suggestions that will help you get the most out of this book and your study of Chios® Energy Healing, whether you study alone, by distance or under the personal instruction of a healing teacher.

You should acquire a professional massage table before you begin this exciting work. It is virtually a requirement for this type healing; it makes it possible to practice healing techniques and give complete treatments in an easy, pleasant manner and without strain. The adjustable-height feature of most brands is necessary, so that you will be able to adjust the height to what is best for you. Generally a table width of 27" to 30" is best (27" works very well). A face cradle, so that your patients will be comfortable when lying on their stomach, is a worthwhile accessory. Many good brands are available, both new and used, and this is an investment that will return terrific benefits for many years.

Learning by doing is the best way to learn energy healing (as with almost anything) and it is very beneficial to study energy healing step-by-step, enjoying and mastering each step before moving to the next. Chios® is structured in three levels: Chios® Level I is a brief introduction to energy healing, in which you will learn basic energy channeling, will begin to sense the human energy field with your hands and then give your first complete healing treatments. Chios® Level II is an intermediate course in energy healing, and introduces techniques for using healing symbols, reading the aura and chakras using intuitive information, learning to view the aura, assessing the basic energy defects in the energy field and many healing techniques for correcting those energetic defects. Chios® Level III (the Chios® Master Teacher Level) offers the full power of this healing system, with advanced techniques for viewing all seven layers of aura, detailed in-depth reading of the chakra system and the full series of Chios® master techniques mentioned above.

As you progress through each of the three Chios® levels, become proficient in each exercise or technique within that level one at a time, in the order given in this book, before moving on to the next. Detailed and complete instructions are given to assist you in learning each technique; use them to learn each technique correctly, the first time. With just a little practice, the technique will become second nature to you, and you will employ it very powerfully and effectively. As you complete each level, also, be sure you feel comfortable and confident with your experience of the entire level, before moving on to the level following. Do not be in a hurry! Approach each step of your study of energy healing with patience, and always learn and practice from a state of relaxed awareness—cultivate a state of *openness* in yourself. It is not any intellectual understanding, nor even any kind of effort, that will enable you to see the aura, sense the condition of the chakras, or effectively channel energy, color and light and practice these techniques. It is your openness—your willingness to let go, expand your awareness and open yourself to the whole of reality that makes these wonderful abilities possible. When it comes time to call in the energy and perform an exercise or technique (or give a full healing treatment) always begin by *setting your ego and intellect aside*, and moving into this state of openness. Always remember to perform your healing work not from any limited state of mind, but with your *whole being*. Never forget that you, your patient and the energy, color and light you use to heal are all ultimately *one*. This spirit of openness, unbiased conscious awareness and oneness is always the real foundation of your energy healing work.

As you perform the exercises and practice the healing techniques within each Chios® level, you will also usually need "patients" upon whom to practice. In the beginning, these will probably be cooperative family, friends and acquaintances—people you already know who agree to assist you in your learning. Generally, most people are comfortable with holistic healing therapies like energy healing and are receptive to the benefits they offer. To have a "live" healing patient is always the best way to learn and practice the Chios® techniques and incorporate them into complete healing treatments. If you have family members, friends or people you meet in your local area who share your interest in learning energy healing, that is ideal: you can work as a group and practice on each other. Group learning brings in a group energy and symbiosis highly beneficial to all; the whole becomes more than just the sum of the parts.

It is also highly desirable to have a variety of patients upon whom to practice. This will expose you to a wide range of phenomena and energetic defects in the energy fields of differing patients upon which to expand and refine your sensing and healing abilities. A word of caution, however: when your practice includes patients with whom you have a close personal relationship, you must strive to set aside any issues that may exist (conscious or otherwise) in your work with them. Otherwise, you may find that your perceptions and the intuitive information you receive can be distorted by issues and ego biases. This is not to say you should not practice energy healing on people with whom you have a personal relationship—often they are your first patients as you begin this work—only that you must be conscious of this potential bias. Later, your circle of patients will expand beyond those close to you, and you may even become a healer offering your services to members of the public. You will find it easy to remain open and unbiased, and you will have benefitted immeasurably from all that practice. You will be a highly competent energy healer!

Chios® Healing Attunements Are Not Necessary, But Are Very Helpful

You should also consider receiving Chios® healing attunements as part of your healing study. Chios® offers a series of three healing attunements—the first, second and third attunements—that correspond to and are ideally included at the beginning of your study of each of the three Chios® levels. These attunements initiate a more rapid acquisition of the ability to channel energy, color and light, and practice the Chios® techniques. Are Chios® attunements absolutely necessary to learn energy healing? Of course not—many have learned without them. You can learn, use and enjoy every technique in this book, from the simplest to the most advanced, without any healing attunements. Without any attunements you will be able to give highly beneficial healing treatments, too. But, the series of three Chios® attunements have been given and made available to assist you in quickly becoming proficient in this work, and many students have found them very beneficial. Chios® attunements are also required if you wish to obtain certification as a Chios® Master Teacher and teach or practice as a healing arts professional.

Attunements from other healing arts (e.g. Reiki) are not interchangeable with the Chios® attunements and will not activate nor add to your ability to practice the Chios® system—it is best to receive the Chios® attunements. If you have already had Reiki attunements, however, you need not worry: Reiki attunements, although not the same as Chios® attunements, will in no way detract or interfere with them. Chios® attunements, should you elect to receive them, will also not interfere with any Reiki attunements you have received. Reiki and Chios® are separate healing arts, with separate attunements that do not substitute for each other yet also do not interfere with each other. If you've studied Reiki, that will not interfere with your practice of Chios® in any way; it is actually ideal preparation (your author got his start as a Reiki Master).

Chios® attunements are available from Certified Chios® Master Teachers at reasonable cost (see "Contact Information," below). Many students prefer to receive attunements in-person, from a teacher in their local area, but the Chios® attunements are also available as distance attunements if you prefer them in that form or if you are not located near an established Chios® teacher or school. The Chios® attunements—both in-person and as distance attunements—are standardized attunement procedures given *only* by Certified Chios® Master Teachers, who perform them in a manner that carefully preserves their purity and effectiveness. Proper preparation for Chios® attunements is important, also, to gain the full benefits they offer (see Appendix #1 - Preparation for Chios® Attunements). The method of performing the Chios® attunements is not included in this book; it is kept private and only given to Chios® Master Teachers. If you decide to pursue certification as a Chios® Master Teacher you will receive your own private copy of the Chios® Attunements Manual, which contains full instructions that enable you to give Chios® Attunements to your own students.

Practice of Meditation Is Not Required, But Is Highly Recommended

From ancient times to our modern day, meditation has been recognized as the fundamental spiritual practice. To learn and practice meditation is one of the most beneficial avenues of personal development available, in this world or any other. Chios® Meditation, included as an integral part of the Chios® system, is especially designed for the energy healer. It fosters not just spiritual growth in general but also the specific abilities useful in energy healing: 1) improved access to intuitive information; 2) activation of the "third eye" and the acquisition of receptive visualization ("psychic sight"), and 3) the ability of active visualization to effectively direct energy, color and light in healing work. As a practice to quiet the thinking mind and contact the deeper state of pure consciousness that is the true source of the knowledge and power we use in energy healing work, it is impossible to overstate the importance and the potential benefits of meditation practice. A separate chapter in this book includes complete instructions for the practice of Chios® Meditation.

Immediately after the instructions for Chios® Meditation is another optional yet highly recommended chapter: The Self Knowledge of the Healer. After learning meditation you may proceed to this chapter and the advanced exercises therein. You will find simple yet highly effective exercises for performing intuitive self-readings, sensing and healing your own chakra system, sensing and directing body energies, developing empathic perception, developing the ability of thought communication, and advanced meditation practice. Practice of Chios® Meditation and these self-knowledge exercises is not necessary to learn the Chios® healing techniques—it is strictly optional—but you may find it very rewarding should you choose to do so. You will find them highly beneficial to your spiritual growth, and they will add greatly to your healing ability, too.

Contact Information—Becoming Part of the Chios® Healing Community

As you learn and practice Chios® healing, you are not alone but are part of the larger Chios® healing community, which is constantly expanding, as students and healers (like you) become involved in this powerful energy healing art. One main resource is the official Chios® website:

Chios® Energy Healing Main Website: http://www.chioshealing.com

The official Chios® website is very popular world-wide and contains many resources. It is the public open source site for the Chios® information, which is made freely available to everyone throughout the world via foreign language translation (yet without the comprehensive series of illustrations, advanced techniques and many other extras that are contained in this guidebook). If you are interested in studying Chios® with a Certified Chios® Master Teacher, for the purpose of obtaining attunements and certification as a teacher and healer, you can locate a teacher from the comprehensive list on the "Contact Chios Master Teachers" page of the site (which is linked from the home page and "home" drop down menu), or examine teachers' own websites from links on the "Links to Chios Websites" page (also linked from the "home" drop down menu). You can obtain more information on Chios® certification from "The Chios Study Program" page, download the Chios® Workbooks used to complete the three levels from the "Download Course Materials" page and examine the process by which you can become a Chios® Master Teacher to teach healing professionally and certify your own students on the "Certification Requirements" page.

You might also want to "like" us on Facebook and become part of the dynamic Chios® Energy Healing Facebook community. We welcome your participation and would love to hear from you here:

Chios® Energy Healing Facebook Page: http://www.facebook.com/chioshealing

You can post questions or comments, and connect with other healers who are learning and practicing the Chios® techniques. We have other social media in development that you may find useful:

Chios® Energy Healing Youtube Channel: http://www.youtube.com/chioshealing

Chios® Energy Healing Twitter Feed: http://www.twitter.com/chioshealing
#chioshealing   @chioshealing

Chios® Energy Healing Google+ Group: http://www.chioshealing.com/g+

We have many other resources and activities planned—please consult the main Chios® website and the Chios® Facebook page for the latest developments. I also do everything possible to make myself available for your questions, comments, special requests or any assistance you may need in your healing or teaching work, and I may always be reached at steve@chioshealing.com. I strive to personally respond to as many inquiries as possible, but if I cannot respond personally your email it will be answered by a member of the Chios® Institute support staff and our group of Chios® teachers and healers.

Chios® is not only a wonderful and complete energy healing art that may provide great benefit to your patients, but also a great tool for your personal spiritual growth; energy healing is often a powerful spiritual path for you the healer as well. The more you put into your learning and practice of Chios®, the more you will get out of it. Welcome to Chios®! I wish you the greatest success in all your work with Chios®, and a happy and light-filled healing journey.

Stephen H. Barrett
Creator of Chios®
December 2012

---

[1]The word "Chios" is from the ancient Bactrian language, and there is no equivalent pronunciation in English. The pronunciation is approximated chee' ohss, and this is the way we commonly write the pronunciation, but the precise pronunciation is approximately halfway between chee' ohss and gee'ohss (the word beginning with a sound halfway between the soft ch sound and the soft gee sound). For details of the origin of the name, see Appendix #3 – The Development of Chios.

1

Chios® Energy Healing – Level One

Welcome to Chios® Energy Healing. Chios® Level I is your introduction to this fascinating and powerful healing art. In this introductory level, you will learn to channel healing energy and also to begin to sense the human energy field. You will use these new skills to give your first complete energy healing treatments.

As you begin your study of Chios®, you may choose to receive the first Chios® healing attunement. It is not at all required that you receive this attunement, should you wish to learn and practice the techniques taught in this level (and throughout this book). The first attunement may assist you, however, in more easily acquiring these healing abilities. If you choose to receive the first Chios® attunement be sure to observe the correct preparatory steps, so that you may receive its full benefits (see Appendix #1 – Preparation for Chios® Attunements).

As you learn these basic healing techniques, and incorporate them into your first treatments, you may find it helpful to refer to the outline of treatment steps for this Chios® level (see Appendix #2 – Outline of Treatment Steps for Chios® Levels I, II and III). This will clarify for you the recommended steps, for your first treatments, and serve as quick and easy reference while learning.

You are about to embark on a wonderful energy healing journey, where you will learn many exciting techniques and discover—within yourself—knowledge and healing power you may not have suspected were available to you. Chios® will be a journey of not merely learning to help and heal others, but a journey of self-discovery, as well. It is important during your exploration of Chios®, however, that you practice your healing skills regularly. Practice is essential to bringing out your healing ability, and practice is essential to proper learning, as well. It is through practice that you will really experience the world of the energy healer.

Introduction: The Role of the Energy Healer

You will begin your study of energy healing by learning to work with the *energy*. Every living thing that exists is permeated by a universal energy that connects and nourishes all life. This energy has been called by many different names, such as prana, mana and chi. An "invisible" *energy field* composed of this energy surrounds every human being. It is this energy field around each person that integrally supports the life process in all its aspects—the material operations of the physical body, the functions of the emotions and mind, and even the spiritual life.

The energy in this energy field is not lifeless or inert—it is active and intelligent. It is conscious energy, a manifestation of the universal consciousness that is the source of each of us and the entire universe. The energy, like everything in the universe, emanates from the *field of pure consciousness*, the spiritual source of life. This field of pure consciousness has inherent within it infinite knowledge and power, infinite love (as a universal creative force) and unlimited health and wellness. It also contains the higher self (or true self) of you, your patient and everyone. We each possess consciousness—each of us is an individuated portion of this universal consciousness—but we are all connected and are ultimately all one. Your connection to this higher spiritual reality lies within you; in your ultimate nature you *are* pure consciousness, with the infinite knowledge and power inherent in it. Many other spiritual and religious words and phrases have been used to refer to this field of pure consciousness, and you the reader may use any of them interchangeably, because it matters not what this ultimate reality is called.

The energy field is composed of the *aura* (which exists in seven layers) and the *chakra system* (which consists of the seven major chakras). It acts as a bridge, a seven-step connection, between the field of pure consciousness and life in this world. From the highest spiritual level, down to the levels of mind, emotions and body, the energy field brings into worldly life—at each of these levels—the powers and potentialities inherent in our spiritual source. The energy field is both an indicator and a regulator of the manner in which the life force and higher potentials that exist within the field of pure consciousness are expressed into the worldly life of the individual. If this energy field is clear, healthy and free from defects, the living person will likewise exhibit good health, at each step—from the spiritual aspects, down to the mental, emotional and physical levels. Innate health and harmony of body and mind, spiritual awareness and higher human potentials will all manifest in the person and in his or her life, by virtue of a plenary connection to the field of pure consciousness from which all these attributes flow. Many times, however, *energetic defects* are present in the energy field. When the flow of energy within this energy field becomes weak, impure, unbalanced or blocked, these energetic defects prevent the pure connection to the higher spiritual reality—the field of pure consciousness and the true self of the person. This prevents the full and healthy expression of the living potential of the whole person and removes the natural condition of energetic health that is a requirement for physical, emotional, mental and spiritual well-being.

The ultimate causes of these energetic defects are often physical and/or psychological trauma. One (or a series) of traumatic experiences, harmful life circumstances or dysfunctional relationships in the past (often including past lives), if they remain unintegrated by the psyche, impress the energy field with energetic defects. These energetic defects in the energy field separate the person from a full connection to his or her higher (true) self and from the whole of reality, leaving rigid existential biases (including core issues in the personality). They also make it possible for unhealthy energies to establish themselves in the aura and chakras, because the strong, healthy energy that the energy field normally possesses, and which resists such energetic invasion, is compromised. And so, these three effects—personality trauma (including repressed memories), fundamental energetic defects in the aura and chakra system (including but not limited to those corresponding to negative thoughts and emotions) and invasion by unhealthy impure energies (either self-generated or imposed by others)—often exist together and are closely related. They produce unhealthy energetic conditions in the energy field, and rigid and unhealthy patterns of emotions, mind and spirit that occlude the full and healthy expression of the true self of the person and that will eventually lead to problems in the worldly life. Diseases or afflictions of a physical, emotional or mental nature often eventually become manifest.

Energy healing is the art and science of sensing and correcting energetic defects in the energy field. As an energy healer, you will seek to restore the condition of your patient's energy field to its strong, natural and healthy state and correct any defects that are present, thereby helping to restore and maintain health to your patient's body, emotions, mind and spirit—to all levels of his or her being. In doing this, you will treat the ultimate cause of afflictions and disease. By treating ill conditions in the energy field, you may work to assist in the resolution of a disease condition which has already manifested in the physical body, or in the mental and emotional life of your patient. Your healing work may also serve to prevent future disease by treating faulty energetic conditions in your patient's energy field which might otherwise result in illness in the future, should they remain untreated. Additionally, your healing work is beneficial simply because it enhances the entire life process of your patient, even if prominent disease or afflictions are not present, improving functioning of body, mind and spirit and enabling your patient to live a healthier, more balanced and fulfilling life.

As you perform an energy healing treatment, you will conduct an extra measure of the energy into your patient. This serves to supplement and enhance the overall health of the energy field. You will also expand your awareness for the purpose of gaining intuitive information regarding the condition of the energy field of your patient, to sense and detect energetic defects of various kinds (and perhaps even their causes). This healing knowledge is not the product of your thinking mind, but comes through you from the unlimited knowledge contained in the field of pure consciousness. You will then heal the energetic defects that are present by using various special energy healing techniques. You do not generate the healing power that makes the healing techniques work, but your proper use of the techniques will enable you to be a channel for the healing power that comes from the field of pure consciousness. By healing the energetic defects in your patient's energy field you offer your patient the opportunity to reconnect to his or her true self (or higher self) and the unlimited health and wellness contained in the field of pure consciousness. Reintegration of the personality, a new vision of self beyond negative thoughts, emotions and self-limiting beliefs, and a healing of the energetic defects in the energy field are the potential benefits. You do not actually accomplish this healing, which is actually performed by pure consciousness and the higher (true) self of your patient, but you will be a catalyst and a pure channel for the knowledge and power that enables healing to take place. This is the role of the energy healer.

Instrumental in your healing work, therefore, will be this ability to act as a pure channel for the knowledge and power inherent in pure consciousness. You already have, within yourself, this ability—you need only discover and make use of it. This book will teach you the healing techniques you will use, in a way that makes you a pure channel for this healing knowledge and healing power. You will employ every technique, not from any specific state of mind, but from a wider awareness—from your *whole being*. This is called *openness*. As afflictions of body, mind and spirit begin in the wider realm of consciousness—the whole being—so do you heal from that level. In this wider realm of awareness, in the state of pure consciousness you seek to become a pure channel for, there is also a unity or *oneness*: you, your patient, the healing techniques you use, and the energy itself are all one. This approach—to heal from your whole being, in a spirit of openness and with a sense of unity and oneness—is the key to powerful, effective practice of every technique you will learn in this book. It is the key to being a true energy healer.

Your first step in becoming an energy healer is to learn *Energy Channeling*. Energy channeling is the practice of bringing extra energy into yourself, allowing it to flow through your body and into your hands, and then conduct it into your patient. You already have inherent within you the ability to channel this energy—it is a natural human ability. You need only open yourself to the energy, to do so. As you begin your practice of channeling energy into your patient, your patient's energy field will use the energy you conduct in the way that is most needed. As you grow in your healing abilities, you will become increasingly more able to sense the energy, more aware of areas in your patient's energy field that harbor energetic defects, and more able to use the energy to heal those defects, using a variety of healing techniques. As your awareness and abilities increase, you will become a progressively more conscious participant in the healing taking place, and you will, should you continue your study of Chios® energy healing, learn some extremely powerful and exciting tools to effectively sense and heal the human energy field.

Learning to Channel the Energy

All around you, and throughout the entire universe, circulates the life energy. It exists not only as an energy field around every living thing, but also circulates through the earth, through the atmosphere around us and throughout nature. The flow of this energy connects everything that exists, and you, as a living being, are taking in this energy at every moment. You are always drawing this life energy into your own energy field, and it is this energy that supports your life, as well as the life of all you seek to heal. In order to practice energy channeling—conducting a greater measure of this energy into your patient for the purposes of performing healing work—you must first learn to bring a greater measure of the energy into your own energy field.

The technique you will use to do this is referred to as *Calling in the Energy*. You call in the energy by using your power of *Visualization*. Visualization will be one of your most important tools as an energy healer because it allows you to direct the energy with your effortless intention alone. To call in the energy, using visualization, you will "see"—in your "mind's eye" or "psychic sight"—this energy begin to flow into you, from all around you, in greater and greater measure. You will also "see" this energy, as it flows into you, move through your body towards your shoulders, down your arms, and collect in your hands, so that you may then channel it into your patient. Calling in the energy, using this visualization, will start the energy flowing through you in this manner when it is time for you to begin a healing treatment. The following exercise will help you in becoming practiced and comfortable in calling in the energy:

Exercise 1-A: Calling In the Energy

1. Each day, for three times or more at various times during the day, summon the energy. Stand with your feet about shoulders-width apart, close your eyes and place your arms at your sides but with your hands not touching your body.

2. Now effortlessly "see," in your mind's eye, the energy coming into your body—up from the earth, down from above you, and from the atmosphere all around you, and thence into you. Really see and feel the energy coming into you, from all around. You may feel a slight tingling beginning, throughout your body, as the energy comes into you.

3. Then "see" the energy moving through your shoulders, down your arms and into your hands. As you hold your hands at your sides, really see and feel this energy coming into you from all around, through your body, down your arms, and then filling up your hands like water filling a glove. (See Figure 1). You should feel a tingling, or even a sensation of heat, as the energy flows to and collects in your hands.

4. This tingling you feel in your body and hands, when you call in the energy, is not just a physical sensation, but is similar to the sensation you experience when emotions flow through you. You can practice calling in the energy anywhere, at various times throughout the day. Each time you practice this should only take a minute or two.

After you have had a little practice calling in the energy, and have begun to feel it in your hands, you can proceed to channel the energy into a "live" patient. For your first experience channeling the energy you will call in the energy, as you have just learned to do, and then channel it through your hands and into one or more of your patient's chakras. The chakras are the primary energy centers or energy junctions within the energy field—the primary points at which energy enters the body, as well as the points within the energy field where important life-supporting energetic operations take place. As an energy healer you will often be working with the chakras of your patient, so this is a good place to start. When you channel energy into a chakra you will place your hands gently, palms down, on the chakra, and then simply allow the energy to flow through you and into that chakra. This is a very simple thing, and you have the innate ability to do this, so do not doubt! This energy channeling through the hands is the essence of the *laying on of hands* method (also called *hands-on healing*) where your hands are placed on your patient's body to conduct the energy. You can see how useful the hands are in transferring this energy; they can be moved anywhere on your patient's body so that the energy can be transferred to each of the chakras

Figure 1: Calling In the Energy

or to any other needed location. As you begin this process of channeling energy into your patient, it is best to follow these important guidelines:

- Remove all rings, watches and jewelry from your hands before beginning a treatment. It is also a very good idea, as a courtesy, to wash your hands.

- Do not let doubt interfere. *Trust, expect and believe* that the energy is flowing. Do not worry—the energy does exist and will flow, if only you allow it.
- Do not press too hard with your hands. You might think that it is better to press firmly when placing the hands on your patient's body, but this is not the case. Use *zero pressure* with the hands to maximize the energy flow. Your hands should just barely be touching your patient's body.
- *Be open* to the energy flow. Energy channeling is not a practice of the intellect; it is a practice of *opening and release to the energy*. Just imagine the energy flowing through you and out of your hands, and you will feel a sense of openness to the energy. You will find, if you simply release yourself to its flow, that it comes easily. Do not try to force the energy, but just open yourself and "see," in your mind's eye, the energy flowing through you. Effortless intention alone is sufficient to call in and conduct the energy.

Now that you are ready to begin energy channeling, proceed as follows:

Exercise 1-B: Energy Channeling

1. Have your patient lie flat on your treatment table, arms at his or her sides. Now, call in the energy as you have learned to do, in steps 1 to 3 of Exercise 1-A: Calling In the Energy, until you feel the energy tingling in your hands.

2. Then place your right palm directly over your patient's heart chakra (between the breasts), and then place your left hand alongside your right hand, and just above it on your patient's body, so that your hands gently overlap. This is called the "hands overlapping" position, which you will often use to channel energy into your patient's chakras (see Figure 2). If you are a male healer treating a woman, you may need to take special care, and vary hand positions somewhat to show courtesy, but try to keep your right palm centered over the chakra.

3. Now simply allow the energy to flow through you and into your patient's heart chakra. As you do this, try not to be self-conscious or wonder if you are "doing it correctly." Don't worry—it will "do itself." The energy is intelligent—it is conscious energy—and has the ability to come into you, to conduct through your hands, and flow into your patient in the manner that is needed, all without you "making" it do so. All you need do is open yourself to being a channel for it. The energy, as a manifestation of consciousness, already knows how to move and where to go. Focus instead on opening yourself to feeling and sensing the energy flow in your patient—being aware of the energy as it moves through you and into the body of your

patient. Allow the energy to flow through you and into your patient's heart chakra for several minutes.

4. You can begin to sense how much energy is flowing: if you do, you may find that the energy "builds up" as you begin to channel it, but will then diminish after a few minutes as this chakra accepts all the energy it needs. After a few moments, or when you sense the energy flow diminish, remove your hands.

5. If you wish, you can then channel energy into another of your patient's chakras—the solar plexus chakra that is two to three inches above the navel, for example. Do you feel any difference in the energy flow, as you channel the energy into this new chakra?

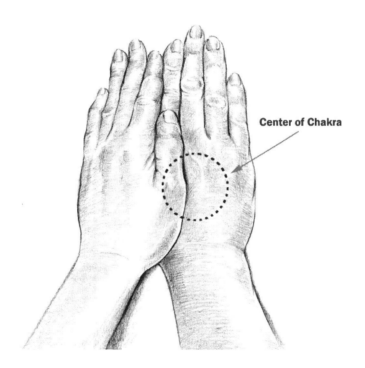

Figure 2: Hands Overlapping Hand Position

As you learn this new skill of energy channeling, do not be too concerned with whatever sensations you may feel or not feel as the energy flows through you. For different healers, and with different patients, there will be times when you definitely sense the energy flow as you channel the energy, and also times when you do not sense it as much or may just barely sense it. The degree to which you sense the energy flow as you channel it into your patient is not necessarily related to the amount or kind of energy you are conducting or the effectiveness of the treatment you provide. You will find, when you gain a good deal of experience in energy channeling, that you will become "transparent," in a sense. You may sense the flow of energy through you, but you will also sense a freedom from your body and mind, a simple awareness of acting as a channel for the energy, as though you were witnessing your own body and the energy transfer. Right now, from the very beginning of your energy healing work, start moving away from worrying about yourself, and instead begin to become aware of the energy, and the energy field of your patient. In energy healing, you must "forget yourself" and instead seek to become one with your patient and the energy, as you work.

As soon as you have had your first experiences calling in the energy and channeling it into one (or a few) of your patient's chakras, proceed through the rest of this chapter to "Putting It All Together: Giving Complete Healing Treatments." Your energy channeling skills are best developed by giving complete healing treatments, and that section will guide you, step-by-step, as you learn the correct hand positions to channel energy into all your patient's chakras.

Beginning to Sense the Energy Field

After learning to call in the energy and channel it through your hands and into your patient, you can also learn to sense the energy—to *feel* the energy with your hands. This skill is useful, for you can use this ability to sense where and how your patient's energy field has acquired energetic defects, so you can correct them and bring renewed energetic health. You will be able to pay special attention to those areas in particular need of healing: you will conduct a greater measure of the healing energy to these locations and work to correct whatever problem exists there. As with energy channeling, sensing the energy with your hands is a natural human ability you already have inherent within you. Opening yourself to the sensations that the energy produces, in your hands, is all you need do. Your hands are very useful in sensing the energy in your patient's energy field because they may be moved through various areas of the energy field to inform you of what areas are in need of healing.

Sensing the energy with your hands takes a little time to learn, as the sensations are often subtle, but the following exercise is a great place to start:

Exercise 1-C: Fingertip Sweep Exercise

1. Call in the energy as you have learned to do in steps 1 to 3 of Exercise 1-A: Calling In the Energy, until you feel the energy tingling in your hands. This

tingling, which means you have brought extra energy into your hands, also means your hands have become more sensitive, and able to feel the energy.

2. Place your hands out in front of you, somewhat less than a foot apart, with palms flat and facing each other, fingers together. Now bend the wrist of your right hand so that the palm of that hand points towards you, and the fingertips of that hand point towards the open palm of your left hand.

3. "Sweep" the fingers of your right hand across your open left palm slowly, with finger-tips about three or four inches away from it. Try sweeping one finger, or a few. (See Figure 3).

4. What sensation do you feel in the palm of your left hand as you do this? Do not try to "think" about what you are feeling, but simply let go and open yourself to whatever sensation comes.

5. Try sweeping your fingertips in different directions (e.g. up and down vs. left and right). Do you feel anything in your left palm, as the fingers of your right hand sweep across it? The sensation will be subtle. You are sensing the energy field emanating from your fingertips as it sweeps across the palm of the opposite hand.

6. Now switch—sweep the fingers of your left hand across your right palm, in the exact same way as before. Do you feel anything? Is one of your palms more sensitive than the other? Experiment with this exercise. Repeat it several times a day to become accustomed to sensing the energy, with your hands. It may take a little practice.

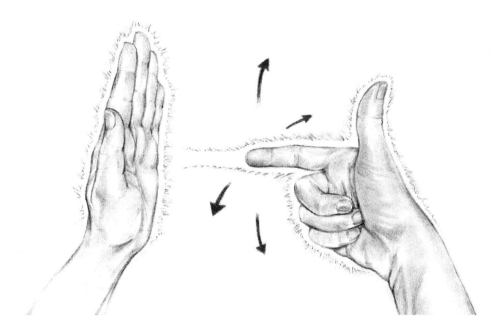

Figure 3: Fingertip Sweep Exercise

After you have begun to sense the energy emanating from your fingertips through practicing this exercise, it is time to try sensing the energy field of a "live" patient. You will do this by using a technique called the *Passing of Hands*. In this technique, your hands are slowly passed palm-down along the body surface of your patient, approximately four to five inches above skin level (see Figure 4). Whatever energetic defects may exist in the energy field around the body of your patient will register as subtle sensations in the palms of your hands. Often, these sensations will be a subtle feeling of a "bump" or "dip," or a subtle sense of heat or coldness. You may receive other subtle sensations as well. It is these sensations in your palms, along with the intuitive impressions which you receive while performing this technique, that will inform you of the condition of the energy field over whatever region of your patient's body you are "scanning" with your hands. Proceed as follows:

Exercise 1-D: The Passing of Hands

1. Have your patient lie flat on your treatment table, arms at his or her sides. Now, call in the energy as you have learned to do in steps 1 to 3 of Exercise 1-A: Calling In the Energy, until you feel the energy tingling in your hands. Once again, this tingling means your hands have been sensitized so they can feel the energy.

2. Now, begin to scan the body of your patient, by using the palm of one hand at a time. Start with your right hand, whether you are right-handed or left-handed (the right hand is "dominant" in sensing the energy in most people). Begin at the top of the head. Hold your hand level, with fingers spread slightly, as if resting. Your hand should be about four or five inches above the body surface. As you scan, move your open palm slowly—two to three inches per second is the ideal speed. "Forget yourself" while you do this, and instead open yourself to any sensation that may form in your hand as you do so. Just be open to *any* sensation which comes. Do you feel anything around the top or sides of the head, over the face or over the throat area? Can you feel any of the head chakras (you can consult Figure 5 for their locations)?

3. Move downwards, to the abdomen. Scan the entire abdomen. Do you feel anything around the shoulders, down the arms or over the center of the chest or belly? Can you feel any of the abdominal chakras? Remember not to move your hands too quickly. Over what areas of your patient's body do you feel something—a subtle sensation in your hands?

4. Continue scanning the entire front of the body in this way, including the hips, upper legs and lower legs. Do you sense something in any of these lower areas?

5. What intuitive impressions did you get, as you passed your hands over the chakras, or over other areas where you felt sensations in your palms? Make note of the areas where you felt sensations in your palms, and the intuitive impressions that came to you as your hand moved over these areas.

6. You can repeat these steps, scanning with your other hand. It is easiest to work with one hand at a time. After you have begun to sense the energy field with your right hand, try this technique with your left hand, too. Is one hand more sensitive than the other? Do your hands feel the same things, over the same areas, or slightly different sensations? Remember to use only one hand at a time, however.

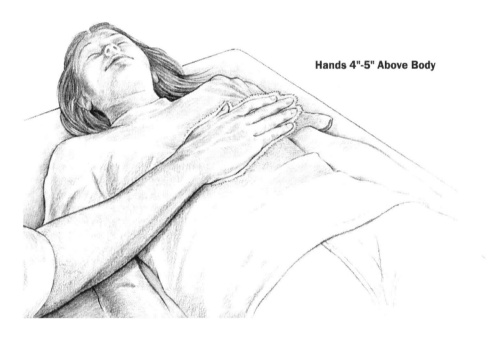

Hands 4"-5" Above Body

Figure 4: The Passing of Hands

Always practice the passing of hands without expectations. To sense the energy effectively you must have faith and believe in the energy, and release your expectations. You will then be able to feel the energy as it is, and receive clear intuitive information on the condition of your patient's energy field. Move away from concentrating on just your hand, or worrying if you are performing this method correctly, and instead simply relax and allow sensations and impressions form in your whole being as you scan the energy field of your patient. You already have the ability to gain these impressions and this information. All you need to do is suspend your thinking process and allow them to come.

Introduction to the Chakra System

As an energy healer, the chakras of your patient will be of central importance to you as you work. Because the chakras are so important, and because you have begun channeling energy into them and sensing their condition by passing your hands over them, it is beneficial to have a basic understanding of them.

There are seven major chakras associated with the human body, and numerous minor ones which are much less important. In Chios®, we concern ourselves with the seven major chakras primarily. These major chakras do not actually exist as "objects" (they are actually energy patterns) but there are certain specific locations on the body that correspond to them, five along the spine, and two on the head. Each chakra is shaped like a funnel or whirlpool of energy. Their vortices lie inside the body, along the spinal cord (which corresponds to a *central energy channel*) and up into the head. Each of the seven chakras has both a front (usually dominant) component, and a rear (usually less dominant) component, which are intimately related. The 1st and 7th chakras, however, are usually represented and thought of as having only the one dominant component, as it is far, far more significant than the weaker component in these two chakras. The seventh chakra extends vertically upwards above the head. The 1st chakra extends forwards from the base of the spine, and downwards, at up to a 30 to 45 degree angle, although its exact position will vary from person to person and often appears to extend mostly downwards towards the feet. The other five chakras, spaced between the 1st and 7th, have at their appropriate locations a front component extending out the front of the body and a rear component extending out the rear of the body (see Figure 5).

Each of these seven major chakras, or primary energy centers, has its own character and corresponds to a unique aspect of our being—from the 1st chakra (physical vitality, or survival) to the 7th chakra (totality of beingness, or spiritual perfection). Because the chakras are spiritual entities, however, it is impossible to convey a true explanation of the nature of each chakra in words alone—each is a *realm of being and consciousness* that cannot be described in mere words but must be experienced. In later Chios® levels you will learn to sense the true spiritual nature of the chakras for yourself. Each chakra also has a certain true color associated with it—from red (1st chakra) to violet (7th chakra). You will also later learn to sense and see the true color of the chakras.

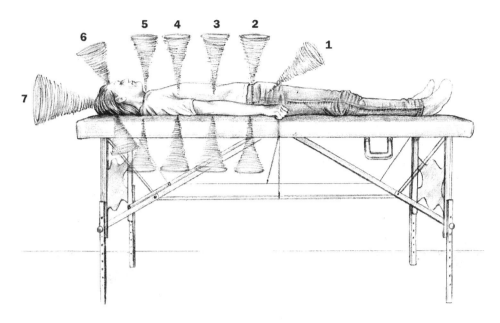

Figure 5: The Chakra System

The chakras are energy processing centers, points of energy flow, and act as the major energy junctions in the energy field. The energetic operations within them are what make every aspect of our bodily, emotional, mental and spiritual life possible. Every chakra is always receiving energy into itself, from all around, and it is this energy that supports the energy field and the entire life process of each individual. Aside from this entry of energy

Number	Name/Location	Character	True Color
7	Crown of Head	Totality of Beingness/Spiritual Perfection.	Violet
6	Forehead	Spiritual Sight ("Psychic Sight"). Visualization.	Indigo
5	Throat	Communication. Creative Expression.	Blue
4	Heart	Universal Love. Compassion. Empathy.	Green
3	Solar Plexus	Creation of Self. Perception & Projection of Self.	Yellow
2	Sacral (Pubic)	Desire, Including Sexual Energy.	Orange
1	Base of Spine	Physical Vitality. Survival.	Red

into the energy field through each of the seven major chakras, there is also an upward flow of energy in the central energy channel, from the lower to higher chakras. This upward flow of energy originates mostly from the earth and then moves through the 1st chakra, 2nd

chakra, etc. as it ascends finally to the 7th (crown) chakra. This energy is processed at each chakra, on its way up, in accordance with the unique nature of that chakra. The lower chakras are simpler-functioning, but as the energy ascends upwards there is a greater degree of sophisticated and more spiritual functioning, intimately related to the life experience and state of being of the individual.

A defect in the energy flow through any given chakra will result not only in a defect in the energy provided to certain portions of the physical body, near to and associated with that chakra, but will also affect emotions, mind and spirit in certain specific ways associated with the nature and character of that particular chakra. Defects in a certain chakra will also often affect many other parts of the energy field—they will impair the entire energy field's ability to process energy. This is because the energy field is a holistic entity: every part affects every other part.

The chakra system is also the way you bring extra energy into yourself so you may channel it into your patient. When you call in the energy, it enters you through your own chakra system. You receive the extra energy at first primarily through your 1st and 7th chakras, but later, with practice, you will draw the energy through all your chakras equally.

The seven major chakras will be of central importance to you as you learn energy healing. It is important to reiterate, however, that an intellectual understanding of the chakra system will not be useful to you in your healing work. The true energy healer learns to expand his or her awareness and experience each of the chakras as a realm of being. Each chakra is a realm with its own nature and consciousness. As you begin to channel energy into the chakras, and practice the passing of hands over them, begin to allow some sense of the unique nature of each chakra to form in your awareness. This is not a thinking process, but one in which you merely open yourself and allow impressions to form in your whole being. You will also begin to gain some insight into the condition of each chakra in your patients, as well.

Putting It All Together: Giving Complete Healing Treatments

Now that you have learned to channel and sense the energy, it is time to begin to give complete healing treatments. Right from the start, however, you should learn to give each treatment in an atmosphere that is genuinely beneficial to your patient. Be sure to conduct each treatment in the proper setting and manner. Healing treatments should take place in a peaceful, restful, calm and supportive environment. It is important that your patient be lying down, and warm and comfortable. You should have a massage table of the proper height (it is virtually a necessity for this type of healing). Some patients enjoy having music playing softly in the background, yet make sure this does not distract you from giving an effective treatment. During the treatment you should maintain an air of calm and confidence, and above all an interest in nurturing the person you are treating. Healing is an act of nurturing, done to aid another human being. Generally, it is best not to carry on a "busy" conversation while healing, but it is acceptable to share a few words with your patient if you feel it is beneficial during the treatment.

It will often be that your patient will enter into a calm, peaceful and relaxed state during treatment and perhaps have experiences of expanded awareness. It is also possible, on occasion, that energy healing treatments may manifest experiences or memories of past traumas, repressed emotions surfacing, physical symptoms, or other things unpleasant to your patient which sometimes accompany the personal healing process. These disturbances in the body or mind of your patient cannot be predicted or controlled by you the healer. It is your responsibility at these times, however, to be a present and compassionate supporter and yet not become "wrapped up" in whatever is coming up—to maintain the openness and clarity necessary for healing while acknowledging and encouraging your patient to express and embrace whatever thoughts, emotions or sensations may appear during treatment. It is also possible for your patient to have peak experiences, unusual or extraordinary experiences in consciousness, and you can again act in an affirming and supportive role.

Calling in the Energy

To begin an energy healing treatment, you always first call in the energy, requesting that it begin to flow. Stand by yourself for a moment, close your eyes and call in the energy as you have learned to do, in steps 1 to 3 of Exercise 1-A: Calling In the Energy, until you feel the energy tingling in your hands. Really see and feel the energy coming in, flowing through you and building up in your hands. Do not try to force the energy, just see it effortlessly building in this way, as you have practiced. Release yourself to the energy.

The Passing of Hands

For a few brief moments, before beginning to channel the energy, pass your hands over your patient to gain some idea of the condition of his or her energy field. Practice the passing of hands over your patient, as you have learned to do, in steps 1 to 5 of Exercise 1-D: The Passing of Hands. Be sure to pass your hands over each of the seven major chakras. Relax your hands as you do this, and be open to sensations in them. What do you feel? Are there certain chakras which you sense are not completely healthy, and are perhaps going to need extra energy during this treatment? Are there certain other areas in which you feel an energy disturbance of some sort—a "bump," a "dip," a hot or cold feeling? Are your hands drawn to certain areas, or are their certain areas you have sensed something and have received the impression that they are in need of special treatment? Make note of all such areas, so you can later give special attention to them during treatment by conducting extra energy to them. Release yourself and be open to any intuitive information you receive about these areas, as you pass the hands over them. Your patient may also find this passing of hands quite soothing.

The Normal Sequence of Treatment Hand Positions

After practicing the passing of hands, begin to channel energy to each of the chakras, in the sequence of treatment hand positions shown below. We refer to this sequence as the *normal sequence of treatment hand positions*, and you will often be following it in your healing treatments. Begin this energy channeling, as you have learned to do, in steps 1 to 4 of Exercise 1B: Energy Channeling, above. It is important to use the proper hand position on each chakra. In each of the positions shown, keep your hands relatively open and flat, with fingers together but relaxed, and remember to use zero pressure. In each treatment hand position, be open and aware of the energy flow. Can you sense when the energy flow builds, and then diminishes, in each chakra? How much energy does each chakra draw—do some "want" more energy than others?

Relax and allow yourself to feel the energy flow through your hands as you treat each chakra, until you feel the flow diminish or until you gain a sense of completeness. This will inform you when it is time to move to the next chakra position. You will often find yourself treating each chakra for three to five minutes, but this will vary, because some chakras will need more of the energy than others. As you work, allow yourself to begin to gain a sense of how the energy is flowing through you and through your patient. Begin to "tune in" to your patient's energy field. What are you sensing or feeling about your patient? Suspend your rational thinking process and simply be aware, and allow impressions to come to you. Healing is best done in a state of openness and holistic awareness. All you must do to access this state is to set yourself free and release yourself to the energy and the healing taking place.

You will notice that the 1st chakra is not treated in this basic standard treatment. This is because to do so would require placing the hands directly on the genital region. In energy healing the hands are never placed on or near the genital region as this might disturb, offend or cause psychological discomfort to your patient. In later Chios® levels you will learn techniques to correct the common energetic defects that may occur in the 1st chakra.

7th Chakra: Place your hands, not on the very top of the head, but on the top sides of the head. This provides for maximum stimulation. Your hands should not be too far apart, perhaps with a gap of two to three inches between the little fingers. You will need to stand at the head of the treatment table for this position (see Figure 6).

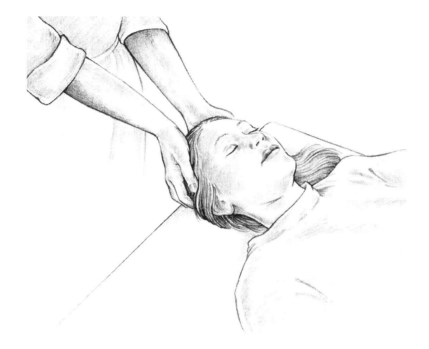

Figure 6: 7th Chakra Treatment Hand Position

6th Chakra: Center your right palm between and just above the eyebrows. At the same time, place your left palm underneath the head, centering it, not directly underneath, but between the back of the head and the neck, just below the curve of the back of the head (see Figure 7). You are treating both the front and rear components of this chakra at the same time, one with each hand. This will require you to stand to your patient's side, usually the right side, for this and the following chakra positions.

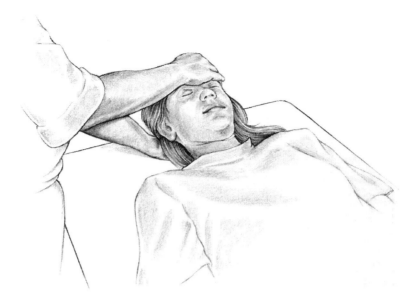

Figure 7: 6th Chakra Treatment Hand Position

5th Chakra: Center your right palm over or just above the pit of the throat, and your left palm below the base of the neck, underneath your patient and directly back from the front palm (see Figure 8). You are again treating both components of this chakra at the same time, one with each hand.

Figure 8: 5th Chakra Treatment Hand Position

4th Chakra (front component): Center your right palm at a point directly between the breasts (between the nipples), and then place your left hand alongside your right hand, and just above it on your patient's body, so that the hands gently overlap (see Figure 9). You are using the "hands overlapping" position you employed when you learned energy channeling. Notice that when the hands overlap in this way that just your thumbs, and part of your index fingers, overlap (see Figure 2). If you are a male healer treating a woman, you may need to take special care, and vary this hand position somewhat to show courtesy. You may need to place your right hand vertically between the breasts (not touching them). Try to keep your right palm centered over the chakra, however your left hand can be vertical, yet overlapping the right somewhat. You are just treating the front component of this chakra— you will treat the rear component later.

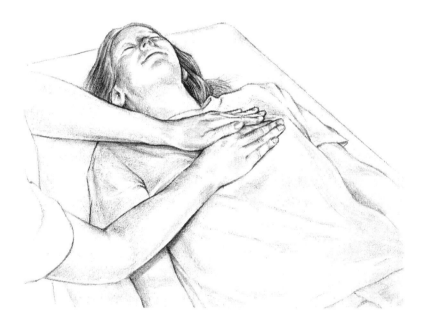

Figure 9: 4th Chakra Treatment Hand Position

3rd Chakra (front component): Center your right palm at a point that is about half way between the depression at the bottom of the sternum (the bottom of the breast bone) and the navel. This point will be several inches above the navel. Place your left hand just above the right, with them gently overlapping, as before (see Figure 10). You are again just treating the front component of this chakra.

21

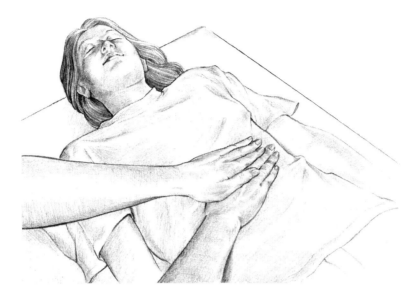

Figure 10: 3rd Chakra Treatment Hand Position

2nd Chakra (front component): Center your right palm at a point about half way between the navel and the protruding front portion of the pubic bone (which is at the top of the genital region). Place your left hand just above the right, and gently overlapping (see Figure 11). You are again just treating the front component of this chakra.

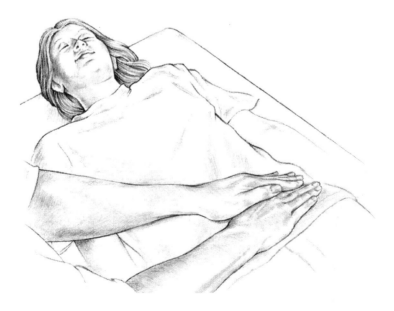

Figure 11: 2nd Chakra Treatment Hand Position

Arms and Legs: It is most important to treat the chakras, but your patient will also benefit from treatment of his or her arms and legs if you wish to do so or have sensed that it is needed. Begin with your patient's right arm, placing your right palm on the inside of the elbow joint, left palm on the outside. Proceed around your treatment table, in either direction, using your right palm on the inside portion of each limb joint (elbows and knees), your left palm on the outside, to channel the energy to each limb.

Supplemental Areas: You may also, at this time, treat any other specific areas that you sensed may have harbored an energetic defect or as needing extra energy, when you practiced the passing of hands at the beginning of treatment. You may have also sensed, with your intuition during treatment, other additional areas that would benefit. Treat all such areas accordingly, by placing your hands directly over these areas. You can either place your hands in the "hands overlapping" position you used with many of the chakras (the right palm centered over the area, with the left hand gently overlapping the right hand), or simply place your hands lightly side-by-side on that area of your patient's body.

In addition, you may also at this time wish to treat any area in your patient's body where injury, illness or disease are present. Place your hands directly over, or adjacent to, the affected area, using either hand position mentioned above. See "Precautions and Special Situations" below, for situations you may encounter and precautions you must always take when treating patients with certain diseases.

In all such additional positions—whether treating the arms and legs, supplemental areas you have sensed require extra healing or areas of the body that harbor disease—allow yourself to be open to sensing the flow of energy, just as you have done while treating chakras. As you channel energy to these areas, be aware how much energy is flowing through you, and allow impressions to come to you regarding where the energy may be going in your patient's body and on what your patient's condition in that area might be.

2nd Chakra (rear component): Ask your patient to turn over, so you may treat his or her back. It is always best to offer a face cradle to your patient, whenever treating the back, because if your patient is forced to turn his or her head sideways it can cause discomfort, over long periods, and even constrain the energy flow in the head and neck. Center your right palm at the base of your patient's spine, on the 4th or 5th lumbar vertebra (one or two vertebra above the sacrum), placing your left hand just above your right hand, gently overlapping (see Figure 12).

Figure 12: 2ⁿᵈ Chakra (Rear) Treatment Hand Position

3ʳᵈ Chakra (rear component): Imagine, first, where the rear component of the fourth chakra is (directly in back of the body from the heart), then center your right palm about half-way between this point and the point where you just treated the rear component of the 2ⁿᵈ chakra. Place your left hand just above your right, gently overlapping (see Figure 13).

Figure 13: 3ʳᵈ Chakra (Rear) Treatment Hand Position

4th Chakra (rear component): Center your right palm at a point directly in back of the body from the front component of the heart chakra (directly in back of the heart). Place your left hand just above your right, gently overlapping (see Figure 14).

Figure 14: 4th Chakra (Rear) Treatment Hand Position

Ending Treatment

End the treatment by standing by yourself for a quiet moment, and requesting that the energy stop flowing. It is a quieting. See it stop its flow into your body, then stopping its flow through your hands. Feel a sense of completeness, and perhaps give a moment of thanks in your heart.

The chakra locations given above are a general guideline for you to use while learning. As you become more proficient at the passing of hands, you will actually acquire the ability to "feel" the exact position of the chakras of your patient, and it is ideal to use that information to center your hands more precisely over each chakra during the treatment hand positions, to maximize the energy flow. The precise positions on the human body that correspond to the chakras may vary from person to person, as each person is unique.

The large majority of healers will find it comfortable to employ the hand positions described above, centering the right palm over the chakra. The right hand is generally a little more active and more attuned to the energy flow. This is true for nearly all healers—whether right or left-handed—and so to place your right palm directly over the chakra position almost always provides maximum stimulation. If, however, you find yourself continuously uncomfortable using this arrangement, try modifying the hand positions above to center your left palm over each chakra. Your right hand will then either be underneath your patient's body (for the 6th and 5th chakras), or gently overlapping your left hand (for the other chakra positions).

Precautions and Special Situations

There are certain situations that require you to take precautions or special measures to increase the safety and effectiveness of your treatments. It is wise to ask every patient, prior to treatment, if there is any physical condition or disease present that you should know about, or if he or she is under a doctor's care for any specific condition. Always include the following precautions or special procedures, when appropriate:

AIDS: Special considerations are not necessary, but after you have gained considerable experience with energy channeling, you may try the following advanced exercise: seek to impart a quality of stillness with the energy, rather than an energizing force. Feel the stillness in yourself, and pass this on, as the energy, through your hands.

Broken Bones, Sprains or Traumatized Areas: Place your hands directly over the afflicted area in addition to normal treatment.

Burns: When your hands may not be placed on the body, as with burned areas, your hands may instead be placed a few inches, up to three to five inches, above the burned area, and the energy will still transfer to your patient in good quantity, although it will not be quite as effective.

Cancer: No special precautions are required, but place your hands directly over the diseased area, or as close as you can, for an extended period (up to half an hour). It is beneficial to, instead of keeping your hands in a static position, vary the position of your hands around the affected area during treatment.

Children: Treat children for one-half to one-third the usual amount of time at each chakra position. Children should not receive more than one treatment every eight or nine days.

Colds and Flu: For patients suffering from colds, passing viral illnesses, etc., you may give frequent treatments, but of shorter duration, one-half or one-third of the usual time on each chakra position. These short treatments are a tonic to the sufferer, but a longer treatment tends to tire the body.

Diabetes: Always treat diabetics from the lower chakras upwards. Start at the lowest chakra you usually treat, the 2ⁿᵈ chakra, when treating the front of the body, and move upwards, as you usually do in the back.

Diseases of the Brain and Nervous System: Treat from the lower chakras up, as with diabetics, and treat the 7ᵗʰ chakra for an extended period.

Diseases of the Internal Organs: Treat as usual, but spend extra time on the chakra(s) nearest the affected organ(s).

Heart Disease: When treating a patient with mild heart disease, give a regular healing treatment (no changes are necessary). For a patient with serious heart disease (including patients on medication for heart disease), always treat the 4ᵗʰ (heart) chakra last. If the person has heart disease in an advanced stage, treat the 4ᵗʰ chakra last, and for an extended period of time (up to half an hour in some cases).

Pregnancy: Pregnant women must always lie on their side for treatment. You may alter the usual hand positions in such a way that you treat both components of the 4ᵗʰ, 3ʳᵈ and 2ⁿᵈ chakras at the same time, if you wish. If you do so, center your right palm over the front component, and your left palm over the rear component, so your palms "sandwich" the body at each of these chakra positions.

Psychological Disorders: It is impossible to predict the effect of treatment. You must proceed with caution. Treat the person for a short time, one-half or one-third of the normal treatment time per chakra, and note any effects. Proceed carefully.

Notes

Notes

Chios® Energy Healing – Level Two

Welcome to Chios® Level II. This level will assist you in greatly adding to your healing power and repertoire of techniques. You will learn to channel larger amounts of healing energy into your patient, to sense many simple energetic defects in your patient's aura and chakras and also many new healing techniques to correct those energetic defects.

As you begin your study of this level, you may choose to receive the second Chios® attunement. As before, it is not at all required that your receive this attunement, should you wish to learn and practice the techniques in this level, but the attunement will assist you in channeling larger amounts of healing energy and will add to your ability to effectively perform the many new healing techniques that you will learn. The second Chios® attunement is a more powerful attunement than the first. If you choose to receive it, be sure to once again carefully observe the preparatory steps, so that you may gain the full benefits (see Appendix #1 – Preparation for Chios® Attunements).

As you learn the many interesting new techniques in this level and incorporate them into your healing treatments you may find it helpful to refer to the outline of treatment steps for this Chios® level (see Appendix #2 – Outline of Treatment Steps for Chios® Levels I, II and III). This will clarify for you the recommended order of techniques, and serve as quick and easy reference while learning.

Introduction: The Importance of Holistic Awareness and Action in Healing

In your study of Chios® Level I, you began to work with the energy—you began to channel the energy and sense the human energy field with your hands. As you have learned, the energy field is composed of the aura and the chakras, and it is energetic defects within them that result in diseases and afflictions of body, mind and spirit. It's time to learn a little more about this energy field and some of these defects that can occur in it.

The aura exists in seven layers or "higher bodies" and each layer of aura corresponds to a different aspect of our being—each aura layer, like each chakra, is a realm of being and consciousness. The 1st layer, or etheric body, is an energy body that closely follows the outlines of the physical body and that consists of the energetic operations that support the biological and chemical processes within it. You have begun to sense the energy of this etheric body through your practice of the passing of hands. In Chios® Level II you will learn to *see* this 1st layer of aura. The *emotional body*, or 2nd layer of aura, and the *mental body*, or 3rd layer of aura—the next two layers above the etheric body—are intimately connected to the emotional life and mental life, respectively. The remaining layers, the 4th through the 7th, have progressively more spiritual functioning. These seven layers of aura interpenetrate (occupy the same area of space in and around the physical body), but each layer extends a little further beyond the body surface than the layer before (at increments of approximately four to five inches). The layers exist upon successively higher level of energetic "vibration," and it is important to understand that these layers are defined by their successively higher levels of vibration and not by their physical location. Energetic defects commonly occur in any or all of the seven layers, and during your practice of Chios® Level II you will learn to sense and correct four common simple energetic defects in the aura. In Chios® Level III you will expand your ability to sense and heal energetic defects in all seven layers of aura.

The chakra system consists of the seven major chakras, each of which also corresponds to a different aspect of our being. Each chakra has an important relationship with its *corresponding layer of aura*—from 1st to 7th. The 1st chakra, for example, is associated with physical vitality and physical life and bears a close relationship to the 1st layer of aura (the etheric body), which is the energetic pattern for the operation for the physical body. The 2nd chakra is associated with emotions, particularly desire and sexuality, and bears a close relationship to the 2nd layer of aura (the emotional body). The 3rd chakra is associated with mind, especially concepts relating to perception and projection of self, and bears a close relationship with the 3rd layer of aura (mental body). The 4th through 7th chakras display successively more complex and more spiritual modes of functioning, just as their corresponding layers of aura likewise progress to higher, more refined and spiritual levels of operation. The seven aura layers and seven chakras form an energy field around the physical body that supports all the various facets of our worldly life and is both a regulator and indicator of our physical, emotional, mental and spiritual states of being. Energetic defects of the chakras are common, and during your practice of Chios® Level II you will learn to sense and treat one very important energetic defect in chakras: blocked chakras. In Chios® Level III you will learn to sense and heal additional energetic defects in chakras using many additional powerful techniques.

There are many exciting healing techniques you will learn in Chios® Levels II and III, but it is important to understand, right from the start, that it is not these techniques alone but the *holistic awareness and action* of you the healer that makes effective energy healing possible. The human energy field is a holistic entity: every part affects every other part. You should never think of the various parts of the energy field—the chakras, and the layers of aura and the phenomena within them—as separate entities, but as *parts of a greater whole that work together*. Each affects all the others, and together they comprise the health and state of being of the individual. The layers of aura, for example, are not entirely separate entities. Not only do they interpenetrate in space, they intimately affect each other. Energetic defects in one layer of aura will often filter through and affect many other layers. Chakras are not entirely separate entities, either. The chakra system is one whole system; it works as one, and defects in one chakra will often affect other chakras and the entire system (and also layers of aura). You must not limit your awareness, as you employ healing techniques to sense the conditions in the aura and chakras, but must remain open to the entire energy field your patient, instead of remaining too focused on any particular part of the energy field you are working on or any particular energetic phenomenon therein.

You may be treating, for example, a patient who has energetic defects in his or her 1st layer of aura, which you have sensed are related to a physical disease that is present. These defects in the etheric layer may have actually "filtered down" from defects on the 2nd and 3rd layers, however, defects that themselves may be related to those in the 5th, 7th or other higher layers. Of course, conditions in one or more of the chakras are often intimately involved, too—it can be an involved pattern. This is a very common situation. If, in treating the condition in the 1st layer, you limit your awareness to this "isolated" energetic condition you are treating, you will not be aware of the intuitive information that would otherwise come to your awareness—information on many related conditions on the higher layers of your patient's aura, related conditions in your patient's chakras, and correlating conditions in the psychology and life experience of your patient. If, however, you remain open in your awareness, allowing intuitive impressions to form in your whole being as you work, you are far more likely to become aware of all related, connected conditions in the aura, chakras, psychology and life of your patient. Maintaining this holistic awareness that allows you to be a clear channel for this healing knowledge, from the field of pure consciousness, is crucial to being a successful energy healer. Always seek to *be aware of, and respond to, the whole being of your patient*.

It is also important to maintain holistic action, as you employ all of the various healing techniques that you will learn and use. These techniques *are not different from yourself*; they are not separate tools that exist apart from your use of them. There is ultimately a unity between you, the energy field of your patient, the healing technique you are using and the healing energy itself as each healing is performed. You, your patient's energy field and whatever healing tool you are using are always *one*. This is required, so you may become a pure channel for the healing power of pure consciousness. Remember this as you learn and practice every healing technique in Chios® Levels II and III. If, in using a specific healing technique on a specific part of the energy field, you allow your awareness to contract into this small, particular area of working, you will not be healing your patient with your whole being. You will not be a completely open, clear channel for the healing power of pure consciousness, as it flows through you. You should never become preoccupied with particulars, but should release yourself into an expanded awareness and becoming a pure, open channel for the healing power. This is what provides you the ability to provide genuine spiritual healing to your patient.

You cultivate this expanded holistic awareness and action through openness. Of all the qualities that you must possess in order to heal effectively, openness is the most important. You must remain open to the healing knowledge and power coming through you, even while sensing or treating one particular area in your patient's energy field. If your awareness and action are limited to one part of the energy field, you are no longer established in a state of unity with your patient nor have the full knowledge and power of the field of pure consciousness available to you. An effective healing treatment is guided by this higher spiritual reality. A complete understanding and awareness of your patient's condition emerges in your whole being, you naturally know what techniques to use, and you use them in the state of openness that makes them maximally effective—it is a beautiful, unitary process. True healing work always begins and ends in this holistic awareness and action that openness brings, and never in technique alone. Always *heal your patient from your whole being*.

To get the full knowledge and power available from the field of pure consciousness—the higher spiritual reality that governs all healing and provides the knowledge and power that makes it possible—always maintain the openness that keeps you a wide, pure channel. As you heal, always allow the knowledge and power of this higher realm to be your guide, and not any specific guidelines or techniques. You are about to learn many powerful and effective healing techniques, in Chios® Levels II and III, but it is not the techniques themselves that are important. They are designed to assist you in contacting and working with the unlimited knowledge and power of pure consciousness that lies within you, in the ways necessary to provide healing. Energy healing is much more than the sum of the many techniques that can be listed or described in this or any healing book; it is a holistic expression of and contained within this higher realm of pure consciousness. True energy healing is not contained within any book; it is found within *you*.

The Chios® Symbols, and Using the Symbols to Call in the Energy

A good first step in learning to give more powerful and effective healing treatments is to learn to call in greater amounts of healing energy into yourself. In fact, the effective use of most of the healing tools you will learn in Chios® Level II also requires that you have the ability to call in this greater amount of energy for use in healing.

In the first Chios® level you learned how to call in the energy by "seeing," in your mind's eye, the energy flowing into you from all around, down your arms and into your hands and then conducting into your patient. In this level, you will also use *healing symbols*, which are tools—vehicles for the focus of energy. Your first important use of healing symbols will be to employ them to greatly add to the amount of energy you call in and channel into your patient. It is possible to call in and channel the energy without using symbols, as you already have done, but your use of symbols will add much to the quantity and power of the energy you are able to bring in and channel. The symbols will have other uses that you will learn, too, such as clearing blocked chakras.

There are three symbols used in this level of the Chios® system: the Circle, the Trine, and the Star (see Figure 15). These symbols are simple and elementary, it is true, but they are also closely related to the elementary essence of all existence—they are simple and close to the essence and this gives them the potential to be powerful and effective. Humanity has had an instinctive understanding of the powers that move in the physical world, the essence of the powers that make existence possible, the powers that build form and give shape to all we know. This instinctive understanding recognizes the shape of these powers, and in the mind's eye these symbols take shape as representative of the most fundamental and important aspects of the creative power of the field of pure consciousness.

These symbols are not merely physical shapes; they are universal symbols that correspond to universal patterns of energy and awareness. There is, in each symbol, an essence linked to the shape. They are, in their essence, representations of the ways in which energy and awareness flows in our manifested world, and are therefore useful in healing work. Do not think that because these Chios® symbols are simple they cannot be powerful. At various times in the past, humanity has been much more aware of the power and uses of simple

The Circle   **The Trine**   **The Star**

Figure 15: The Chios® Symbols

symbols than we are today, in our modern technological civilization, where it is often mistakenly assumed that something must be complex to be powerful. These three symbols have been known and used as symbols of power in virtually every culture on earth, and in the magical tradition as well. While there are other symbols that have been used in healing work, these particular symbols are as powerful, and potentially more powerful, than any.

It may interest you to have some idea of the meaning and the essence behind each of these symbols—indicative of the energy patterns they represent—and this is given below. Do not be bound by these descriptions, however, because a true understanding of the essence of these symbols transcends description. The description is only an approximation of an essence to each symbol that is beyond words or ideas. It is important, therefore, not to think of any meaning when using these symbols, but just to be aware of the symbol itself. The true meaning and power is inherent in each symbol.

The Circle

The Circle, which is the outline of a circle (not filled in), is the symbol of wholeness, unending life force, and the unity of creation—the beginning and end of all things. It attunes with the all. It is complete, and draws together and encompasses all that is. It also represents duality, inside and outside, but shows, in its completeness, that apparent duality resolves itself in unity, in one being. This is the pattern of energy and awareness inherent in the shape of the Circle.

In healing, one often works with separated (polar) energies—energies not completely connected or harmonious. The Circle not only calls forth polar energies; it pulls them together and resolves them. You will shortly learn to use the Circle (in combination with the Trine) to call in a greater amount of the energy, at the beginning of treatments. When calling in the energy using these two symbols, the Circle is used first, to draw life energy from the earth and all around, using the body life force to receive the universal life energy, the two energies meeting. It uses the energy that is already in the body to receive the energy that exists all around. It assists you the healer in opening yourself to, and in bringing in, the energy.

The Circle creates an opening of the spirit, a balanced harmony between the spirit and the earth.

The Trine

The Trine, which is the outline of an equilateral triangle (not filled in), is the symbol of penetration to higher levels of existence. It increases the rate of vibration of the energy and the vibrational level of your awareness, and awakens the mind to the higher levels. It points upward and connects this world to the higher worlds. This is the pattern of energy and awareness inherent in the shape of the Trine.

Its three sides correspond to the many trinities in spiritual systems, but especially as a symbol of the passing, from one to the other, between incarnation and discarnate life (the base points of the Trine), with the goal of spiritual growth and rising above the world towards a state of self-realization and spiritual liberation. As a symbol of this ascension, it represents a heightened and broadened awareness, and a refined perception: an ascension to a higher level of reality.

When the Trine is used at the beginning of healing treatments, it takes the universal life energy that has been brought in, by the Circle, and moves it upwards towards higher vibrational levels—it raises the energy to a higher rate of vibration. This lends a more powerful and purifying effect to the healing energy, and also increases your sensitivity to the energy.

The Trine leads the spirit towards growth; it is an elevation of the personal spirit as it relates to this existence, a rising from the earth.

The Star

The Star, a regular five pointed star filled in to a solid shape, is a channel for energy between our physical world and the field of pure consciousness which is the spiritual source and essence of all creation. It is different from the Trine, but can be thought of as the Trine symbol focused and combined with this earth (trine shapes spaced around a circular outline). The Star has five points pointing in, and five pointing out, indicative of this use as a channel for energy between this world and the higher spiritual reality. This is the pattern of energy and awareness inherent in the shape of the Star.

One way the Star is used in Chios® is to draw and focus energy from the higher level into this physical world: to tap the healing power inherent in pure consciousness and channel it down into the physical body to correct major disturbances in energy flow which would otherwise be very difficult to correct. The Star is also very effective when used to treat the 7th chakra. The Star (as a channel between our worldly life and the realm of pure consciousness) has a close correspondence with the nature of the 7th chakra (our spiritual totality—the total relationship we have between the world of spirit and our material existence). The energetic pattern inherent in the Star conforms with the spiritual nature of the 7th chakra, and so the 7th chakra can be powerfully cleared and energized through use of the Star.

The Star is beyond the earth—it is where there is no beginning and no end, to a broader existence, not even existence, beyond existence. As we all exist on this earth now, we also exist above. As you might stand on the shore and watch the waves on the ocean, feeling a stirring within, the Star calls forth the beyond and all times. It is our higher self, the totality of our being. The Star is a channel to a realm beyond time and space. It is the light above us, and in us, and leads to an understanding of eternity.

Using Visualization to Direct Energy

The ability of these three Chios® symbols to direct energy is activated by visualizing them. Visualization is a very useful tool in healing, because it enables you to direct energy in many different ways. "Energy follows thought" is a well-known maxim, and the meaning of this saying is that the proper visualization of energy flow, in your mind's eye, is sufficient to direct the energy in whatever manner you desire. This may be done by visualizing the flow of the energy itself, in whatever pattern desired, or through other methods—the use of symbols which represent patterns of energy flow being an important example. When you visualize a pattern of energy flow, in your mind's eye, the energy is activated to flow in that manner. When you visualize a symbol in your mind's eye, the nature of energy flow that is contained in the essence of that symbol is activated, and the energy flows according to that nature. Both of these uses of visualization are important and will be used in Chios® Level II.

In order to make effective use of this ability to direct energy through visualization, however, you must visualize in the proper way. When you visualize an energy flow, for example, it is important to understand that visualization is not the same as "thinking about" the desired energy flow, or "pretending to see" the energy flow, but is a process of *sensing and becoming* the energy flow, in your mind's eye. Visualizing in the proper way, by sensing and becoming the desired energy flow, allows you to become a pure channel for the healing power of pure consciousness, which is what actually directs the energy in the manner visualized and causes it to heal the energy field of your patient in the manner required. When you visualize a symbol, it is similarly important that you sense and become one with the symbol, and not merely "think about" or "pretend to see" it. This proper visualization of the symbol is what activates the inner essence, the inherent power of the symbol from the field of pure consciousness, and sets the energy flow into motion according to the pattern of energy flow that the symbol represents. Visualization is the process of maintaining a particular symbol or a pattern of energy flow in your awareness, in a complete and effortless way. It must be effortless, because you are creating a pure channel in yourself—effort is an imposition of your mind, and clouds the real power which flows through you. This is this proper practice of visualization: an effortless sensing and becoming. You *are* the flow of energy. You *are* the symbol. In visualization, as with every healing tool you will learn in Chios®, the power ultimately comes from the connection to pure consciousness that lies within *you*.

In Chios®, you will learn techniques that will often require you to visualize a desired flow or pattern of energy, a symbol, or even both at the same time. Every technique that you will learn and use to heal the various defects that you will encounter in the energy field of your patients will require you to use your visualization ability in some way. *Every time you will need to use visualization in this correct manner, during Chios® Levels II and III, we will specify that you "visualize, sense and become" whatever is required, so you become a pure channel for healing power,* in whatever form you need it, to heal.

You began to use your visualization ability in Chios® Level I when you learned to call in the energy at the beginning of treatment—you began to see, in your mind's eye, the energy flowing into you, conducting through you, and then into your patient. Now you will employ your power of visualization to add the visualization of two Chios® symbols—the Circle and the Trine—to more powerfully bring in and raise the vibrational rate of the energy so that you can channel a greater quantity and quality of energy into your patient. It is your natural ability to call in the energy and refine it, in this way. Your visualization of the energy coming into you, and the visualization of the symbols, merely activates this ability.

If you have begun to learn the practice of Chios® Meditation, you will have a good understanding of the process of visualization already, and your experience of it through your meditation practice will be of great benefit to you in your use of these symbols and the various other healing techniques in this level. If you have not yet studied Chios® Meditation, that's fine. The following exercise will give you some practice in this correct method of visualization, by visualizing the Chios® symbols:

Exercise 2-A: Visualizing the Chios® Symbols

1. Sit comfortably with your eyes closed, and seek a calmness, a quietness in your mind.
2. Now imagine, in your mind, the Circle. Now, do not merely think about, or pretend to see the Circle, but begin to feel its circular shape with your mind. Ask yourself, how does it feel to be that shape? Feel that you are the Circle, and should other feelings or thoughts come up, simply drop them—allow them to become unimportant as you just return your focus of awareness to sensing only the circular shape of the Circle alone.
3. Seek to merge with the Circle, feel your entire being sensing, moving into and *becoming one* with the Circle. If you find yourself thinking about the Circle, stop thinking and just *be* it. If you find yourself pretending to see the Circle, release the visual portion of your awareness of it—the portion of your awareness that "sees" it as if you were using your eyes—and just become it. Do not think about or pretend to see the Circle. Be the Circle. Sense it effortlessly.
4. Continue sensing yourself as the Circle for a moment, then end the exercise by stopping your sensing of the Circle and resting for a moment, with your eyes closed.
5. Repeat this exercise with the other two Chios® symbols to gain a sense of them, also. The Trine is sensed in its outline shape, but the Star is sensed more as a solid (filled in) object, with its points.

Calling in the Energy Using Visualization of Symbols

You are now ready to call in the energy using the Circle and the Trine In visualizing the energy begin to flow into you, and in visualizing these symbols in order to increase and refine its flow, be sure to remember that your visualizations must be done effortlessly, and with a release to the energy. To call in the energy using visualization of these symbols, follow this procedure:

Exercise 2-B: Calling In the Energy With Symbols

1. Stand by yourself for a moment, eyes closed, and visualize the energy beginning to flow into you. Really see and feel it coming into you from all around, coursing through your body, through your shoulders and arms and down to your hands. Feel it begin to collect in your hands. Visualize this energy flowing into you—not by thinking or pretending to see—but now by effortlessly sensing and becoming this energy flow, in your mind's eye.

2. Now, visualize, sense and become the Circle. Sense yourself as the Circle, and then feel the Circle as being composed of a white light, brought to a dazzling, flaring brightness of light, and held in the mind for about ten seconds, and then dimmed. Bring the Circle to brightness in this way for two additional times, for a total of three times, and then dimmed.

3. Visualize, sense and become the Trine. Sense yourself as the Trine, and then feel the Trine brought to a dazzling, flaring brightness, held in the mind for about ten seconds, and then dimmed. Bring the Trine to brightness in this way for two additional times, for a total of three times, then dimmed.

4. Now visualize, sense and become the Circle again, brought to a final, single, quieting brightness, unlike a flare, a brightness that is held in your mind for about ten seconds, and then swells and fills out into you, a warm light suffusing into your entire body.(See Figure 16).

You will sense the greater energy as a stimulating feeling in your body and hands. The harnessing of the energy provides a sensation in the body similar to what you experience when feeling strong emotions—you should feel a definite tingling and some degree of heat, in your hands, now that you've learned to call in greater amounts of the energy and raise its vibrational rate. Note that the Star is never used at the beginning of treatment when calling in the energy.

You have now opened yourself up to channel much larger amounts of the energy into your patient, and will also experience more power in performing the many healing tools you will learn in Chios® Level II. From now on, begin your healing treatments by calling in the energy using visualization of symbols, using the steps above.

Figure 16: Calling In the Energy With Symbols

Simple Energetic Defects of the Aura and Chakras

After learning how to call greater amounts of energy into yourself for use in healing, your next step is to begin to learn how to sense and then treat some of the common energetic defects you will encounter in the aura and chakras of your patients. The nature of these energetic defects will be discussed first, then you will learn several new techniques for detecting them, and finally, during the remainder of Chios® Level II, you will learn various specific techniques for their correction.

There are a total of four potential energetic defects of the aura that you will learn to treat in this level. They are: energetic impurities in the aura, leaks and tears in the aura layers, energy depletion in the aura and disturbance of energy flow in the body energy. The fifth condition you will learn to treat is blocked chakras.

Blocked Chakras

Blocked chakras are chakras in which the upward flow of energy that usually ascends in the central energy channel through the entire chakra system has become restricted or stopped at one or more particular chakra points. Blocked chakras do not just restrict this upward flow of energy, however, but restrict the entire flow of energy through that chakra. Each chakra does not merely conduct the energy upwards through the central energy channel, to the next chakra above it, but also brings energy into itself from all around, conducts it through itself and then sends it to the entirety of the energy field (including the physical body). Blockage of a chakra affects both aspects of the energy flow, through the chakra, and so a blocked chakra has a very deleterious effect on the entire energy field of your patient. Generally, a patient will usually exhibit at least one, and often more, blocked chakras.

Blocked chakras usually coincide with certain psychological core issues—with certain existential biases that your patient has adopted in his or her relationship to reality. These existential biases inhibit the wider range of self-awareness and action available to your patient, restricting it to a limited range of expression. Often they are tied to the emotions, although mental and spiritual aspects of the being are invariably involved (and often relationships with other persons). The entire life process of your patient becomes restricted. Because the operation of the chakras is so central to the healthy functioning of the entire being it is very important to become aware of and correct any defective conditions in them.

It is very common to find blocked 4th, 5th and 6th chakras on patients. Blocked 2nd, 3rd and 7th chakras are also fairly common, while blocked 1st chakras are somewhat less common. Some patients will have only one blocked chakra, and many other patients will have two or even more blocked chakras—very often a low one and a high one, for example. When two or more blocked chakras are present in your patient, it is usually indicative of more than one cause at work—different issues in different chakras—although they may have some relationship to each other. Sometimes patients will exhibit a chakra that is chronically blocked, as well as another chakra or chakras that are blocked occasionally, with changes in the individual's life. Unblocking chakras, in concert with other techniques, often provides a great deal of emotional, mental and spiritual clearing for your patient, and prevents physical disease, too.

Leaks and Tears

The aura is composed of seven discrete interpenetrating layers, as previously described. *Leaks* and *tears* of the aura are areas where the "fabric" of one or more aura layers has become damaged. Leaks and tears are treated using the same technique, but have important differences.

Leaks generally occur primarily on the 1st layer of aura, the layer closest to the physical body. They are regions where the energy of the energy field is being slowly dissipated—leaking away—instead of being retained in its normal pattern. Leaks may be likened to a "wearing thin" of the aura layer. As a wearing thin of fabric might allow for a loss of protection and weakening of a fabric garment, resulting in a loss of body heat, leaks of the aura reflect a weakening and loss of integrity of the aura layer, resulting in a loss of energy. This loss of energy that results from leaks is detrimental to your patient, because it lessens the strength of the life energy upon which every aspect of health depends.

Leaks are generally found over areas of the physical body that have been subject to wear, strain or physical trauma of some kind, and are often found over joints. Usually they are found on the front of the body: the knee, shoulder and hip joints are very common places to find them. They are also sometimes found near the neck, the ankles and the elbows.

Tears (unlike leaks) usually occur in the higher layers of aura, above the 1st layer, and often extend through multiple layers. Tears are similar to leaks, in that they are regions where the aura layers have become damaged, resulting in energy loss. Tears, however, are a more severe form of damage; they can be likened to an actual "tear" of the field. As a tear in fabric might serve to completely destroy the covering, tears in the aura are more like complete openings: they are "holes"—regions of complete loss of field integrity—and are more harmful to your patient. Whereas leaks are a smaller and more gradual loss of energy, tears are usually a more serious loss of energy. Tears can also allow for invasion of unhealthy energies from outside your patient and into your patient's energy field. Tears are therefore a double hazard for your patient: they are a loss of energy (dissipating from inside your patient's field and flowing out) and a loss of protection (from undesirable energies flowing from outside your patient's field and coming in).

Tears can exist on any layer of aura, but most often occur in the middle layers. They can begin on the 1st layer, but this is not common. They usually begin on the 2nd, 3rd or 4th layer (or even higher layers), and frequently extend through two, three or more layers above. It is not uncommon for tears to extend all the way to the 7th layer of aura. Each patient is unique, however, and tears can begin on any layer and extend through any number of layers. Tears, like leaks, are often related to stress of some kind, but tears (as a more severe form of damage) are often related to emotional, mental or spiritual stresses or past traumatic experiences. Some traumas are severe enough to cause tears in two, three or even more of the higher aura layers—including most of the layers and up to the 7th layer. Large tears on multiple layers of aura result not merely in serious energy loss, but also in further psychic vulnerability. These tears are often related to traumas, of various kinds, and/or issues from past and/or present dysfunctional relationships.

Tears are usually found only on the front of the body, and can be large or small. The large, catastrophic tears that extend through a number of layers are usually found over various parts of the torso—the abdomen or chest area—although they can sometimes occur elsewhere, too. It is of great benefit to your patient to correct these damaged areas of the field layers: it prevents both the serious energy loss and the psychic vulnerability tears create.

Auric Energy Impurities

Auric energy impurities are unhealthy, stagnant dark energies which have accumulated in the aura, in certain areas. They are energies which are not necessary for the normal, healthy energetic functioning of the energy field. They do not function according to the laws and normal flow of healthy energies, but instead inhibit or act as blockages to the free flow of bright, clear healthy energy. Areas of auric energy impurities can exist on any of the seven layers of aura. These unhealthy energy impurities can contribute to physical disease or problems in your patient's emotional, mental or spiritual life.

In Chios® Level II you will remove auric energy impurities that have accumulated in various locations down near the body surface of your patient (within a maximum of 1 to 1 ½ feet above the body surface, yet usually closer). These auric energy impurities are often associated with the 1st, 2nd, 3rd and 4th layers of aura, but can be associated with any layer. These areas frequently appear as, and are often likened to, "clouds" of dark energy, and such clouds of energy impurities often include energies on several layers of aura—the energies on one layer are associated with energies on adjacent layer(s) that exist in the same zone or cloud. Auric energy impurities in these areas, or clouds, are "stuck" to the energy field at certain locations, almost as though with static electricity. Because the aura layers also exist inside the space occupied by the physical body, these areas of energy impurity can be partially "inside the body," as well.

Auric energy impurities, on the aura layers, relate to ill conditions in your patient's body, emotions, mind and spirit. On the 1st layer, they can be the "energetic leftovers" of physical trauma or conditions of ill health inside the body. On the 2nd or 3rd layers they are patterns of unhealthy negative emotions or negative thought-forms that are being "held" by your patient and are the "leftovers" of trauma, or psychological issues and negative feelings and beliefs your patient has otherwise acquired during life. On the higher layers, these impurities have affected your patient's spiritual state of being. Often, impurities on one layer will be closely associated with those occupying the same general area yet on other layers: impurities on the 4th layer that interfere with the expression of love, for example, will be associated with impurities on the 3rd layer corresponding to negative thoughtforms about self and other, impurities on the 2nd layer corresponding to core negative emotions, and unhealthy energies on the 1st layer that have caused physical affliction or disease. Sometimes unhealthy energies that have invaded your patient's energy field from outside (from other people) can contribute to and become enmeshed with these auric energy impurities your patient has generated in his or her own energy field.

Auric energy impurities are commonly found on patients. They generally appear on the front of the body—often around the head, face, neck, shoulders, chest, lower abdomen or hips. They are also sometimes found over one or more chakras—often the 4th, 7th or 2nd. It is very desirable to be able to detect and then remove these unhealthy and detrimental energies from your patient's aura. Removing these energies, in conjunction with the unblocking of chakras, provides a great deal of emotional and mental clearing for your patient.

Energy Depletion

Energy depletion is a weakness in the overall (global) energy of the energy field—it is a lack of sufficient energy to give the energy field vibrant health and to adequately support the life process of your patient, on all levels. It usually manifests as a condition of low or depleted energy on the entire aura—on all layers of the aura. *Some* weak chakras may be present as well, yet these are treated separately (as you will learn in Chios® Level III).

When the strength of the life energy in your patient's energy field becomes too low, the body, emotions and mind become less integral in their operation and your patient becomes more susceptible to illnesses and afflictions of various sorts from this weakened energy alone. This condition of weakened natural energy also makes it much easier for unhealthy outside energies to invade the energy field at whatever points are weakest: the unhealthy outside energies often lodge themselves in the aura layers and filter through them, and will also eventually affect some of the chakras. The healthy, protective function a strong aura normally provides is lost. This not only results in the condition of diminished overall health in the individual, but can be an important contributing factor to serious illness—physical, emotional or mental. Even when serious illness is not yet present, energy depletion, if left untreated, will make it considerably more likely that serious illness will eventually result.

This condition of energy depletion can occur not only in the entire energy field but also sometimes in those portions of the field over certain bodily areas. This condition, which can sometimes be found over the lower legs or arms, is termed *local energy depletion* to distinguish it from the more common, and more serious, overall or *global energy depletion*. This local energy depletion is most commonly found in the lower legs, although it sometimes occurs in the lower arms as well. It is very desirable to correct the condition of energy depletion when it is found, and to do so is a great contribution to your patient, especially if he or she is suffering from or susceptible to serious illnesses.

Disturbance in Energy Flow

Disturbance in energy flow is a condition of irregularity or disruption in the pattern of the flow of the life energy in and immediately around the physical body. It is not a condition that exists in the layers of the aura above the body, but in the body energy system.

The energy in your patient's body (actually to a level about one inch above the skin) flows in a normal, healthy pattern—in a pattern of energy channels—upon which energetic and bodily health depends. This pattern has been described in acupuncture and various meridian-based energy therapies. The central energy channel along the spine is the largest (and by far most important) of these channels, but there is a system of smaller channels that bring the energy to all organs and tissues of the body. Sometimes the pattern of energy flow in many or most channels in the body becomes erratic and uneven, from various disturbances in your patient, or even completely disrupted from its normal, healthy paths. This disturbance in the flow eventually results in physical maladies and other unhealthy consequences for your patient, should the condition remain untreated. This is a *global disturbance in energy flow*, which affects the flow of energy in the most or all of the body and is not tied to any particular location.

Disturbance of energy flow can also occur in specific regions, too. The energy can become disrupted and diverted from certain specific pathways. This disturbance of energy flow in certain particular areas is called local disturbance in energy flow, to distinguish it from the somewhat more common global (or overall) disturbance in the flow of the life energy.

In Chios®, these two forms of disturbance in energy flow are treated using the same technique. The disturbance is treated either globally—all over the body—or more specifically, according to the pathways that have become disrupted. When disturbances of energy flow are sensed they can be corrected, and it is beneficial to the energetic health of your patient to do so. This acts to prevent potential afflictions and disease in the organs and tissues of the body.

Sensing Simple Energetic Defects in the Aura and Chakras

Now that we've learned about some of the energetic defects that can be present in your patient's energy field, it is time to learn to detect them. You will begin each healing treatment by calling in the energy using symbols, as previously described, but after this your next step will be to "read" the energy field of your patient to assess his or her energetic condition. Each patient will present him- or herself to you with specific energetic defects in the energy field and specific treatment needs. You will therefore need to treat each patient as unique, and seek to come to an understanding of his or her condition prior to treatment. You must remember, however, that this process of becoming aware of the condition of your patient also continues throughout treatment—that you will use the perceptual techniques you will learn in Chios® throughout each healing treatment to continually refine and add to your understanding of your patient as you work.

In Chios® Level II you will use three main perceptual tools to inform yourself of your patient's condition: 1) Intuitive information you receive regarding the condition of your patient's aura and chakras. You will shortly learn the Chios® technique for receiving this intuitive information; 2) Your direct observations of the aura of your patient. You will also soon learn the first Chios® technique for beginning to view the aura, and 3) Sensations in your hands as you practice the passing of hands over your patient's energy field. You have already learned this passing of hands technique, and will now refine it for use in sensing energy defects. The information you receive from these three sources will be combined and used together.

One primary and very important tool of the energy healer is visualization, and you have learned much about visualization already. Another primary and very important tool of the healer is the ability to obtain intuitive information. You will now learn to acquire this intuitive information by performing an *Intuitive Reading*.

Beyond the level of our everyday awareness, with our busy thinking mind, which preoccupies itself with the surface level of reality, lies a larger realm of awareness within which lies great knowledge. Each of us has, by virtue of our intuitive mind, a connection to this larger realm—the unlimited knowledge of the field of pure consciousness. This deeper knowledge already contains whatever information you might ever seek to know—including details of the condition of your patient's aura and chakras, contributing factors in the psychology and life experience of your patient, and the most beneficial way for healing treatment to proceed. This information can be accessed by developing and refining the connection you already have to this wider realm. You do this by cultivating your intuitive abilities, through practice using the proper technique. You will be able acquire this useful information, use it to become more aware of your patient's condition and thereby be able to plan and give a more effective and beneficial treatment. It is the development of your intuitive ability that will make possible your reception of this information.

The technique that you will use to receive this intuitive information is to perform an intuitive reading, and the steps are described below. This technique effectively assists you in asking for and receiving the desired information, and provides a beginning to a process that will become (after a little practice) the effortless reception of the information you need to heal. As you practice, you will find that your receptive ability will progressively increase and become more accurate, and you will naturally receive more information as you work.

The first step in learning to do intuitive readings is to understand how your mind works to obtain this information. The human mind is often thought to be composed of two differing functions: the intellect, or rational mind, which thinks along specific avenues of thought, and the intuitive mind (or intuition), which is able to access information from the larger realm of intuitive awareness. These two functions correspond (not perfectly, but in an essential way) to the two cerebral hemispheres, and each has its part to play in life, by virtue of its unique abilities. The rational mind, corresponding to the left hemisphere, is deductive, active, concentrates, and assists us in living in this world. It excels at focusing on specifics—at formulating, analyzing, interpreting things and taking specific action. The intuitive mind, corresponding to the right hemisphere, is expansive, passive, receptive, and possesses an inner awareness beyond time and space. It excels at receiving impressions and coming to intuitive understanding of things and is able to access information from the wider realm of awareness—it is our personal connection to this realm.

These functions of your mind are termed the *active principle* (the rational mind) and *receptive principle* (intuitive mind), and you use them in a certain way to obtain intuitive information. You use the active principle, with its ability to focus and formulate, to ask for the information that is desired—to focus the awareness upon the subject of the inquiry. The active principle is then "dropped," or left behind, so that the receptive principle may receive the information desired. Before the information comes, the rational mind (active principle) focuses the attention and intention, and then control is relinquished, so that your intuitive mind (receptive principle) may effortlessly receive the needed information. You can practice this method of intuitive reading—asking for and receiving information about energetic defects in your patient's aura and chakras—as follows:

Exercise 2-C: Intuitive Reading: Sensing Simple Energetic Defects of the Aura and Chakras

1. Before beginning a healing treatment, and with your patient lying down on your treatment table, stand with your eyes closed.
2. Imagine in your mind's eye the shape of your patient's body—a body outline. Focus your awareness on a "blank" outline of your patient's body alone, allowing all other thoughts and emotions to become unimportant. Create this shape in your mind. Do this with the awareness that you will shortly receive information on the energetic defects that may be present in your patient's aura and chakras. This concentration on the body outline will probably require a little effort, at least while learning. For a short moment let your attention concentrate and focus on this shape alone.
3. Then *release* all effort, *relinquish all control*, and open yourself up to effortless reception of information that will just come. Let your mind drift. Let go of all thoughts and preconceptions and suspend your thinking. Do not strive to "see" anything. You may still "see" the body outline, although now other information will appear as patterns upon it—blotches or patterns on the body, fuzzy areas or other appearances in the aura, colors, or in many other ways. Let whatever comes just come, without placing any judgment or thinking bias upon it. Just see whatever is coming effortlessly. It is not the same as pretending to see, or as seeing with the physical eyes, it is "seeing" information intuitively, with the "third eye"—information that is seen with your intuitive sight and felt in your whole being.
4. It is not possible to tell you exactly what you will "see," because you (like all healers) are unique, and each "sees" differently. You must experience and interpret for yourself your own unique perceptions. Perhaps you will "see" a discoloration or blotch over a chakra location, and know, at the same time,

that it is a blocked chakra. Perhaps you will "see" leaks (damaged areas in the lowest field layer which are leaking energy) or tears (more catastrophic "rips" in one or more aura layers, often extending through multiple layers). Perhaps you will "see" areas of dark energy around the head that you know to be auric energy impurities, and at the same time sense a gummy or mucky feel to the energy. Perhaps you will sense energy depletion in the field—a weakness in the energy. Perhaps you will sense and even feel a disjointed, jagged feel to the energy—an overall disturbance of energy flow in your patient's body energy, or in specific pathways. You will sense any or all of these conditions in your patient, in various combinations, depending on your patient's unique condition. You may, at the same time, receive information regarding the proper treatment for these areas. (See Figure 17).

5. As you receive the intuitive information, the important thing to understand is that you will not be "seeing" as you normally do with your eyes. It will be something like remembering a distant memory, or like a dream you have decided to dream, without knowing exactly what it will be. It will not be information you "think," but information which just comes, automatically. You will not be limited, in your reading, to your "seeing," as information may come also through sounds or feelings, even in your own body. It can even be "inner knowings" that come without any quality of sight, sound or words. The information will come in whatever form is best for you.

6. If, while receiving the information, you find yourself distracted by thoughts, or doubt, do not react to them, just drop them and continue receiving the information effortlessly. When you are receiving clear intuitive information you are free from thoughts and emotions—free from the excessive activity of your thinking mind—and are allowing just the information coming from beyond yourself to emerge. This information coming from the realm of wider awareness has a different "flavor" or a different feel than the thoughts from your own mind. You must learn for yourself how this difference feels.

This technique for performing an intuitive reading will take just a moment or two, before beginning a healing treatment, and you may repeat it for a second or third time, if you feel it would benefit, although once will often be enough, especially after you have gained some experience in this basic technique. Whether performing one round of this technique, or several, allow all the information coming to begin to integrate into an overall understanding of the condition of your patient, as well as inform you of whatever of the various energetic defects we've discussed may be present.

Doing an intuitive reading in this manner allows you to access the potentially unlimited information in the field of pure consciousness, which lies beyond your thinking mind and

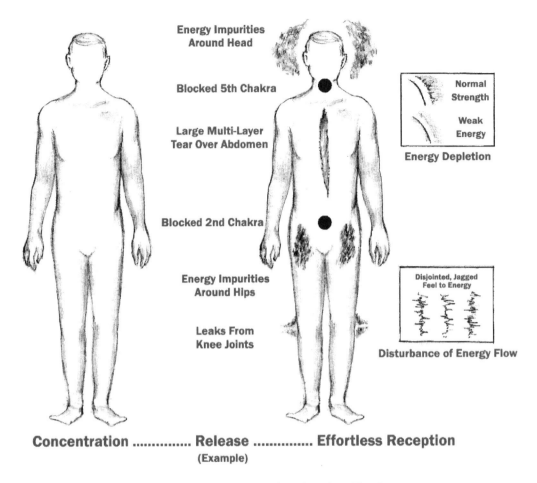

Energy Impurities
Around Head

Blocked 5th Chakra

Large Multi-Layer
Tear Over Abdomen

Blocked 2nd Chakra

Energy Impurities
Around Hips

Leaks From
Knee Joints

Normal
Strength

Weak
Energy

Energy Depletion

Disjointed, Jagged
Feel to Energy

Disturbance of Energy Flow

Concentration .... Release .... Effortless Reception
(Example)

**Figure 17: Intuitive Reading: Sensing Simple
Energetic Defects in the Aura and Chakras**

five physical senses. The basic technique, using the active and receptive principles, is your tool to specify and then receive whatever healing information you need. You focus on just the healing information required, during the active phase—you focus and rest your awareness on that only. Then, in receptive phase you release all effort, relinquish all control, let go of all thoughts and suspend your thinking, to allow the healing information coming from beyond yourself to emerge. These steps are what allow you to become a pure channel for this information. It is a very powerful technique.

This fundamental procedure of doing an intuitive reading is a very useful training tool, and it will be a key element in all the other perceptual techniques you will learn in the remainder of Chios® Level II and in Chios® Level III—you will use this basic technique, with many additions and variations, to completely read the entire energy field of your patient. You will use it to read and see all seven layers of aura and also sense the condition of all seven chakras, in a very complete way. When you become very advanced in the technique, however, you will no longer have to consciously follow these steps. You will direct your awareness to whatever healing information you need, and the information will come automatically. This is true for this basic technique you are learning now, and all the more advanced techniques you will learn later. The key to advancing in the use of the intuitive reading technique is *practice*. It is with repeated practice that your ability to obtain intuitive information will develop to this desirable degree.

As you practice this important ability and perfect its use in the series of Chios® techniques that follow, always simply allow the information to emerge as it is and trust your first impressions. Do not allow your thinking mind to question or modify what emerges. Trust the information you are receiving and learn to trust your intuitive sense—it is as valid a tool as your rational mind.

Beginning to View the Aura

Another primary and very important tool for you the healer is to learn to see the aura. Viewing the aura directly is an important additional source of information, and will often confirm and add to the intuitive information you receive from your intuitive reading. To learn to see the aura can require practice at first, for the eye not accustomed to seeing it, but do not worry if you have not seen an aura before. Virtually everyone who persists in practicing viewing the aura can succeed at it, although it may take a little time. Actually, you already have this ability within you, and just do not realize it. The aura is actually visible to all, although we do not teach ourselves to recognize it, cultivate our ability to see it, or consciously acknowledge its presence. It is very possible that you have had experiences in which some portion of the aura has been visible to you on some level of your awareness but your conscious mind did not recognize it as such. There have often been times when you have been aware of the emotional or mental state of other persons, for example, and have "known" so on a deep level from your unconscious awareness of their aura.

Attempting to view the aura is best done in an environment conducive to viewing it, an environment in which there is not bright or harsh lighting, nor lighting that is too dim. Soft light in a room that is neither very bright nor too dark is ideal. The background color against which you will practice viewing the aura should be neither very dark, nor very light, nor a strong color. A light to medium neutral color will work the best, gray being ideal, yet the background color is not critical. You may wish to cover your treatment table with a suitable color if it is not that color already, so you can more easily view the aura of your patients during treatments. It is always best to use a human subject when you practice viewing the aura, and it is not necessary to use external devices such as special glasses to learn.

It is important to approach viewing the aura with the proper attitude. Attempting to view the human aura is not something to "work at" or concentrate on, in fact, the gaze itself must be soft, you must soften and slightly de-focus your gaze, as though you were looking at something off-center or with the eyes slightly out of focus. This is using your eyes in accordance with the receptive principle—your eyes relax and allow whatever visible information wants to come in to just come, instead of reaching out to notice details. Learning to see the aura is not something you work at but something you *relax to*. It is another form of openness. You should strive before practice to achieve a quiet within your mind also and be devoid of expectation.

Release all preconceptions of what it will look like or feel like to see an aura and be aware that it will be a subtle experience with fine perceptions. Have faith also, and believe that you will see what exists, and do not doubt. Do not allow yourself to fall into the common trap of doubting, and then discrediting what you see. You have learned to trust your first intuitive impression when practicing intuitive readings, trust your impressions now in your efforts to learn to see the aura.

There is a Chios® technique that will assist you in beginning to learn to view the aura—the "glancing technique." In learning to see it you will use the same basic concepts you employed in learning to perform intuitive readings. In learning to view the aura, you will use a similar alternation between active and receptive principles. You will concentrate (with the active principle) upon the shape of the area over which you wish to see the aura (either a part of the body or the entire body), as you see it with your eyes. You will then release (into the receptive principle) to allow impressions of the aura to form in your mind's eye, at first, and then will attempt to confirm this intuitive impression with your physical eyes. It is easier to learn to see the aura in this way, because *the aura is seen first with the mind's eye*, and then with the physical eyes. To learn to see the aura in this way makes perception easier and serves to perfect the ability. In actuality, as you become more and more able to see the aura you will see it with the mind's eye in conjunction with the physical eyes.

The first portion of the aura you will probably be able to see is the 1st layer of aura, or etheric body. It will appear to you as a light gray, light blue, or colorless "haze" around the surface of the body, from one-half inch to an inch or so above the skin surface. This haze is a superphysical light, a very fine perception, and may not appear the same as a physical light would. If you approach viewing the aura with the proper attitude, you should find that it is not very difficult to begin to see this first layer.

It is sometimes easiest to learn to see this first layer of aura by attempting to view it around specific parts of the body. The exercise below is a good start at perceiving the etheric layer, and may assist you in viewing this 1st layer of aura around your hands. To see this 1st layer around your hands:

Exercise 2-D: Viewing the Aura Around Your Hands

1. With your eyes open, hold out one of your hands (perhaps your right hand) in front of you with fingers gently spread, and relaxed, palms toward you. Concentrate—gaze for a brief moment, with your active mind, on the outline shape of your hand and the area immediately around it. Just your hand, and the area immediately around it, should occupy your attention.

2. Now release; relax into receptive phase as you have learned to do, while at the same time glancing away from your hand to an area of empty space, to the side. Allow an impression to form in your mind's eye—let your mind's eye perceive in the same way you did when learning to receive intuitive information with your eyes closed (yet now with your eyes remaining open). Trust your first impression. Notice that an impression can form in your mind's eye independently from whatever your physical eyes are looking at. What impression do you get in your mind's eye? Do you "see" anything around your hands—like a fuzziness, a haze or a layer of light surrounding your hands?

3. Now, with your gaze softened, de-focused and relaxed, look back at your hand with your physical eyes and try to see the aura around your hands with your physical eyes, too. Try (effortlessly) to confirm with your physical eyes what you have seen in your mind's eye. (See Figure 18).

4. Repeat this cycle several times, to begin to allow a stronger impression to form in your mind, and perhaps make the aura around your hand easier to see. Remember: seeing the aura is a subtle experience. Do not doubt, and do not discredit what you see.

After attempting to view the aura around your hand in this way, call in the energy using symbols (using steps 1 to 4 of Exercise 2-B: Calling In the Energy With Symbols), to bring in the energy more powerfully into your hand, feeling it build. Then repeat the glancing technique again, now, using steps 1 to 4 above, to attempt to see the aura around your hand. Perform several rounds, allowing impressions to form. What do you see? Is there any difference between the apparent size or intensity of the aura around your hand? Did

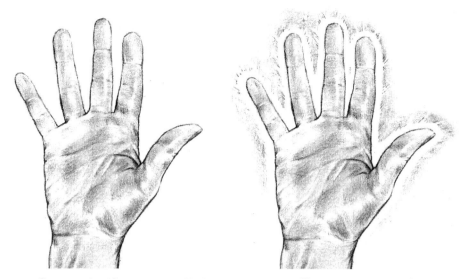

Concentration .... Release .... Effortless Reception

Figure 18: Learning to View the Aura

bringing in the energy into your hand make the aura easier to see? By calling in the energy, you intensified the intensity of the aura around your hand. This may make the aura around your hand bright and more easily visible. Try using this technique to look at the aura around both of your hands after calling in the energy—can you see the light around them?

It is also possible to practice seeing the aura around other specific parts of the body, especially the head, where the etheric layer is sometimes also easily visible. This is an excellent next step in your practice, after you have become able to see the aura around your hands. Repeat the glancing technique once again, using steps 1 to 4 of Exercise 2-D above, but this time using the head of a patient or friend. Can you see the aura around the head? This is not difficult to learn to do with a little practice. Practicing this basic glancing technique at various times throughout the day will serve to assist you in gaining the ability to see this first layer of aura. After gaining some success in this effort, it is time to attempt to view the entire first layer of aura of your patient, prior to treatment:

Exercise 2-E: Viewing the Aura Around the Body of Your Patient

1. With your eyes open, have your patient lie flat on your treatment table, arms at his or her sides. Now, gaze with your "active mind" at the outline shape of your patient's body and the area just above the body surface (where the 1ˢᵗ layer of aura should be), for a brief moment.

2. Then release into the receptive phase, while at the same time glancing away at an area of empty space, to the side, and allow yourself to become aware of what your mind's eye perceives. What do you see in your mind's eye? You might still see the shape of your patient's body in your mind's eye, but is there perhaps something around or near it—a shell, a haze or a layer of dim light near the surface of the body?

3. After getting some impression of your patient's 1st layer of aura, in your mind's eye, look back at your patient with your physical eyes—with your gaze softened and in the receptive phase. Do not strive to see anything—just relax, de-focus your eyes, and allow whatever visual impression is forming just come. Do any of the impressions that formed in your mind's eye appear to your physical eyes as well?

4. Repeat this cycle several times, each time giving yourself a brief moment for an impression to form in your mind's eye. This is a bit like taking a quick glance into a darkened room, and then looking away—after some number of rapid glances, you will begin to get an impression of the room that lingers in your mind, after such glances. It is in this way that you will get some impression, in your mind's eye, of the aura of your patient. Then look back with your physical eyes, to see if you can view with your physical eyes what you are seeing in your mind's eye. If you remain completely open, it is possible that you will begin to gain some sense of the energetic defects in the aura of your patient, as you practice.

It is with this repeated glancing, with the use of the active and receptive principles, that an impression will form in your mind's eye, and it will require practice for more than a general impression to form, and especially for the aura to then begin to appear to your physical eyes. Do not be afraid to invest a little time in this practice. Virtually everyone who invests a little time to practice this technique learns to see this 1st layer of aura.

After you have succeeded in seeing the 1st layer of aura (the etheric body) of your patient, it is possible that with time you may begin to see the colors of the emotional body, the 2nd layer of aura. During your attempts to view the aura, you may, as you release into receptive phase and glance away, have the impression of a certain color over some part of your patient's body, in your mind's eye. You may not think that your eyes see anything, but in your mind's eye you may see a certain area over your patient's body and have the sudden impression, "yellow!" Do not discount this impression, for this is the beginning stage of becoming aware of colors in the aura, and if you effortlessly maintain your openness to this perception, you will at some point begin to glance back and see the color with your physical eyes. It will be a very fine perception—it is very subtle at first—but it will be real. Trust your impressions of color, and you will find that you saw more than you consciously realized. It may take some time and much practice before you are able to glance back and gain some vision of the colors of the aura around your patient.

For now, just let the colors come. Continue your practice, and you may eventually see various colors around the body surface, and specific details as well. First, in your mind's eye, and then, with much practice, perhaps with your physical eyes also. Do specific darkened or colored regions appear? Patterns? You are beginning to see the colors of the second layer of aura, the emotional body. You may see movement in the patterns or colors.

Remember that the aura is not something that is seen with the eyes alone. You may look at a hand, for example, and see patterns that have a shape, form and movement, but you may not see them in the same way that you would see a table or chair because the colors and patterns are not seen only with your eyes. If the awareness required to see the aura was a product of the physical eyes alone, everyone would always see auras. You will begin to see the aura and its phenomena with your mind's eye, and then begin to see it with your physical eyes, too. As you begin to see the aura with your mind's eye, you will detect everything you imagine you should see with your physical eyes, and there is ultimately no difference in these two kinds of seeing. In Chios® Level III you will learn an expansion and refinement of the basic "glancing technique" that will enable you to see—first in your mind's eye and then eventually with your physical eyes—all seven layers of the aura.

As you learn to view the aura, you should integrate what you see with the intuitive information you receive during your intuitive reading of your patient. Consider the intuitive reading, the aura viewing, the passing of hands and the other ways you will receive information, not as separate techniques, but as part of a single continuous process of perceiving the energy field of your patient. You may wish to begin your healing treatments with just the intuitive reading, using just the body outline, as you begin learning. This may make it easier for you to gain the information you need to give treatments, in the beginning. You might then proceed to also attempting to view the aura, at the beginning of your treatments, using the glancing technique above. It is also possible to combine the two techniques, perhaps after you have had some success in viewing the aura, so that you concentrate on your patient's body with your eyes open, and then release and glance away, to see in your mind's eye the aura of your patient and whatever energetic defects may appear. You can then look back with your physical eyes to attempt to confirm and the information you received in your mind's eye. You can use the intuitive information appearing in your mind's eye to plan treatment and incorporate your own visual viewing as it develops. These are all steps—stages in a single process of learning to see and assess the health of your patient's aura. You may use whatever form of reading is best for you, given your own abilities at the particular time.

If you are attempting to corroborate your intuitive information with your aura viewing, it is important to understand that, at first, the two information sources may not convey identical information. This is because you may be receiving intuitive information on energy defects in the aura that have not yet become visible to your physical eyes. The intuitive methods are a starting point, and entry, into viewing the aura directly—it is good to eventually gain the ability to see the energy field directly with your eyes.

It is ideal to use your intuitive and aura viewing abilities all throughout the treatment, employing them later, as well, after taking your initial readings and beginning to treat. You may see that these two techniques are really the same, and that there is really no difference between seeing with the mind's eye and with the physical eyes—they are one. It is not necessary to incorporate direct viewing of the aura in your treatments at all, at least while you are learning Chios® Level II, but it is an excellent skill to begin to practice and will prepare you for Chios® Level III and the advanced aura viewing techniques. All that is important is that you do what makes it easiest for you to sense and learn.

Refining the Practice of the Passing of Hands

Now that you have learned to perform intuitive readings to obtain intuitive information, and begun learning to see the aura with your physical eyes as well, you will refine your use the passing of hands technique and then employ it as your third main information source for becoming aware of your patient's treatment needs. You will take the results of all three sources of information and integrate them into an interpretation of your patient's needs. You will do this, not in an exclusively rational way, but in a manner through which each information source, and all of them, work together to give an awareness of the condition of your patient that will form in your whole being.

In Chios® Level I you began to practice the passing of hands. It is worth discussing the passing-of-hands technique further, however, so you can be sure you are practicing it with maximum effectiveness. Pass your hands only over the front of your patient's body, but including the limbs, and all around the head area. They are passed palm facing downwards, with the fingers spread slightly. Your hands should be relaxed, as if resting, so that they are receptive to the sensation of the energy. Notice how this is similar to the idea of "receptive phase," as you have learned it. They should remain about four to five inches above the body surface of your patient, and should be moved slowly, approximately two to three inches per second, while sensing the energy.

The delicate sensations you may feel as you pass your hands over your patient's body might manifest as a hot, cold, attracting ("dip") or repelling ("bump") feeling in certain areas, or in some other way. You will commonly feel such sensations over areas that harbor the energetic defects we have recently discussed. The sensation in your hands is not necessarily related to the type of energetic defect being sensed by your hand, however. It is the impressions that emerge in your whole being that will inform you of the nature of the energetic defect you may be sensing, as you pass your hands over certain areas. It is important to remain free of any preconceptions of what you may sense, during the passing of the hands. Once again, openness is the key: release any expectations you may have, and you will then be free to sense the energy as it is and receive these impressions.

The fingertip sweep exercise you practiced in Chios® Level I began to make you aware of the subtle sensations of the energy as you sense it with your hands. There is another exercise you may practice now that will help you in *Tuning Hand Sensitivity*—the sensitivity your hands have when sensing the energy—and refining your ability to practice the passing of hands technique. Here is this beneficial exercise:

Exercise 2-F: Tuning Hand Sensitivity

1. With your eyes open, call in the energy using the symbols, using steps 1 to 4 of Exercise 2-B: Calling In the Energy With Symbols.
2. Now hold both of your hands out in front of you, relaxed, with palms open and fingers slightly spread, one palm facing upwards and the other palm facing downwards and over it.
3. Then, pass your palms over each other, at about the same relative speed as when you pass them over the body of your patient (two to three inches per second), and with the palm surfaces four to five inches apart. Do not try to figure out whatever you may be sensing as you practice this exercise—just pass them over each other while remaining open to the sensation and experiencing it with your entire being. You are passing each of your hands, over the other hand. (See Figure 19).
4. You can then reverse your hands, so that the hand that was above becomes the hand below, and vice versa. Pass your palms over each other again, in just the same way as before.

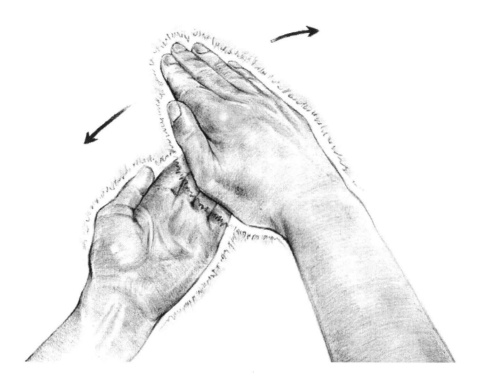

Figure 19: Tuning Hand Sensitivity

This is a "feeling" exercise, and a very experiential one—you are sensing and experiencing things you may not be fully aware of, in your conscious awareness, as you perform it. When you practice this exercise you are tuning your sensitivity—you are practicing the integration, at a deep level, of the delicate sensations the energy produces in each of your palms and also the entire perception that it forms in your whole being. You are "scanning" each of your hands with the other hand; each hand is "reading" the other hand. You are comparing, refining and integrating the "separate" sensations in your hands with your whole being. This exercise will increase the sensitivity and capability of your hands.

After you have practiced this exercise for a bit, to tune your sensitivity, you may also use this concept of comparing and integrating the sensations in your hands to examine the energy field of your patient. To do this, while practicing the passing of hands, first pass one hand by itself over a given area in your patient's energy field where sensation is detected, then pass the other hand over the same area. One hand may feel a sensation, and then the other hand may feel something slightly different. This experience will expand your sense of your patient's energy, as if gaining more perspective. Do not try to mentally figure out the differing sensations, however; simply allow the experience to give you a more complete intuitive understanding of your patient's energy that (once again) emerges in your whole being. As before, you are "tuning" your sensitivity, increasing your sensitivity and understanding of the energies, but you are not merely interpreting the sensations with your mind.

You can then experiment with other variations of the passing of hands, to "scan" each area of your patient's body. You can keep both your hands close together, passing them together over a given area of your patient's body, at the same time. You can even move your hands over different areas of your patient's body, at the same time. There is not any particular advantage to any of these alternate methods of passing the hands, but it is wise to experiment a little, with the passing of hands technique, because you may find a method that particularly suits you. Often it is easiest and best to work with a single hand at a time, but you should do what makes it easiest for you to sense.

As you examine your patient using the passing of hands technique, open your sensitivities to your patient's energies. Try to sense each area of your patient's energy field where the flow is disturbed. For each area, then "merge" with the sensations in your hands and your patient's energy field, at that location. Become one with the energy field of your patient, in each area, and you will receive intuitive impressions about the energetic defects that exist there. These impressions will then emerge in your whole being, as you "scan" each area with your hands.

It is especially wise to pass your hands over whatever areas your intuitive reading and/or aura viewing has indicated an energetic defect may exist in order to gain this additional information. Use the passing of hands to substantiate and add to your intuitive reading and your viewing of the aura. Combine and compare the information you get from all three sources. Should your hands give you information that is not confirmed by your intuition or physical eyes, do not discount it, however. Your hands are accurate "scanners" of the energy in your patient's energy field, and they may sometimes indicate conditions not revealed by your intuitive reading or physical sight. This is true for your patient's entire energy field, and especially the chakras: passing your hands over chakras will often give you important information not highlighted by your intuitive reading or physical vision.

Although you may, while you learn, practice the intuitive reading, aura viewing and passing of hands as a separate steps at the beginning of your treatments, there is no reason why they cannot be performed at various times, as needed—alternating from one information source to the others to explore and confirm your perceptions, all throughout treatment. These are perceptual tools for you to use, in whatever way and at whatever time is best for you.

Integrating an Interpretation of Treatment Needs

After calling in the energy using symbols at the beginning of treatment, you will use your three perceptual tools—performing an intuitive reading to obtain intuitive information, viewing the aura, and passing the hands—to sense and then integrate information on the energetic defects present in your patient's energy field. All three sources of information are compared with each other and used together, to obtain a complete and overall understanding of your patient's condition, and the result is a deep knowledge of your patient's energy field that emerges in your whole being. The impressions come at a deep level and integrate into a deeper knowing. This process begins as you start each healing treatment but continues throughout.

As you practice and gain experience using these perceptual tools, you will begin to be able to discriminate between normal, healthy conditions in your patient's energy field, and unhealthy ones. Unhealthy conditions in the aura and chakras will always have a different feel and a different appearance than normal, healthy energies. You will always use this *unhealthy feel or unhealthy appearance* as a prime indicator of energetic defects in your patient's energy field. You will find that healthy energies in the aura, for example, will feel smooth, healthy and clear as you pass your hands over them, and will appear as clear, bright colors when you learn to see them. Unhealthy energies will feel unhealthy, gummy or mucky as you pass your hands over them, and will also appear as dark and unhealthy as you see them during your intuitive reading and as you view the aura. Healthy chakras will have a sensation of health and energy associated with them when you pass your hands over them, but with blocked or diseased chakras you will feel an unhealthiness to their energy and that it ends abruptly where it should flow—a stoppage in the energy that flows upward through the chakra and into it from outside. You may even sense or see darkness or impurity in an unhealthy chakra—a blackened, muddied or smeared appearance accompanying this unhealthy feel. This sense of unhealthiness will be easier to sense, after a little practice—you must be clear and open to it—but it will always be a very important indicator to you of areas that require treatment.

Blocked chakras will usually be first sensed during your intuitive reading, when you "see" a discoloration or blotch over a chakra location, and know, at the same time, that it is a blocked chakra. You will likely "see" a blackened, muddied or smeared appearance to the chakra's energy, during your intuitive reading, but it will be seldom that you are able to see blocked chakras while viewing the aura with your physical eyes. You will often be able to confirm a blocked chakra with the passing of hands, however—the chakra will feel unhealthy and you will sense the stoppage and "blockedness" of the energy. Blocked 4th, 5th and 6th chakras are very common, while blocked 7th, 2nd, 3rd and 1st chakras are progressively less so. You will notice that some chakras will be chronically blocked on certain patients, while other chakras will be blocked occasionally, varying with the life circumstances of your patient. They are corrected using a Chios® technique called *Unblocking Chakras*.

Leaks and tears in the aura layers will usually be first sensed during your intuitive reading as well. Leaks will usually appear as a "jet" of energy flowing out from the body, usually near the knees, shoulders, neck, elbows or ankles. You may, after practice viewing the aura, be able to see these "jets" of outwardly-flowing energy on the 1st (etheric) layer with your physical eyes. When passing your hands over them you will additionally almost always be able to feel leaks, as energy flowing in an unlikely direction (outwards). Tears are usually seen, during your intuitive reading, as rips in the field layer or layers. During the passing of hands tears are felt more as a complete "break" or openness in the aura layers—like a "hole." Tears are often found over the abdomen, including large tears that extend through several (or many) layers of aura. When you sense a large tear, you can pass your hands at levels successively higher above the body, at four to five inch increments, as an aid to sensing the location and extent of affected aura layers. Tears can also occur over any other area, including the face and any of the chakras. With both leaks and tears you will, during the passing of hands, get a sense of a break or rupture in the harmonious flow of energy—an unhealthy feel to its flow. Leaks and tears, although differing in these ways, are treated with the same basic technique, which in Chios® is referred to as *Sealing Leaks and Tears*.

Auric energy impurities, like blocked chakras and leaks and tears, will also usually be first sensed during your intuitive reading. You will "see" areas of dark energy around certain areas of the body that you know to be auric energy impurities, and this dark energy can appear as clumps of material or as fuzzy, cloudy or otherwise discolored regions. As you view the aura, you may (as with tears) not be able to see auric energy impurities with your physical eyes at first, but only after much practice. You will nevertheless find them fairly easy to confirm with your passing of hands, during which you will feel a sticky, gummy, mucky and generally unhealthy sensation over these areas. As with blocked chakras and leaks and tears, auric energy impurities will usually have this "unhealthy" feel to them as you practice the passing of hands over them. This will feel like heaviness, discord or impurity—excess energy material in a place where it is not supposed to be. Usually, passing your hands four to five inches above the body will suffice, to confirm the presence of auric energy impurities, but when you sense that they are present further above the body surface you can pass your hands at successively higher levels above the body, at four to five inch increments, as an aid to sensing the location and extent of aura layers that harbor the impurities. These impurities are commonly found around the head, face, shoulders, torso, hips and other areas. They also occur over chakras. The Chios® technique for removing these auric energy impurities is *Aura Clearing*.

Energy depletion can often be sensed during your intuitive reading, as an absence of the energy, a lack of robustness in the overall feel or appearance of the energy field. During your viewing of the aura you may also notice that the brightness of the aura of your patient seems low—that the first layer (and higher layers, if you have begun to see them) seemed dimmer and harder to see than usual. This condition will cause a weakness and dimness of the aura, on all its levels. As you practice the passing of hands, you will sense a lack of vitality in the body energy, and thereby confirm your perceptions. While energy depletion usually affects the entire aura, sometimes this dimness and lack of vitality will occur only in certain areas of the aura, usually at the extremities (the lower legs or arms). In Chios®, energy depletion is corrected through a technique known as *Aura Charging*.

Disturbance in energy flow is usually not sensed visually, during your intuitive reading, but you may nevertheless receive an impression of overall disharmony in your patient's body energy—you will get this specific intuitive information even though it does not come visually. You will almost never be able to see this condition while viewing the aura with your physical eyes, either (although this is possible). During the passing of hands, however, you may very well experience a disjointed, jagged or unbalanced feel in the energy flow over the entire body. You may sense, in your entire being, an uneasy, unpleasant or uncomfortable sensation, something like the sensation that screeching on a blackboard presents to your sense of hearing. This disturbance in energy flow is often global—affecting the entire body—but can also occur in specific areas or pathways, which you may "see" with your intuition, especially if you are already familiar with the pattern of the energy channels in the body (from your other studies). This condition of disturbance in energy flow is corrected through a Chios® procedure known as *Correction of Energy Flow*.

After coming to a good understanding of the energetic defects in your patient, you will then proceed with treatment. The various techniques that you will use, and the proper method of their practice, are detailed in the remaining sections of Chios® Level II. You should learn and master these techniques one at a time. You can incorporate these techniques into your healing treatments at whatever pace is best for you, however: you can learn one (or a few) and then incorporate them into your treatments, or study and learn them all and then incorporate all. Do whatever is best for you, and your own preferred learning style. Enjoy your learning and practice of these powerful techniques to heal the energy field of your patient!

Sealing Leaks and Tears in the Aura

During energy healing treatments, it is often beneficial to your patient to perform the healing techniques in a certain order. As you begin to use specific techniques to heal the energetic defects in your patient's energy field, it is a good idea to first repair any leaks or tears you have detected. The Chios® technique for sealing leaks and tears repairs the affected layer(s) of aura, brings back the field integrity and prevents the energy loss and vulnerability of the energy field that would otherwise remain. This is an excellent foundation for further healing work.

Sealing of leaks and tears is performed by moving one of your hands over the region where you have detected the leak or tear, in a position similar to the passing of hands, yet with some important differences. Where the passing of hands is a receptive technique—you simply open yourself to the sensations and intuitive impressions that come—sealing leaks and tears is an active technique. You will use your power of visualization, in a specific way, to *seal* each leak and tear you have detected. The same basic technique is used for both leaks and tears, but with some important differences. Leaks generally occur on only the 1ˢᵗ layer of aura, in localized regions. Tears often occur on multiple layers, in the aura, and are longer "rips" in the layers. The steps for sealing leaks and tears are therefore given separately.

To seal each leak you have detected, follow these steps:

Exercise 2-G: Sealing Leaks in the Aura

1. With your eyes open, and your patient lying down in front of you on your treatment table, hold one of your hands over the first leak you wish to seal, in the same general position as during the passing of hands (palms about four to five inches above the body), but with your fingers gently held together, palms open and held flat (instead of relaxed, as in the passing of hands). Begin with your right hand, as you learn this technique (whether you are right-handed or left-handed), the right hand is "dominant" and more active with the energy in most people.

2. Now begin to slowly move your hand in a gentle back-and-forth or circular motion, over the area where you have detected the leak. You will find that your "felt sense," your intuition, will often tell you how to move it. While

moving, your hand should travel at a speed of about two to three inches per second—if it is moved much slower or much faster than this the technique will not be as effective. Because leaks occur over a localized area—usually over joints—your hand will thus move in a small region perhaps half a foot in diameter, over the leak.

3. As you move your hand all over the area in which the leak occurs, begin to seal the leak using your power of visualization. Visualize, sense and become an intense layer of energy, under your hand, as it melds, fuses and seals the leak shut. Really see, in your mind's eye, the weakness or thinness of the energy field at that point being supplemented, resupported and repaired as you move your hand over it. This is an intense, active technique, using your power of visualization—your power of visualization directs the energy flowing through your hand to seal the aura layer at that point.

4. Continue until you sense that the leak has been repaired. This may take from one to three minutes, per leak, but allow your intuitive sense inform you when your repair of the leak is complete.

5. Repeat steps 1 to 4, above, for each leak you have detected in your patient's aura.

6. After you have learned this basic technique, and if you have an affinity for using light in healing, you can modify it for use with the light. For full details see Exercise 2-R: Beginning to Use Light in Healing.

To seal each tear you have detected, follow these steps:

Exercise 2-H: Sealing Tears in the Aura

1. With your eyes open, and your patient lying down in front of you on your treatment table, hold one of your hands over any portion of the first tear you wish to seal, in the same general position as during the passing of hands, but with your fingers gently held together, palms open and held flat (instead of relaxed, as in the passing of hands). Your hands should be at the level, above the body, of the lowest layer of aura affected, at four to five inch increments. If the tear begins on the 2nd layer, for example, your hand will be four to five inches above the body surface. If the tear begins on the 3rd layer, your hands will be eight to ten inches above, and so on. Begin with your right hand, as you learn this technique (whether you are right-handed or left-handed), the right hand is "dominant" and more active with the energy in most people.

2. Now begin to slowly move your hand in a gentle back-and-forth or circular motion, over the tear. You will find that your "felt sense," your intuition, will often tell you how to move it. While moving, your hand should travel at

a speed of about two to three inches per second—if it is moved much slower or much faster than this the technique will not be as effective.

3. As you move your hand over the tear, begin to seal the tear using your power of visualization. Visualize, sense and become an intense layer of energy, under your hand, as it fuses and seals the tear shut. Really see, in your mind's eye, the gash or rip (the tear) in the aura layer at that point being repaired as you meld, fuse and seal it shut (as if you were sewing shut a rip in fabric), as you move your hand over it. (See Figure 20). This is an intense, active technique, using your power of visualization—your power of visualization directs the energy flowing through your hand to seal shut the aura layer at that point. Although you are sealing the tear by moving your hand at the top of this particular layer, focusing your sealing of it at that place, be aware you are not merely sealing this layer, at this level, but sealing all affected layers (including this layer) in the entire area below your hand, all the way down to the body surface. The affected layers exist not just at their top levels, but all the way down to the surface of the body.

4. Proceed along the entire length of the tear, at this level, fusing it shut from one end all the way to the other end. This will take two or three minutes, for a long tear, but only a minute for shorter tears. Continue until you intuitively sense that the tear has been repaired, on this level.

5. If your intuitive reading has indicated that the tear occurs on multiple layers, you must now move your hand up to the next level, four to five inches above the level you just sealed. Seal the tear on this higher level in exactly the same way, using steps 1 to 4 above.

6. If the tear extends to yet higher layers, you must move your hand up to each successively higher layer that the tear occurs and seal that layer, again using steps 1 to 4 above. You will know from your intuition how high tears must be sealed. It is possible for the tear to extend up to any layer of aura. Remain open to your intuition to sense when this is the case, and seal the layers to as high a level as necessary. Your hands should be 12 to 15 inches above the body for the 4th layer, 16 to 20 inches above for the 5th layer, 20 to 25 inches above for the 6th layer and 24 to 30 inches above for the 7th layer.

7. Repeat steps 1 to 6, above, for each tear you have detected in your patient's aura. If the tear is a large tear extending through many layers there will often be only one, but there can be more.

8. After you have learned this basic technique, and if you have an affinity for using light in healing, you can modify it for use with the light. For full details see Exercise 2-R: Beginning to Use Light in Healing.

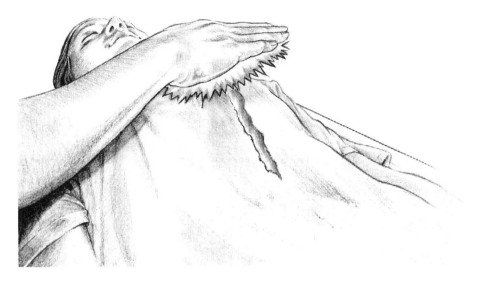

Figure 20: Sealing Leaks and Tears

Sealing of leaks and tears is generally performed using only one hand at a time. Although you may choose to use the right hand, at first, with even a little practice both hands can become equally effective at this technique.

The Importance of Active Openness (Transparency)

Now that you are actually learning specific techniques for healing the energetic defects which you find in your patient's energy field, it is important to briefly reiterate an important aspect of openness—the central quality you the healer must maintain in yourself as you heal. We have discussed at length this openness as it applies to receptivity—the open, receptive quality you maintain in yourself as you use the perceptual tools you have learned to gain information about your patient and his or her energy. You must also remember to maintain openness whenever you practice an active technique to heal these energetic defects. When sealing leaks and tears, for example, as with all the specific healing techniques you will learn in Chios® Level II and then in Chios® Level III, it is important at all times to be open, aware and in a state of unity with your patient and his or her energy field, and not to distance yourself from them and focus just on whatever technique you are using at the time. Although your hands are the instruments you use, when practicing any of these healing techniques, *you are really actively using your whole being through your hands*. You must be open and acting as your whole self, to the entire energy field of your patient, and not just consider that it is your hand alone working with some small area of energy. It is necessary to set aside your self-consciousness of your hand—to forget about yourself and your hand, and seek to instead visualize, sense and become the energy, according to whatever healing technique you are using, at the time. When openness is practiced in this active sense, it is also sometimes called *transparency*. The healing power of pure consciousness will then transmit through you, like light shining through a clear window. Always remember, as you learn and practice each of these techniques, that you perform every aspect of energy healing with your whole being.

Aura Clearing

It is vital to the health of your patient that the flow of energy in his or her aura be free from interference or corruption from stagnant, unhealthy and impure energies that can block its normal, healthy flow. If you have detected such auric energy impurities in the aura of your patient, they may be cleared out and removed using a procedure known as aura clearing.

This technique is performed over whatever areas of the body these auric energy impurities are detected. It removes these energies from the layers of aura in which they have become lodged—often this will be the 1st through 4th layers, buy any layer of aura can be affected. Aura clearing uses your hand (including your fingers) to remove these undesirable energies. When performing this technique, your hands are used to attract these impurities—like a magnet—and then "draw them out" away from the body of your patient, removing them from your patient's aura layers. Your hand draws only the unhealthy auric energy impurities: the energy impurities obey different laws than the healthy energies, and it is only these energy impurities that are drawn to your hand and then removed. The auric energy impurities are simultaneously removed from all aura layers that harbor them. The "drawing out" movement is done in a slow, deliberate manner—you must concentrate on the act during aura clearing. Notice how this technique, like sealing leaks and tears, is also a more active (as opposed to receptive) healing technique. To clear away auric energy impurities that you have detected, follow these steps:

Exercise 2-I: Aura Clearing

1. With your eyes open, and your patient lying down in front of you on your treatment table, place your hand palm-down over the first area to be cleared, with your fingers spread a moderate amount (wider apart than during the passing of hands). Your fingers should extend straight out, level from the

hand, or perhaps be slightly pulled up above level. Note that this hand position is different from the one you use in the passing of hands and also different from the one you use to seal leaks and tears. (See Figure 21). Your hand, at the start of this technique, should usually begin about one inch above the body surface. Begin with your right hand, as you learn this technique (whether you are right-handed or left-handed), the right hand is "dominant" and more active with the energy in most people.

2. Now visualize, sense and become the energy around your hand and fingers expanding and growing strong. Visualize, sense and become this powerful energy around your hand and fingers attracting the dark auric energy impurities from all around it, pulling them towards it and capturing them as they stick to it. Your hand is acting like a magnet, to pull in and capture the cloud of dark energy impurities, which may exist on multiple layers of aura, from all around your hand (including above it, all around it, below it and possibly even below the body surface of your patient). Really see and feel all these energy impurities detaching from the aura of your patient, and being pulled in and sticking to the area around your hand. You are actually using your etheric hand and fingers, to capture the impurities. Your hand and its outspread fingers are a magnetizing, attractive device—like an "energy magnet"—that attracts these impurities and causes them to detach from the area of your patient's aura they are lodged in and instead "stick" to the energy around your hand and fingers.

3. Now begin the "drawing out" motion. With the impurities stuck to the energy around your hand and fingers, draw your hand slowly and deliberately up, starting from one inch above the body surface of your patient, and at the end of the motion perhaps 15 inches above the body, the entire motion taking approximately five seconds. You are detaching and removing these auric energy impurities from the energy field of your patient—visualize, intend and sense them being removed (see Figure 21). They are pulled out and away from your patient's aura, by the upward motion. You are removing part, or all, of a cloud of dark energy impurities that may exist on multiple aura layers. Apart from your patient's body, all these energy impurities lose their charge, their ability to cling to the energy field of your patient. The impurities dissolve, become as dead, and have no further effect on your patient. You must actively visualize all these things, as you perform this technique.

4. After your hand has completed the "drawing out" motion, you should shake your hand—you should "shake off" the impurities and visualize them drawn to and reabsorbed into the earth. Visualize, sense and intend this, and do not allow them to remain around your hand and fingers. Your hand may then be

relaxed, slightly so, so that the fingers slant slightly downwards, and then returned to the correct starting position one inch above the body once again.

5. Repeat steps 1 to 4 above, over the same area, to ensure that all auric energy impurities in that location have been removed. This will usually involve between two and ten motions and take between one and three minutes, in each location, depending on the quantity of energy impurities to be removed there.

6. While you will usually begin the "drawing out" motion approximately one inch above your patient's body, there will occasionally be times that you will feel guided to begin the motion at a higher level—five to six inches above the body surface, or even (very occasionally) up to 10 to 12 inches above. In these cases, perform the technique just as given above, yet with the motion beginning at the higher level and ending higher than before (e.g. beginning five inches above and ending 20 inches above body level). You are removing energy impurities remaining at these higher levels.

7. Repeat this entire technique—steps 1 to 6 above—for every area over your patient's body that you have detected auric energy impurities. After you are done, be sure to "shake off" your hand well, to rid it of any residual negative energies.

Aura clearing is done using only one hand at a time. It may be done with the right hand

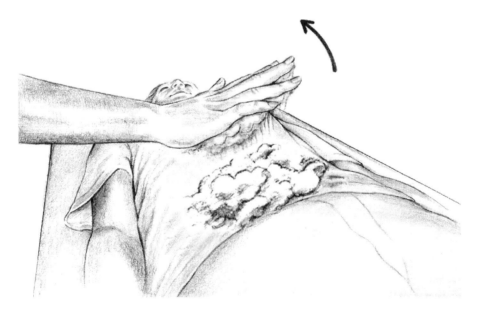

Figure 21: Aura Clearing

in the beginning, if desired, as it is usually somewhat more effective at first, but with experience both hands will usually become equally effective at removing impurities. It is performed with the eyes open.

You will find that aura clearing will sometimes be required over specific chakras fairly often to remove stagnant or discolored energies over them. The 7th, 4th, and 2nd chakras are particularly susceptible to these sorts of stagnant energies, although they can occur over the other chakras, as well. When performing aura clearing over chakras, be aware that you may also be smoothing the energy flow in the chakra, as well as removing impurities. With some chakras you may detect what appears to be a poisoning, and you can correct this by drawing out the impurities and smoothing the flow at the same time. Draw the hands up over the chakra as if you were cleansing and smoothing the flow in a "funnel" of energy.

Unblocking Chakras

It is vital to the energetic health of your patient that the upward flow of energy through the chakra system and the flow of energy into and through each chakra be maintained. If you have sensed that a chakra is blocked—that the energy stops its normal flow through that chakra—it is possible to restore that flow using the Chios® technique for unblocking chakras.

Unlike sealing leaks and tears and aura clearing, which are performed at the beginning of each healing treatment over all areas that require it, unblocking of chakras is performed during the main portion of the treatment itself—during the normal sequence of treatment hand positions that you learned in Chios® Level I. For each chakra that you have sensed requires unblocking, you will channel energy into that chakra, with your hands on the chakra in the same position as you have before, but you will unblock that chakra by also using the following technique:

Exercise 2-J: Unblocking Chakras

1. With your eyes open or closed, and while you are channeling energy into a chakra that requires unblocking, visualize, sense and become the Chios® symbol related to that chakra (see Figure 22) during the full time you channel energy into that chakra.
2. *At the same time* visualize, sense and become the energy that is flowing upwards through the central energy channel, at that chakra point, flowing

through the chakra, the blockage in the chakra being removed as it does so, *and* the energy that flows into the chakra from all around passing easily through it, with any blockage to that flow likewise being removed (see Figure 23).

3. You are really seeing, in your mind's eye—you are actively visualizing, sensing and becoming—not only the Chios® symbol, but the energy flowing freely and clearly in both these ways. With just a little practice it will not be difficult for you to visualize all this, if you visualize, sense and become just the symbol and these two energy flows alone. You will find it easier to visualize the symbol and the chakra clearing with your eyes closed, as you learn. With a little practice you should be able to visualize both the symbol and the energy flows with your eyes open, as you practice this technique. If you have trouble visualizing both things at once—the Chios® symbol, and the energy flowing smoothly through the chakra and clearing the blockage— try making the energy flowing smoothly through the chakra your primary visualization, yet with an awareness that you are also using the symbol. This may make it easier to learn this technique.

4. Repeat steps 1 to 3 above, for each chakra in your patient that you have sensed is a blocked chakra.

5. After you have learned this basic technique, and if you have an affinity for using light in healing, you can modify it for use with the light. For full details see Exercise 2-R: Beginning to Use Light in Healing.

The Chios® symbols are each related to a fundamental pattern of energy flow, as we have discussed, and the progressive energetic nature of the three symbols is related to the seven major chakras in the chakra system as they progress from the more simple physical level, at the bottom, to progressively more spiritual functioning. The 1st, 2nd and 3rd chakras bear a relationship to the Circle (associated with physical earth) in their energetic functioning. The 4th, 5th and 6th chakras bear a relationship to the energetic nature of the Trine (associated with rising above the earth, and spiritual ascension). The 7th chakra bears a close energetic relationship to the Star (associated with spiritual totality). Accessing the energetic nature of these symbols (which corresponds to that of the corresponding chakras) through visualization, combined with the visualization of the energy flows necessary to clear the chakra, provides the effectiveness of this technique. The chakra is cleared: the blockage is removed and the energy flow through it is restored.

If you have perceived that a blockage of the 1st chakra exists, it must be treated in a slightly different way, as placing your hands on the corresponding body area of your patient

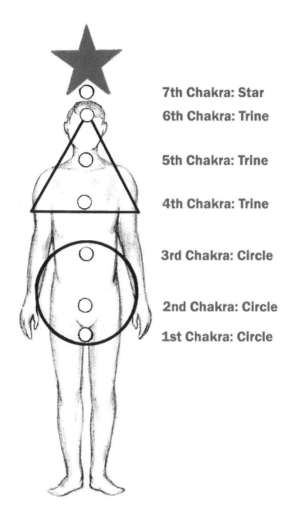

7th Chakra: Star

6th Chakra: Trine

5th Chakra: Trine

4th Chakra: Trine

3rd Chakra: Circle

2nd Chakra: Circle

1st Chakra: Circle

**Figure 22: Chios® Symbols Related to
Chakras and Regions of the Body**

(the genital region) is not done. The hands of your patient, however, are receptive channels for the body energy—there are minor chakras in the palms of the hands—and your patient's hands may be used to treat this chakra. To clear the first chakra:

Exercise 2-K: Unblocking the 1st Chakra

1. Place your hands on your patient's hands, with each of your palms on a palm of your patient. If you are standing to the right of your patient, alongside

your treatment table, your right palm will be placed over the left palm of your patient, and vice versa.

2. Channel the energy into the palms of your patient, while you visualize, sense and become the Circle.

3. *At the same time* visualize, sense and become the energy that is flowing upwards from the earth, flowing through the 1st chakra, the blockage in the chakra being removed as it does so, *and* the energy that flows into the 1st chakra from all around passing easily through it, with any blockage to that flow likewise being removed. This will not be quite as focused a clearing as would be provided with direct hand placement on the 1st chakra, but will assist considerably.

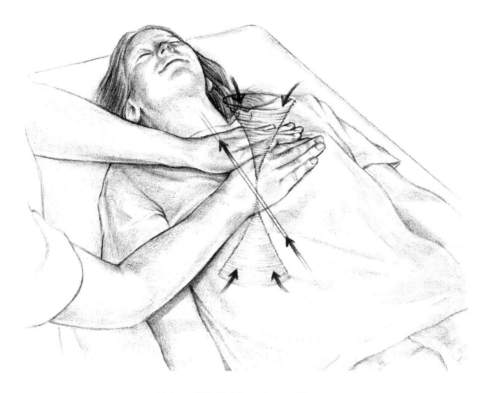

Figure 23: Unblocking a Chakra

The Chios® symbols are also associated with regions of the body. The Circle is associated with the abdomen below the diaphragm, the Trine with the area above the diaphragm up to the third eye, and the Star with the crown of the head. Visualization of the appropriate symbol during energy channeling to supplementary areas may also be done. For example, when treating a problem in the lower abdomen, you may, if you have sensed that it is appropriate, use a visualization of the Circle while placing the hands and channeling energy there. Use of the symbols during treatment of positions other than blocked chakras will not be required on most patients, however, but if you feel guided to use one of the symbols for a particular condition you encounter, use it. It may interest you to know also that while one symbol predominates in each of these body areas, elements of the others are also present.

Aura Charging

Although it does not occur in the majority of patients, energy depletion is a serious condition of weakness in the energy in the entire energy field of your patient and makes your patient more susceptible to diseases and afflictions. This fundamental weakness of energy can also inhibit the ultimate effectiveness of whatever other healing work you perform in your patient's aura and chakras. This condition can be corrected by adding energy to the aura, through a procedure known as aura charging.

You have already been adding energy to the aura of your patient, as you channel energy into the chakras during the sequence of treatment positions you have learned; the energy not only moves into each chakra, but also into the entire energy field (including the area of aura in the general region around that chakra). When the aura is especially weak, however, it is necessary and very beneficial to add larger amounts of energy to the aura in the much more direct and specific manner that aura charging provides. Aura charging provides this supplementation of the life energy in the energy field, and is especially critical for certain patients: those with depression, cancer, AIDS, heart disease and many other serious illnesses. It provides the re-energization and sense of well-being that is necessary for healing these patients. It is also useful for those who are just run down, and may prevent illness and induce well-being in these patients, too. To charge the aura of your patient:

Exercise 2-L: Aura Charging

1. With your eyes open or closed, and your patient lying down in front of you on your treatment table, place your hands on the body of your patient in position 1 (see Figure 24). Your left palm is held directly on your patient's right knee and your right palm directly over the minor chakra in the sole of your patient's right foot.

2. Now channel the energy into your patient, using this hand position, but in a more active way than you usually do during regular energy channeling. Transfer the energy in a more intense way, by intensely visualizing, sensing

and becoming the energy as it intensely radiates into your patient's aura, in this section between your two hands. Visualize a bond between the energy and that section of your patient's aura, as you do so. You are radiating the energy from both of your hands equally. Really see, in your mind's eye, this active radiation of energy, and the bond between energy and aura, as you fill that section of aura with energy. See in your mind's eye, and perhaps with your physical eyes, the aura in this region filling and expanding with energy. (See Figure 25).

3. Continue intensely channeling the energy into this section of your patient's aura, in this way, until you get a sense of completion. This will require one to two minutes. Your intuitive information will inform you when you have radiated enough energy and filled this portion of your patient's aura.

4. Now, move your hands to position 2. Your left palm will now be on your patient's left knee and your right palm directly over the minor chakra in the sole of your patient's left foot. Channel the energy into this section of your patient's aura in exactly the same way given above, until you sense it is complete. You should also get a sense of balance, between this position and position 1—you should sense an equal strength of energy between them, a balance between the two sides of the aura, when done.

5. Continue with all remaining positions, 3 to 11, radiating the energy into each of these sections of your patient's aura in exactly the same way. In each position, your left palm is held at the point on the higher end of your patient's body, your right palm at the point on the lower end. These points are either directly over joints (knee, hip or shoulder joints) or directly over chakras (2nd, 3rd, 4th, 5th or 6th chakras), as shown. Each position should only require between one and two minutes of treatment, although certain positions may require a little longer, depending on your patient's particular needs. In each position that treats a second particular side of the body (positions 2, 4, 6 and 10), be sure to radiate the energy until you obtain a feeling of balance between the two sides. You are leading the energy up the body deliberately, and in such a way that it is balanced on both sides.

As you proceed up your patient's body performing this technique, may see, in your mind's eye and perhaps with your physical eyes, his or her aura fill, brighten and expand. You may feel the energy radiating outward as it fills. It is your intense visualization of radiation of energy, combined with the visualization of the bond between the energy and aura of your patient, which directs the energy to fill and charge the aura in this manner. You may find it easier to have your eyes closed while learning aura charging, but you should find it easy to perform this technique with your eyes open with just a little practice.

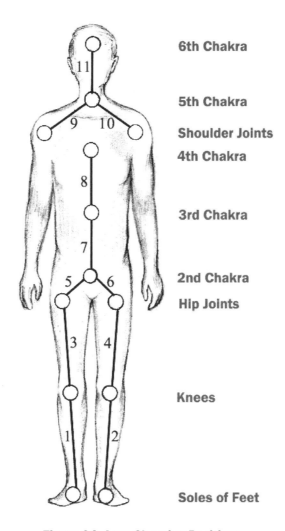

6th Chakra

5th Chakra

Shoulder Joints

4th Chakra

3rd Chakra

2nd Chakra

Hip Joints

Knees

Soles of Feet

Figure 24: Aura Charging Positions

It is sometimes found that only certain regions of the body will exhibit energy depletion. This is not a particularly common condition, nor one remotely as serious as overall (global) energy depletion, but occasionally the extreme portion of the limbs (the lower arms and hands, and/or the lower legs and feet) display a condition of energy depletion, although the overall vitality of the energy field is not particularly low. This condition may be corrected with aura charging of that region only.

For energy depletion in the lower legs, charge from the foot to the knee (as in positions 1 and 2 in the full procedure above), as well as from the knee to the hip joint (as in positions 3 and 4), if you sense it is necessary. For energy depletion in the lower arms, charge each

Figure 25: Aura Charging

arm from the hand to the elbow joint, by placing your right hand palm-to-palm with your patient's hand, and your left palm on the inside of the elbow joint. The arm to the shoulder may be charged on each arm also, if needed. The arms may also be included in this way in a full aura charging treatment, if you feel it wise, yet this is not usually necessary.

Correction of Energy Flow

Disturbance in energy flow is a condition of irregularity or disruption in the pattern of the flow of the energy in the body energy system, which can become erratic, uneven, or even completely disrupted from its normal, healthy paths. This condition can sometimes be of a transient (non-lasting) nature, but it is nevertheless detrimental to the energetic health of your patient and can be a contributing factor to or coincident with various specific diseases and ailments. Disturbance of energy flow is treated by using a Chios® procedure called correction of energy flow:

Exercise 2-M: Correction of Energy Flow

1. With your eyes open or closed, and your patient lying down in front of you on your treatment table, sit or kneel at the head of your patient so that your shoulders are approximately at the level of your patient's head. Facing the crown of your patient's head in this way, hold your hands out in front of you such that your fingers are slightly curved, but with palms open, and with palms facing away from you towards the head and body of your patient. Place your fingertips on the crown of your patient's head, your thumbs pointing down, palms facing directly towards your patient's body (and away from you), but palms not touching the head surface. There should be about a two inch gap between the fingertips of one hand and the fingertips of the other. (See Figure 26).

2. Now visualize, sense and become the Star, while the energy emanates from your hands and flows towards the entire body of your patient. Energy will flow from your palms as well as from your fingertips, even though your palms are not contacting the body surface.

3. *At the same time*, visualize a correction and healing of the entire energy flow in your patient's body. Visualize, sense and become the energy flow in your patient's body becoming regular, even and harmonious, and the energy returning to its correct pathways throughout the body.

4. Send forth the energy for one to two minutes in this manner as you perform this visualization of the Star and a healthy, corrected energy flow. Having your eyes closed may make this visualization easier to practice, at first, but you should then acquire the ability to perform this technique with your eyes open.

5. If you have detected a disturbance of energy flow that is located in only a certain section of your patient's body, a specific channel or area where the energy may have become deviated from its normal, healthy patterns (especially if you are familiar with energy meridians from your other healing studies and sense these specific pathways), visualize the Star while you also visualize, sense and become these energy pathways corrected. Visualize yourself as merging with whatever energy flow has been disrupted from its normal path, and then visualize, sense and become the flow as moving the proper way.

6. After you have learned this basic technique, and if you have an affinity for using light in healing, you can modify it for use with the light. For full details see Exercise 2-R: Beginning to Use Light in Healing.

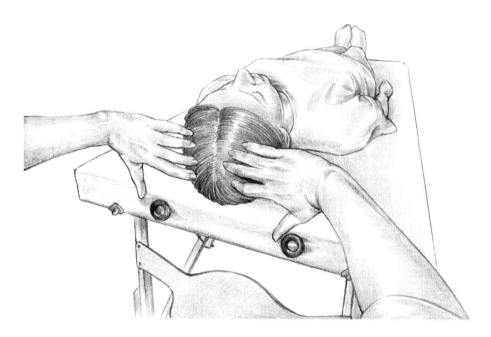

Figure 26: Correction of Energy Flow

flow in the body of your patient, acts to focus the healing power of pure consciousness through the 7th chakra (which also corresponds to this higher realm) and into your patient, providing the large and powerful correction of energy flow needed.

Additional Treatment Positions

Now that you have studied three important perceptual tools for detecting five basic energetic defects in your patient, and powerful techniques for correcting those defects, it's time to add a few additional hand positions you may need to treat further specific situations which you may encounter with your patients. Not every patient will need energy channeling using these additional hand positions, and so with many or even most patients you will not need to include these additional hand positions in your treatment, but if you receive intuitive information that your patient would benefit, or otherwise sense the need for one or more of them, incorporate one or more of them into your healing treatment in the places recommended in Appendix #2 – Outline of Treatment Procedures (Chios® Levels II and III).

The Shoulder Position

The shoulder position is a hand position (your hands on your patient's shoulders, channeling energy into your patient) that is not used to correct any specific energetic defect in your patient's energy field, but is included here because it serves an unrelated yet potentially very beneficial purpose. You will sometimes encounter patients who are not merely unfamiliar with energy healing treatments (having perhaps never had one before) but are also anxious or nervous at the very prospect of receiving one. When you sense this in your patient—often a patient you are seeing for the first time—use this position at the beginning of treatment. Channeling energy into your patient, using this position, has the effect of relaxing and creating trust in them. Perform this technique as follows:

Exercise 2-N: The Shoulder Position

1. Standing at the head of your patient, place your hands on his or her shoulders, such that each hand gently rests between the neck and the outer end of the shoulder.
2. Channel the energy for several minutes, allowing the energy to transfer equally through both your arms and into both your patient's shoulders. Allow yourself to relax, too, and begin to bond with your patient and sense the state of his or her energy field.

The shoulder position is not a necessary position for healing, but you should use it when you sense it will benefit. It is a good starting position, not only if you have noted that your patient is somewhat anxious or nervous, but if you yourself feel a little difficulty in beginning to bond with and sense your patient's energy field.

Using the Star on the 7th Chakra

The Star is used on the 7th chakra to unblock that chakra, when necessary, but you may also use the Star while channeling energy into the 7th chakra during the normal course of hand positions, if you receive intuitive information or otherwise sense it would benefit your patient. The 7th chakra, which corresponds to our spiritual totality, is powerfully cleared and healed by using the Star in this way, and this has far-reaching benefits to your patient at every level. To use the Star on the 7th chakra:

Exercise 2-O: Using the Star on the 7th Chakra

- Visualize the Star while treating the 7th chakra during the normal sequence of hand treatment positions. It is not necessary to visualize the energy flow becoming unblocked (as you would do if performing the unblocking technique on this chakra)—merely visualize, sense and become the Star while you channel energy into the 7th chakra in the normal way.

This technique acts to clear the whole spiritual totality—the whole being and spiritual process of your patient. The energetic nature of the Star is related to the nature of the 7th chakra, and adds to the effectiveness of treating this chakra and specifically connecting your patient to his or her spiritual essence. Clearing it this way is a fine analogy for the whole healing process. This is an effective addition to your healing treatment.

Grounding

Some patients will come to you with the specific need of being better grounded to the physical world. You will usually sense this through intuitive information. These patients—often victims of past trauma, and hence dissociation from the physical—will benefit greatly from grounding. Grounding adds earth energy to your patient's aura and creates a bond between your patient and the earth, to assist your patient in remaining connected to the physical world. It is also simply refreshing and balancing to your patient, and in a sense may be thought of as a simpler version of aura charging in that energy is added to the aura and the aura is balanced (although it does not provide the more profound and intense charging of the aura that occurs during aura charging). While aura charging is only required on some patients, however, grounding is beneficial to all and is especially important for those who you sense are not fully grounded. Grounding is performed as follows:

Exercise 2-P: Grounding

1. Have your patient lie flat on your treatment table, arms at his or her sides, but on his or her stomach, for this position. Be sure to provide a face cradle to your patient. Now stand at the foot of your patient, as he or she lies on your healing table, and place your hands so your palms rest on the minor chakras in the middle of the soles of your patient's feet.

2. Now channel the energy into your patient, through his or her feet. Intensely visualize, sense and become the energy coming up from the earth, into and through your body, out your hands and into the feet of your patient, filling your patient with energy. Channel the energy equally through both of your arms, and also see the energy intensely filling your patient's body and aura in a balanced way that is equal on both sides.

3. *At the same time*, visualize, sense and become a connection and lasting bond between your patient and the earth.

4. Continue until you get a definite sense of completeness. This should take between two and five minutes.

5. After you have learned this basic technique, and if you have an affinity for using light in healing, you can modify it for use with the light. For full details see Exercise 2-R: Beginning to Use Light in Healing.

Spine Cleaning

There is a central energy channel that runs along the spine: an energy channel that serves as the main conduit for the upward flow of energy through the chakra system. This energy channel is a very important part of the anatomy of the energy field. Often you will unblock chakras, by clearing the upward flow of the energy through whatever chakras require it, but sometimes the flow of energy through this central energy channel can itself become blocked and restricted. Only some patients will exhibit this condition, which is usually revealed to you through intuitive information, but for these patients cleansing and purifying this central energy channel is of great benefit. This is done through a position known as spine cleaning. Spine cleaning is usually performed near the very end of treatment, as follows:

Exercise 2-Q: Spine Cleaning

1. As with grounding, have your patient lie flat on your treatment table, arms at his or her sides, but on his or her stomach, for this position. Standing at the side of your patient, place your left palm over the rear component of your patient's 5th chakra, and your right palm over the rear component of your patient's 2nd chakra.

2. Now channel energy into your patient through both of your arms and hands, equally, and visualize, sense and become the energy washing up and down the spine, in both directions, cleansing and clearing the central energy channel and removing any blocks or impurities that may be present. Each hand's energy travels both up and down from that hand's position: the

energy flowing into the 5th chakra flows downwards to the bottom but also up to the 7th chakra, and the energy flowing into the 2nd chakra flows upwards all the way to the 7th chakra but also down to the 1st chakra. Where the energies from your two hands meet in the middle they do not end, but both energies cross and continue on in both directions, washing and cleansing the entire central energy channel from the 1st chakra to the 7th.

3. Continue until you get a definite sense of completeness. This should take between two and five minutes.

4. After you have learned this basic technique, and if you have an affinity for using light in healing, you can modify it for use with the light. For full details see Exercise 2-R: Beginning to Use Light in Healing.

Becoming More Aware of the Energy During Energy Channeling

Now that you have learned many specific hand positions that are used for channeling energy, it is beneficial to revisit (yet another) important aspect of openness. As you channel energy into your patient using the various hand positions you've learned (whether into your patient's chakras during the normal sequence of treatment hand positions, or during the additional hand positions just discussed), it is good to remain open to and become more aware of the energy as you channel it into your patient. Remember: this energy is active and intelligent. It "knows" all about your patient's energy field and the energetic defects in it that require healing. As you channel energy in these various hand positions, you may experience delicate sensations in your hands and may also receive important intuitive information. Visualize, sense and become the energy, as you channel it, and you may get important information regarding where the energy is flowing, in your patient, the energetic defects that may exist there, and how the defects relate to all other aspects of your patient's condition. Becoming more aware of the energy in this way, as you channel it, is merely another aspect of openness, where you use the holistic interconnectedness of all as a way to effortlessly gain information on all aspects of your patient and his or her energetic condition. You, your patient and the energy are one.

Learning to View the Chakra Colors

Congratulations on your study of Chios® Level II, which is now nearly complete. You have learned many useful techniques that, when incorporated into healing treatments, will allow you to perform powerful energy healing for your patients. Like many healers, you may feel content to practice energy healing at this second Chios® level. To work with the energy, using the many different techniques you have studied in this level, is an extraordinary and valuable endeavor. Or you may find yourself, like other healers, feeling a desire to travel beyond this point. If you do, an additional stage of this great adventure awaits you: the mastery of energy healing. If you choose to proceed beyond this point, you will work not just with the energy, but with *color* and *light*. The realm of the master healer will be your destination. Our healing journey continues, in Chios® Level III, to places we could scarcely have dreamt of when we began. But before we leave Chios® Level II we will explore a small part of this new territory. We will begin to use color and light in our energy healing work.

Our first foray into this new territory shall be to begin to learn to view the chakra colors. As you know, each of the seven major chakras has an associated true color, from red for the 1st chakra up to violet for the 7th. Healthy chakras show a strong, pure healthy glow of their corresponding true color. Colors other than the native true color of the chakra are also commonly present (usually to a lesser extent than the native true color), but these, too, normally display a pure, healthy glow. Diseased chakras, however, display a darkened, discolored, faded, watery or streaked appearance—an unhealthy appearance with colors or hues that are not visually appealing. Healthy and appealing-looking chakra colors indicate healthy conditions, and unappealing and unhealthy-looking colors indicate energetic impurities, in the chakra. It is important to learn to view the chakra colors (with these impurities) so that you know when a chakra is diseased and needs treatment (you will learn many powerful tools for healing chakras in Chios® Level III). For now, begin to learn to see the chakra colors with the following technique:

Exercise 2-R: Intuitive Reading: Learning to View the Chakra Colors

1. With your eyes open, and while performing energy channeling to each chakra, during the normal sequence of treatment hand positions, perform an intuitive reading to look for the true color of that chakra *as it illuminates the skin on the back of your hand*. Concentrate briefly on the surface of the skin on the back of your right hand (which is centered over the middle of the chakra) during the active phase. For a brief moment, look at and focus upon the skin of the back of your hand.

2. Now release into the receptive phase, while glancing away (as when using the glancing technique to learn to view the aura). You may still "see" the skin on the back of your right hand, in your mind's eye, yet may also receive an impression of the chakra's color, either strong and fairly pure or weakened,

darkened or discolored with impurities, on the surface of the skin on the back of your hand. (See Figure 27).

3. Look back now, with your physical eyes, at the top surface of your right hand, to attempt to confirm the color hue you saw, in your mind's eye, with your physical eyes (just as you do while practicing viewing the aura). The general tone of the chakra color, with any impurities or discolorations, will appear as a subtle yet discernible hue, to your mind's eye at first, and eventually to your physical eyes also. The color illuminating your skin is from your patient's chakra field, and penetrates your "solid" hand illuminating the skin on the back surface of it to your subtle sight.

4. As you perform this technique, allow intuitive information to come to you. The colors are intelligent energy and consciousness and may speak to you. You may receive sounds, images or feelings, from both healthy and unhealthy colors, with important information. Begin to be open to the colors, and what they will tell you about your patient's condition.

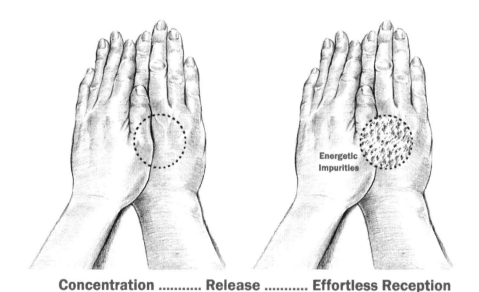

Concentration .... Release .... Effortless Reception

Figure 27: Learning to View the Chakra Colors

You may not see the chakra color at first, it may require substantial practice. After practice, however, you may be able to view the color directly, without looking away, as the chakra color effortlessly appears to your psychic sight. Colors other than the native color of the chakra may also appear—you will learn much more about colors in the chakras, and their meaning, in Chios® Level III.

This is a good technique to begin to incorporate into your treatments. Briefly assess the color of each chakra as you treat it during the regular sequence of hand positions. You will have impressions of the true color of each chakra, as you move from chakra to chakra, but may get differing indications of impurity for each of them. Some chakras in your patient will be basically healthy, and appear such, but other chakras will show indications of diseased functioning. Those chakras that show a poor color hue should be treated with extra energy during the normal sequence of treatment hand positions to help restore their hue. You may be able to view changes in the hue, and work to restore it.

As you become more aware of chakra colors, you may also get information of this sort during your initial assessment of your patient during your reception of intuitive information. Be open to the chakra colors, and you will find that information regarding the strength of their color, and their purity (or impurity), will come to you at various points during treatment. The colors will "speak to you" and inform you (as does the energy) regarding your patient and his or her energetic condition.

Beginning to Use Light in Healing

In addition to beginning to sense the chakra colors, you can also begin to incorporate the use of light in your healing treatments. It is possible that you have already had the natural urge to use light—many healers do. You may have even begun "seeing" the light as you have channeled the energy. If you feel it is natural for you to use light—if you feel an affinity for it—it is very beneficial for you to begin to use it in your treatments. You can begin to use light in your healing work as follows:

Exercise 2-S: Beginning to Use Light in Healing

- Begin by visualizing a cloud of light below your hands as you channel energy during the normal sequence of treatment hand positions you have learned. The light may appear to your mind's eye either as a brilliant pale white, or a brilliant pale light bluish-white light. While brilliant pale white light is perhaps more common, you should use whichever of these two appearances seems natural to you. See the light not as coming from your hands, but as a brilliant cloud of light around your hands and a brilliant illuminated layer of light below your palms, gently penetrating into the chakra of your patient. This will require proper visualization: you must visualize, sense and become the brilliant light around and below your hands in this way, as you allow the energy to conduct. *Always visualize the brilliant light effortlessly.* It is your calm, effortless and persistent visualization of the brilliant light that makes you a pure channel for the extraordinary healing power of pure consciousness. Be sure to remain open to conducting the energy as you visualize the light—do both as one act. The energy and light are not fundamentally different; actually they are the same thing in two apparently differing forms (you will learn more about this in Chios® Level III).

You may begin to use the light while using some of the specific healing techniques you have learned in Chios® Level II to correct the energetic defects you have sensed in your patient. To do so will lend greater effectiveness to those techniques; visualizing the light lends a greater focus and power to the energy.

- To seal leaks or tears using the light, for example, perform the technique as completely described before, but instead of visualizing just the energy visualize, sense and become a brilliant, dazzling layer of light just below your open palm, fusing shut and sealing the break as you move the hand over the damaged area of the aura layer you are treating—like a surgeon using a laser.

- To treat blocked chakras using the light, perform the unblocking technique as usual, but again substitute a visualization of the light for the visualization of the energy. Visualize, sense and become a brilliant cloud of light around your hands and a layer below your palms, and visualize, sense and become the appropriate Chios® symbol composed of the light. *At the same time*, visualize the light flowing upwards through the spine through that chakra, the blockage in the chakra being removed, *and* also the light flowing into the chakra from all around passing easily through it, with any blockage to that flow likewise being removed. See the light as the energy that would flow through a clear chakra, and visualize the chakra clearing in this way.

- To correct disturbances in energy flow using the light, perform the technique as before, but visualize, sense and become the Star composed of the light while *at the same time* visualizing, sensing and becoming the brilliant light flowing through your patient's body, making the energy flow become regular, even and harmonious, and the energy returning to its correct pathways. Should the disturbance in energy flow be in a local area, visualize the light in that area in particular, seeing the light/energy flow of that area being restored to its proper, smooth flow and correcting any disruption and diversion of the energy pathways.

- To ground your patient using the light, perform the grounding technique as described, but visualize, sense and become the brilliant light as coming up from the earth, into your body and out your hands and into the feet of your patient, filling your patient's body and aura. Visualize also the light as creating a connection and lasting bond between your patient and the earth.

- With spine cleaning, again perform the technique as usual, but visualize, sense and become the brilliant light washing up and down the spine, in both directions, cleansing and clearing the central energy channel and removing any blocks or impurities that may be present, from the 1st chakra to the 7th.

You may find it easier to close your eyes as you first learn to visualize the light in these ways, as you lay on the hands and employ the various techniques, but after a little practice you should be able to keep your eyes open while using the light. Note that the use of light is not necessary when performing aura clearing or during aura charging.

You may use light visualizations at your discretion in your regular healing treatments. You may wish to use it at every chakra position, or save it for chakras in which you have detected unhealthy conditions. You may wish to visualize the light, and the Star composed of the light, when treating the 7th chakra. It is also especially beneficial and important to use the light in areas of your patient's body that harbor disease, as per suggestions given in the section describing disease treatments. Simply visualize the brilliant light—using the correct principles discussed above—in place of whatever energy visualization is recommended. The light is a higher, and more powerful, form of the energy.

Practice in viewing the chakra colors and using light in your healing work are excellent preparations for Chios® Level III.

Ending Treatment

End each healing treatment as follows:

Exercise 2-T: Ending Treatment

1. End treatment by standing for a moment and visualizing the energy flow you started by calling in the energy—the energy flow into you from all around, through your body and shoulders and into your hands—now stopping. See this entire energy flow shut down; quiet to stop the flow.

2. Use, then, a very quiet visualization of the Circle to close the passing of the energy. It gives a sense of completion, to return at the end of treatment to the starting point. It also pays homage to the energy: to the circular flow of the universal life energy.

Specific Treatment Suggestions for Disease

There are certain situations that require you to take precautions or special measures to increase the safety and effectiveness of your treatments. It is wise to ask every patient, prior to treatment, if there is any physical condition or disease present that you should know about, or if he or she is under a doctor's care for any specific condition. Always include the following precautions or special procedures, when appropriate:

AIDS: During the standard treatment, it is important to impart a quality of stillness to the energy flow, feeling the stillness in yourself, and passing this on as the energy, instead of as an energizing force. Seek to strengthen your patient. There will usually be energy loss from leaks and tears in the auric field, all over the body and over chakras, and these should be sealed. Aura charging, to replenish energy, will almost always be required. Certain chakras will also exhibit an irregular or diseased energy to them, poor color hue, and will therefore require extra energy treatment for a longer period.

Your patient will often possess a weakness of the lungs and chest, and treatment of the lungs, as detailed under Lung Diseases, should almost always be included. Complications are common, and they should be treated by placing the hands on affected areas, if localized. The AIDS patient should be treated two to three times per week, and may require even more attention if the disease progresses into more frequent and severe complications and your patient weakens.

Broken Bones or Sprains: Place your hands directly over the afflicted area, channeling energy into it, in addition to normal treatment.

Burns: When the hands may not be placed on the body, as with burned areas, the hands may instead be placed a few inches, up to three to five inches, above the burned area, and the energy will still transfer to your patient in good quantity, although it will not be quite as effective as when the hands lie directly on the body surface.

Children: Treat children for one-half to one-third the usual amount of time at each chakra position. Children should not receive more than one treatment every eight or nine days, also.

Cancer: Employ in your treatment unblocking and extra energy to related chakras—chakras that are close to the area containing cancer and related to the disease. These chakras may display an unhealthy feel, be blocked, show poor color hue, or draw extra energy during energy channeling. For some cancers, more than one chakra is given extra treatment, as shown:

Brain Tumors	7th chakra.
Lung Cancer	5th and 4th chakras.
Cancers of Thyroid, Larynx, Esophagus	5th chakra.
Breast Cancer	4th chakra.
Cancers of Stomach, Liver, Intestines, Pancreas	3rd chakra.
Cancers of Cervix, Ovaries, Uterus, Colon/Rectum	2nd chakra.
Prostate Cancer	2nd and 1st chakras.

After treating the related chakras, assist the cancer patient as follows:

Channel energy, for an extended time, into the area containing the cancer. It is effective to vary the position of your hands, as you channel energy to the affected areas. When treating a certain area containing cancer, place your hands on the body in specific position, with your hands on opposite sides of the cancerous area. Treat the area for a while, using this first hand position, according to the instructions above. Then, move your hands to another, different position, yet again with your hands on opposite sides of the cancerous growth. Repeat this for a total of three to four different positions, close to the cancer, shifting your hands but keeping them roughly opposite each other. This may require 10 to 15 minutes of total time, for each affected area. Varying the hand position, in this way, is more effective than keeping the hands in one static position.

Some areas, e.g. prostate, colon and breast, may require that your hands not be placed directly on the area, in consideration to the comfort and modesty of your patient. In these cases, place the hands on opposite sides of the area as near to the area as comfortable, and vary the position as described. For breast cancer, for example, place the hands on opposite sides of your patient's breast, for colon or prostate cancer place one hand on the lower abdomen below the 2nd chakra and one on the upper leg as near the genital region as comfortable. Auric energy impurities near the affected area may require removal, on some patients. Aura charging is almost universally indicated in serious cases. Sealing of tears will be needed often, especially for patients who have received radiation therapy. End cancer treatments by again treating the 7th chakra, and finally by grounding. A positive attitude on the part of the healer is important, also. Patients with cancer will benefit from a treatment regimen that provides for very frequent treatments—two to three times per week, or even every day in serious cases.

Care For the Dying: For patients who are dying, treatment is still very beneficial. To give regular basic healing treatments, with energy channeling, is a comforting measure. Seek to provide rest and comfort to your patient. Should any chakras in the chakra system have an unhealthy feel, show unhealthy color, or seem to require extra energy, channel energy to all such chakras for an extended period. Treat your patient, in any way you intuitively feel is beneficial, or feel guided to do. The patient who is dying benefits from treatments twice a week.

Colds and Flu: For persons suffering from colds, passing viral illnesses, etc., you may give frequent treatments, but of shorter duration, one-half or one-third of the usual time at each treatment hand position. These short treatments are a tonic to the sufferer, but a longer treatment tends to tire the body.

Diabetes: Always treat diabetics from the lower chakras upwards (start at the lowest chakra you usually treat, the 2nd chakra, when treating the front of the body, and move upwards, as you usually do in the back). Treat the pancreas by sandwiching it with the hands, one palm over the pancreas on the front of the body, one hand on the back of the body, while sending the energy into it. Treat the pancreas, and the 2nd and 3rd chakras, for an extended period. Treat diabetics two times per week.

Diseases of the Brain and Nervous System: Treat from the lower chakras up, as with diabetics, and treat the 7th chakra for an extended period, using the Star. Treat any auric energy impurities around the head or neck. Treat one to two times per week.

Diseases of the Internal Organs: For diseases of the kidney, liver, stomach, pancreas, gall bladder, intestines, etc., treat as usual, but spend extra time on the chakra nearest the affected organ. This related chakra will often give off an unhealthy feel, show poor color, be blocked, or draw extra energy during hand placement. This will often be the 3rd chakra, but it will be possible that the 2nd chakra may require attention as well (with the lower intestine, for example). Treat the diseased organ directly, also, by having your patient sit up, if possible, and placing the right palm directly over the organ on the front of the body, and the left palm on the back of the body directly behind it. See the energy penetrating into the body, between your sandwiched hands, to the affected organ. Treat one to two times per week, depending on severity.

Diseases of the Lungs: After completing the normal sequence of treatment hand positions, you can treat diseases or weaknesses of the lungs as follows:

Ask your patient to sit up, if possible. Place your right hand on the front upper left side of your patient's chest, below the shoulder and directly above the left nipple. The palm should be between the nipple and the shoulder, and two to three inches above the nipple. Place your left palm on a position on your patient's back directly opposite your right palm (such that the left lung is "sandwiched" between your hands). Maintain this position, sending the energy through the hands and into the chest cavity, into the left lung area. Once this is finished, treat the right side of the chest in a similar manner, placing your right palm on the front side and your left on the rear, in the same position as before. These are the ideal hand positions for treating each lung and its side of the chest cavity, and serve not only to treat disease but also to generally energize and strengthen the respiratory system. After treating both sides in this way, treat your patient's heart chakra by placing your right hand over the front component and your left hand over the rear component of the chakra, for several moments.

Some critically ill patients will not be able to sit up, and this lung treatment may be conducted with your patient lying down, by placing your right hand as described, and placing your left hand under your patient's body directly below your right hand, as you treat each side. Place both of your hands, gently overlapping, over the front of the heart chakra to treat it, at the end.

With all diseases of the lungs, the 4th chakra is likely to require extra energy channeling. The 5th chakra may also require this.

Disorders of the Ears and Eyes: For diseases or conditions of the eyes, have your patient close the eyes, and place your hands over the eyes, one hand over each eye, with the palms over the eyeball. Channel the energy in this position.

For diseases or disorders of the ears, place your hands on the sides of your patient's head, one hand on each side, with the palms over the ears. For patients with hearing loss or similar hearing problems, also treat the 7th chakra for an extended period.

Heart Disease: Heart disease will often be indicated by a heart chakra that is blocked, has an unhealthy feel as you pass the hands over it, or has a color contaminated with energy impurities. When treating a person with mild heart disease, give a standard healing treatment (no changes are necessary). For a person who is on medication for heart disease, treat the heart chakra (4th chakra) last. If the person has heart disease in an advanced stage, treat the heart chakra last, and for an extended period of time (up to 15 minutes in some cases). Aura charging is almost always necessary for patients with serious heart disease. The heart chakra may require unblocking and removal of auric energy impurities around it, as well as extra energy during regular energy channeling.

For a patient with serious coronary heart disease (including heart attack victims), give two or three complete healing treatments, employing the special considerations above, and you may then try the following advanced technique:

Stand by the side of your patient, with your hands on opposite sides of the heart chakra. Place all ten of your fingertips lightly on the body surface over the heart, with fingers gently curved but without the palms on the body. The fingertips of one hand should be two to three inches away from the fingertips of the opposite hand. Now draw energy from the entire body of your patient, through the body of your patient, from all of the chakras in your patient's chakra system and also the legs and arms, and into the heart simultaneously. See the energy flowing powerfully from all over the body and collecting in an area all around the heart. Draw and collect the energy there. Maintain this for two to three minutes.

Now simultaneously draw your fingertips and hands up above the heart and away from the body outward, as if the fingertips were tracing the lines of a funnel away, and at the same time visualize, intend and sense the energy coming forth in this way from the body—as a sign of the strength of the heart and a cleansing of the illness from it. Draw the hands at least three or four times in this way, at a moderate speed, taking perhaps three to five seconds to draw outward along a funnel 12 to 15 inches high. Your hands will begin with the fingertips of the opposite hands two to three inches apart, at the body surface, yet end with each hand at the opposite ends of the funnel shape, with the hands now approximately one foot apart.

Hypertension: Incorporate in your standard treatment the correction of energy flow technique. Then, channel energy into your patient's arms, one at a time, by placing your right palm on the inside of your patient's elbow joint, and your left palm on the outside of the elbow joint. After treating both arms in this way, treat your patient's hands, one at a time, by sandwiching each hand between your palms (your palms inward, with your patient's hand between them), for a few moments. Hypertensive patients should be treated in this manner about twice a week, if possible.

Infectious Diseases or Infections: Treatment must always be in addition to conventional medical treatment using antibiotics, etc. The patient under siege by one of these microorganisms will be weakened, and will require aura charging for all patients. Fever, when present, requires that the treatment be of shorter duration, half the usual time at each position.

Certain chakras may display an unhealthy feel, be blocked or show poor color hue. These chakras will require extra energy during energy channeling, as listed:

Poliomyelitis	5th Chakra.
Herpes	Chakra nearest affected area.
Mononucleosis	4th chakra. Arms also.
Candida	4th chakra, 3rd chakra, and 2nd chakra.
Syphilis or Gonorrhea	2nd chakra.
Tuberculosis	Treat as under Diseases of the Lung.
Pneumonia	Treat as under Diseases of the Lung.

Stroke: There is no regeneration for the tissue damaged by stroke, but prevention of stroke, or further stroke, is possible, and it is also possible to assist stroke victims in their work to regain use of affected parts of the body. Regular treatments are necessary for either endeavor. To treat or prevent stroke, ask your patient to sit up. Place your hands on your patient's shoulders, in the shoulder position, with one hand on each shoulder. Channel energy in this position for several minutes or more, until you get a sense of completion. This may last up to five or ten minutes in some cases. Treat both the arms and the hands, also, as detailed under hypertension, which is often present. The 5th and 6th chakras may require extra treatment, during energy channeling. Aura charging is indicated for all patients who have suffered a stroke. Auric energy impurities near the head and neck may require removal. Regular treatments are necessary.

Pregnancy: Pregnant women must always lie on their side for treatment. You may alter the usual hand positions in such a way that you treat both components of the 4th, 3rd and 2nd chakras at the same time, if you wish. If you do so, center your right palm over the front component, and your left palm over the rear component. A mother who has given birth will benefit from a treatment after recovering the birth process, with extra attention to the areas of the lower abdomen affected, and 2nd chakra, but it is not necessary to also treat the newborn.

Psychological Disorders: For patients with psychological disorders, it is impossible to predict the effect of treatment. You must proceed with caution. Treat the person for a short time, one-half or one-third of the normal treatment time per chakra, and note any effects. Proceed carefully.

For emotionally or mentally disturbed patients, perform a shortened treatment first, and then check with your patient, during a 24-hour period afterwards, to ensure no unsettling effects manifest. Should treatments prove safe, you will find that a standard treatment will benefit these persons. Should any chakras seem to require extra energy or display an unhealthy feel or poor color to their functioning, treat them with the energy for an extended period.

Recovery From Surgery: Treat the affected areas with extra energy, and then treat the chakras nearest the area affected for an extended time. Auric impurities near the affected area may require removal. This procedure, as part of a general treatment, is restorative and highly beneficial.

Notes

Notes

Notes

Chios® Energy Healing – Level Three

Welcome to the Chios® Level III. This level contains some very advanced, powerful and extraordinary energy healing techniques that will make available to you the full power of Chios® and lead you toward mastery of energy healing.

As you begin your study of this level, you may choose to receive the third Chios® attunement (the Chios® Master Teacher attunement). As with Chios® Levels I and II, it is not required that you receive this attunement, should you wish to learn and practice the techniques in this level, but the attunement will assist you in practicing them to maximum effectiveness. This third attunement elevates your energy, color and light channeling abilities to the highest level provided by the series of three Chios® attunements. It also accomplishes one other purpose: it gives you the inner ability to attune others. You will be able to perform the attunement procedures used in the Chios® system—the attunements you yourself have received—to attune and teach your own healing students, if you wish. These attunements may be given in person or by distance attunement, and you will be given the information on exactly how to perform the attunements upon your completion of the Chios® Master Teacher degree. Because this third attunement is the strongest attunement of all, and the attunement that gives you the ability to attune others, it is of great importance that you prepare very carefully for it, so that you will receive the full benefits (see Appendix #1 – Preparation for Chios® Attunements).

One highly recommended adjunct to Chios® Level III is the practice of the Chios® Meditation technique. To learn Chios® Meditation is not at all required, to practice all the new healing techniques in this level. It will assist you, however, in learning to contact the state of pure consciousness—the source of all your healing knowledge and healing power—and in acquiring the visualization, perceptual, intuitive and other abilities that are so beneficial for your successful practice of energy healing. It is impossible to overemphasize the benefits to you and your healing work that regular practice of this meditation practice will bring. After you have learned Chios® Meditation, it is also suggested that you practice the self-realization exercises in the chapter that follows the meditation instructions: The Self-Knowledge of the Healer. These exercises will accelerate your personal growth and further add to the advanced abilities useful in healing work. That is why meditation and these advanced exercises are provided as part of the Chios® system.

As you study this series of powerful and exciting new techniques in Chios® Level III, and incorporate them into your healing treatments, you may find it very helpful to refer to the outline of treatment steps for this Chios® level (see Appendix #2 – Outline of Treatment Steps for Chios® Levels II and III). This will clarify for you the recommended order of techniques, and serve as quick and easy reference while learning.

Introduction: The Master Healer as a Tool, a Vehicle for Pure Consciousness

In Chios® Levels I and II we talked a great deal about openness, and this openness came in many forms: 1) simply being open to the energy as you first learned energy channeling; 2) being open to whatever sensations and information comes, as you practice the passing of hands; 3) remaining open to the entire energy field of your patient; 4) releasing yourself and being fully open to receiving intuitive information; 5) openness as the key to learning to view the aura; 5) remaining open to the sensations and information that comes, during energy channeling; 7) remaining open and transparent while using specific active healing techniques, and 8) becoming open to the chakra colors and the information they bring. Every time we mentioned this openness, it was to encourage you to develop the holistic awareness and action so important in healing, and to reinforce the fact that every aspect of your healing work is performed with your whole being. The knowledge and power contained in the field of pure consciousness is the ultimate source of all healing, and it is you, as an open and clear channel to this higher realm, that makes your healing work possible, whether you are using receptive (perceptual and informational) healing tools to gain healing knowledge or active healing techniques to channel the healing power in the specific ways needed. Every single healing technique you employ is simply a tool to make this connection clearer and more effective, in the specific way needed at that time, as you bring this healing knowledge and power into manifested worldly life to heal your patient.

We also talked much about the fact that ultimately you, your patient, your patient's energy field (and every energy flow or energetic phenomenon within it) and every healing tool you use are ultimately one. This ultimate unity is not just the reality of energy healing, but of all existence. In the apparent multiplicity of the manifested world we live in, there is actually only one thing that exists. There is only one unitary, holistic entity behind everything, and that is pure consciousness. It may appear to us that the specific "parts" of the universe—the objects and entities we see in the world—have a "separate" existence, but this is only an appearance and illusion. All is one. Everything we see, sense and feel emanates from this field of pure consciousness, as a particular form materialized from the infinite knowledge and power that resides within it. The state of awareness of this ultimate reality is called *self-realization*. In this state, this essence of all creation—this unity containing the infinite knowledge and power we use in healing—often appears as a light that shines from in and around everything.

When you the healer perform a healing treatment in the spirit of openness we have recommended you begin to gravitate towards this state of self-realization. You naturally begin to leave your worldly self behind as you open yourself to the energy, your patient and your patient's energy field and merge with them, and instead become this state of universal awareness, more and more. You may have noticed small steps toward this already in your healing work, and this is the beginning of your journey into this larger reality. As you practice energy healing you gain momentum; healing itself accelerates your own personal growth towards this state. As you move into this state—where you and your patient and all the healing tools and techniques are one—you the healer tend to "disappear" as an individual entity and instead become this state of pure consciousness. This state, and the infinite knowledge and power that exists within it, has actually always been inside you, waiting to be discovered. The more you are able to realize and move into this state, the more of its infinite knowledge and power will be available to you as you heal.

In Chios® Level III you will work extensively with the energy field—the chakra system and the higher layers of aura--using a new series of very powerful techniques. The chakra system is a seven-step connection between the field of pure consciousness and the individual—it is a "rainbow bridge," a series of receptors and transmutors of incoming energy/consciousness from this higher realm, each with its own color and its own domain of influence over the entire life process of your patient. The chakras are each a way things work and a realm of being and consciousness, and yet they all relate to each other, and are all one. The higher layers of aura relate to the chakras—each layer of aura corresponds to a chakra— and just as each chakra is a realm of being and consciousness, a realm of existence with its own nature and function within the overall being of the individual. This is true for the *astral body*, the *etheric template body*, the *cosmic body* and the *ketheric template body*—the remaining 4th through 7th layers of aura that we hadn't mentioned thus far but that you will now learn to see and work on in this Chios® level. The layers of aura mirror the chakra system, and like it are a seven-step bridge of translation between the realm of pure consciousness and physical life. And yet all these parts of your patient's energy field are one—they intimately influence each other and are not really separate entities. In Chios® Level III you will practice sensing and becoming these apparently different parts of your patient's energy field—you will come to know these realms of being and consciousness, and also access the maximum power available to you to heal them. And yet, they are (and will ultimately appear to you as) *all one*.

To achieve your maximum effectiveness as a healer, you must continue the process of openness that we have introduced. You must practice all these new healing tools with the same spirit of openness you have learned, and continue to move towards the unity of yourself, your patient, your patient's energy field and whatever specific healing tool you are learning and using. Remember this as you learn and practice the exciting and extremely powerful new series of techniques you will soon learn here. You will thereby employ them to your fullest potential.

As you use the powerful techniques of Chios®, you may not only treat the ultimate causes of whatever disease or affliction your patient may have, but may also benefit your patient's entire life process. When you remove blocks, impurities and disturbances in your patient's energy field, you create a clearer, purer connection between your patient and the realm of pure consciousness, in which his or her ideal health, higher awareness and higher potentials reside. By healing defects in the energy field of your patient, you provide the opportunity for your patient to connect to this greater reality—to break free of the physical, emotional, mental and spiritual limitations which might otherwise remain—and thereby enhance his or her entire life process, on all levels. You heal your patient's whole being. This includes facilitating your patient's overall spiritual growth, too.

Your own openness, expanded awareness and connection to pure consciousness is the tool you will use to effect these changes—you heal with your whole being, as well. As we have said, you the healer heal, and your patient receives healing, each with your entire being. But it is pure consciousness that heals, with you acting as a clear, open channel and conduit. You are not acting as an individual personality but only as a clear channel for the knowledge and power; consciousness itself accomplishes the healing. And yet—as with everything that exists—you, your patient and your patient's energy field are one. It is ultimately consciousness itself, acting upon itself, performing healing. Your healing work offers the opportunity to your patient to contact this greater reality, heal and advance his or her spiritual growth, as well as for you to come into greater contact with and act as a channel for this realm. Your role as a healer also facilitates your own growth process, and your healing ability is dependent upon this growth. You, your patient and your healing activities are all aspects of a *unitary spiritual growth process*. You will experience this in your healing work at a practical level, if you have not already: patients will come to you with specific needs for which you have the qualities necessary to provide the catalyst to heal, and your work with them will also facilitate your own growth by catalyzing issues you yourself need to resolve, to grow. You will effect changes in consciousness (and spiritual growth) in your healing patients, and you will also find that your healing work will induce these same things in you. And yet, there is ultimately no difference between you and your patient—it is all consciousness working on itself, in this growth process.

The techniques of Chios® Level III will assist you in this process and will further accelerate you toward becoming a master healer. As you become a master healer, you will gravitate towards working directly with this realm of pure consciousness, not only in your patient, but also in yourself—the realm from which you draw your healing knowledge, the healing power, and the awareness you allow to guide you, as you heal. In your healing work, you are a vehicle for this higher consciousness, as it works through you to do everything we have discussed. When healing, *you the master healer temporarily move away from your personality and individual identity, and instead into a state of self-realization—becoming a tool, a vehicle through which consciousness operates on itself*, in certain ways, so as to effect healing and changes in consciousness.

Implicit in this is the necessity to be guided, in your work, instead of being limited by your own mental ideas or preconceptions. You the master healer are an artist and not a mere technician. In practical terms, this means you must begin to break free of all standardized treatment orders, pre-conceived content of healing treatments, and instead use all your tools, all your knowledge, and the entire power and perception of your consciousness to create the work of art that is each individual healing session. Although Chios® Level III contains many extraordinary tools, you must cut your own path and not be afraid to individualize your use of them, as your individual patients require. It is inevitable, also, that you will encounter many situations not specifically described in the Chios® healing levels, sometimes with patients who are seriously ill. You must therefore use your own judgment, your expanded awareness and your ability to assess each unique patient as your ultimate authority in treatment.

You must master all the healing tools given you but then move beyond all rules, to a wider realm—a realm in which your unitary holistic awareness and action exist as a pure expression of the knowledge and power of the field of pure consciousness and pure spirit.

You must move to a realm in which you, as you have previously known yourself, disappear and are instead guided by, and become, the dream flow of the light. This is the realm of the master healer.

Learning to Channel Color and Light

In Chios® Levels I and II you worked primarily with the energy. You learned to channel the energy and begin to sense it with your hands, and to work with it in specific ways as you performed healing techniques to heal simple energetic defects in your patient's energy field. In Chios® Level III you will also make extensive use of *color* and *light* in your healing work. You will learn to sense and see color and light, and will channel energy, color and light as you perform many new healing techniques.

It is important to understand that these three entities—energy, color and light—are not fundamentally different from each other. They are all the same fundamental thing in three apparently different forms; they are all emanations of the essence, emanations of the field of pure consciousness. It is as if the essence of reality—the field of pure consciousness—exists at three different domains of vibration or radiation. Light is the highest and most refined, color is a slower vibration than light, and energy is an even slower one. Although energy, color and light may appear different, they are all manifestations of pure consciousness and so actually there is a unity. As when you practice energy channeling, when you channel color or light you act as a channel and conduit for this pure consciousness, now in the form of either color or light, respectively. Energy, color and light are ultimately the same, but they differ, however, in their method of perception and application.

The energy that you have sensed and conducted during your healing work thus far works on a grosser level than color or light, yet it is more all-pervasive. Energy is found throughout the body, all around us in the atmosphere and permeates all living things and the environment in which they live. Color and light are also found in the human energy field— in the chakras and layers of aura—but they are more localized entities with a specific manifestation and meaning. They are successively rarer, more concentrated and refined entities of a higher vibration, and their application in healing is similarly more topical: they are applied only in certain specific areas and in specific ways. This is not to say that color and light are less important than the energy in healing work; they are actually successively more significant and refined manifestations of the essence, and are also more powerful. They are a more specific channeling to your patient of the power of healing that is present in the field of pure consciousness.

Energy ——————▶ Color ——————▶ Light

Each step up, from energy to color to light, denotes a more refined state of the same basic form, an entity that works and is applied on a finer vibratory level. When we speak of the light, we are not referring to physical light—the light that exists in the physical world that can be split into the spectrum of physical colors—but to the higher spiritual light. This spiritual light is a higher manifestation, beyond color, and does not include the colors. The light itself is a bridge to the essence—to the field of pure consciousness and the ultimate unity of everything that exists.

When you worked primarily with the energy in your two previous Chios® levels, your method of sensing it was primarily tactile, such as using the passing-of-hands or focusing on the sensations in your hands as you practiced energy channeling. In Chios® Level III, when you use color and light, which have a more visual and radiant nature, you will sense both of them in a more "visual" way. You will make more focused and greater use of your power of visualization in your healing work using color and light, both in sensing these entities and in sending them. This is one of the many reasons that practice of Chios® Meditation is so highly recommended. The treatment steps you employed in Chios® Level II will not be discarded—you will still treat your patient using the energy. You will, however, supplement your treatments with new methods that also make use of color and light—treatments of a more refined nature, which use these more refined entities.

Color Visualization and Its Uses

Channeling color and light are done in a somewhat different way than simple energy channeling, and it's important to learn the correct techniques right from the beginning. We will start with color. Many of the techniques that you will learn in Chios® Level III will require you to properly visualize color, so you can both sense and channel it effectively. The ability to visualize color correctly will be critical to your ability to learn to see all seven layers of aura, and also to heal energetic defects you sense in the layers of aura and the chakras, using the powerful techniques you are about to learn.

The first step in beginning to use color in healing is to become aware of the seven true colors—red, orange, yellow, green, blue, indigo and violet—by learning to visualize, sense and become each of them. Each color has a unique essence to it, and is a realm of being and consciousness unto itself. Each of the seven colors corresponds to both a specific chakra and a specific layer of aura (or higher body)—from red (1ˢᵗ chakra and 1ˢᵗ layer) up to violet (7ᵗʰ chakra and 7ᵗʰ layer). These seven true colors are pure and unadulterated—they are the beautiful colors you would see in a rainbow, or in the spectrum of sunlight as dispersed by a prism. When you visualize, sense and become one with one of these colors you thereby contact its essence and access the specific power of that essence of the color. This makes you a clear conduit to sensing and seeing that color, as well as channeling that color into your patient in order to heal. Note how this is similar to visualizing, sensing and becoming a Chios® symbol, for the purpose of contacting its essence and thence channeling its power to direct energy in a certain pattern. The following exercise will assist you in beginning to properly visualize and become familiar with the essence of these colors:

Exercise 3-A: Visualizing the Seven True Colors

1. Sit comfortably with your eyes closed, and seek a calmness, a quietness in your mind.
2. Now, imagine, in your mind, one of the true colors. Do not merely "think about," or "pretend to see" the color, but try to visualize, sense and become the color, using the understanding and proper practice of visualization you have gained. Ask yourself, how does it feel to be that color? Feel the color in its purest state—as a true color—and then seek to merge with the color, feel your entire being sensing, moving into and becoming one with it.
3. If you find yourself "thinking about" the color, just let go of your thoughts—visualization is not a mental phenomenon. If you find yourself "pretending to see" the color, release the "visual" portion of your awareness of it, the portion of your awareness that "sees" it as a visual sensation. As you visualize the color, note the purity and begin to get a sense of the color's being and power.
4. Continue visualizing, sensing and becoming the color for a few moments, and then end the exercise by stopping and resting for a moment with your eyes closed.
5. Repeat this exercise with each of the true colors, and with each seek to gain a feel of each color's purity, being and power. Note that it is as if each color has its own identity, and that the sense you get from red, for example, is different than that from green.

As you perform the exercise with each color, however, do not try to differentiate between or sense any of the colors on the basis of any particular mental notion, such as vibration, for instance. The true colors are realms of being and cannot be understood purely on the basis of particular ideas but must be visualized and experienced in their essence, with your whole being. Become familiar with the true essence of each. You must learn to know them and become them, and this is done by bringing out a knowledge and sense of the power of each color that you already have inside yourself.

After you have practiced visualizing, sensing and becoming the true colors, it is time to combine your visualization of the colors with your visualization of the Chios® symbols. Some of the important advanced techniques you will learn in Chios® Level III require that you visualize a Chios® symbol in color. This is done so that the color-channeling ability that your color visualization activates will be combined and magnified by the energy-directing ability that your symbol visualization activates, so that in certain applications you will have even greater power and effectiveness as you sense and/or treat your patient's aura layers and chakras. In many of these techniques you will use a symbol in color from the *basic progression*, a series of the Chios® symbols in color each of which corresponds to a particular chakra and a particular layer of aura (see Figure 28). The following exercise will provide practice in the proper visualization of the symbols in color:

Exercise 3-B: Visualizing the Chios® Symbols in Color

1. Sit comfortably with your eyes closed, and seek a calmness, a quietness in your mind.
2. Now, at random, select a colored symbol from the basic progression. Visualize, sense and become the symbol, in color, in your mind's eye, using proper visualization technique. Combine your visualization of the color, as you just practiced above, with your visualization of the Chios® symbol, as you have practiced before. Visualize, sense and become a single object of this shape and color.
3. Do not attach any concept or mental ideas to the symbol in color, or "think about" it or "pretend to see" it. If you find yourself "thinking about" the symbol in color, just let go of your thoughts. If you find yourself "pretending to see" the symbol in color, release the "visual" portion of your awareness of it. Just visualize, sense and become the symbol in color for a minute or two.
4. Rest for a moment, then select at random another Chios® symbol in color, from the basic progression. Now visualize, sense and become that symbol in color for a minute or two, just as before. Continue for about five to ten minutes, employing all the colored symbols one or more times, in random order.

SYMBOL IN COLOR	CORRESPONDING CHAKRA	CORRESPONDING AURA LAYER
★ Violet Star	7th Chakra	7th (Ketheric Template) Layer
△ Indigo Trine	6th Chakra	6th (Cosmic) Layer
△ Blue Trine	5th Chakra	5th (Etheric Template) Layer
△ Green Trine	4th Chakra	4th (Astral) Layer
◯ Yellow Circle	3rd Chakra	3rd (Mental) Layer
◯ Orange Circle	2nd Chakra	2nd (Emotional) Layer
◯ Red Circle	1st Chakra	1st (Etheric) Layer

Figure 28: The Basic Progression of Chios® Symbols in Color

This ability to visualize symbols in color will be used in several important Chios® Level III techniques, and it is beneficial that you begin practicing the above exercise at various times throughout the day in preparation. It is not necessary to employ the symbols when visualizing color—you could perform the powerful color channeling techniques in Chios® Level III by merely visualizing the color itself—but using the symbols in color will add much power to the practice of the techniques.

You will use this visualization of symbols in color for three things: 1) viewing your patient's higher layers of aura; 2) treating your patient's chakras, and 3) treating your patient's chakras *and* higher layers of aura at the same time. When viewing your patient's higher layers of aura, you will visualize a symbol in color to merge yourself into that color—into a certain higher vibratory rate—so that you can sense and view its corresponding higher layer of aura. You will "see" in the color—sense and see in its realm of being—and view the aura layer and whatever phenomena exist within it. Practice in visualizing the symbols in color opens your awareness to the colors and their realms. It prepares your "psychic sight" for viewing all seven layers, in this way, so it's important to prepare now using the exercise above.

You will also use visualization of symbols in color for the purpose of performing specific healing techniques on your patient's chakras. When doing this, you will visualize, sense and become a symbol in color, and will at the same time visualize, sense and become a cloud composed of that color surrounding your hands. You will not see the color as coming from your hands, but just surrounding them—as a *cloud of color around the hands and a layer of color below them, the color penetrating into your patient's chakra*. This will again enable you to "be in the color"—this time to be an open and clear channel for that color, so you can powerfully channel it into the chakra you are treating.

Finally, you will additionally use visualization of symbols in color to treat chakras *and* the aura layers of your patient at the same time. When you do this, you will visualize, sense and become a symbol in color, and at the same time visualize, sense and become a cloud composed of that color surrounding your hands. You will not see the color as coming from your hands, but just surrounding them—as a cloud of color around your hands and a layer of color below them, the color *penetrating down into the chakra but also dispersing all around— laterally in all directions—into the layers of aura you are also treating*. Notice the difference between channeling color into a chakra (where you see the color penetrating into the chakra below your hands) and channeling color into the chakra *plus* aura layers (where you see the color dispersing down but also all-around, into the aura layer). You are again acting as an open and clear channel for that color as you channel it into the chakra and the aura layer.

It is possible and beneficial to practice the visualization of symbols in color with your eyes open, as you will be able to do after some practice, but you may wish to close your eyes while learning the techniques that follow. After a little practice, you will easily be able to visualize the symbols in color with your eyes open. You will find it beneficial to keep your eyes open as you treat your patient.

This method of visualizing the Chios® symbols in color is the one that is recommended and that will be effective for the large majority of healers, but it is possible that you may find it more appealing to visualize a white light-colored symbol against a solid colored background (a background that is the color required). As an alternative, this method is basically the same, and accomplishes the same purpose—it contacts the essence of both the color and the symbol, combining their power. If you feel continually uncomfortable with the symbol in color, as described, and find in yourself a much greater affinity for this alternate technique instead, use it with the following Chios® Level III techniques.

Before moving on, we should again mention the importance of unity. Although we name these colors, their corresponding chakras and their corresponding higher bodies, and ascribe to each a general function or involvement in the being, none of these are to be thought of as separate entities. These are merely a way to describe and work with the whole being of your patient. The aura layers and chakras, like energy, color and light, are not really separate entities at all. Everything always works together and is one. When we treat a patient, we treat and heal the entire energy field and whole being of that patient, even when it may seem we are working on one part. The chakras and higher bodies, as well as the physical body, are one organism. It is always *one being*.

Light Visualization and Its Applications

In Chios® Level III you will also often use light, especially in situations where a more powerful application of healing power is required. Light is the highest and most refined manifestation of the essence, and visualizing light provides the most powerful channeling of the healing power of pure consciousness, as it is brought into this world to heal. The proper visualization of light also increases the specificity of the healing power—it focuses and directs the healing power to a specific area or location. Visualizing light acts to powerfully direct the energy to a certain location, or to flow in a certain manner, because ultimately the energy and light are the same thing. The light is a higher manifestation—and therefore able to direct—the energy. Light visualization is thus a very powerful and useful technique, although it is used for different things than color visualization.

You will use light for four specific things, in healing work: 1) to lend greater healing power while treating chakras during the normal series of treatment positions; 2) to lend greater power and focus to other specific energy healing techniques; 3) to direct healing power to specific parts of the physical body, when treating serious illness in those locations, and 4) to perform distance healing. You may see the light either as a *brilliant pale white light*, or as a *brilliant pale, light bluish-white light*. It may appear to you in either way; the brilliant pale white light is perhaps more common, but you should use whichever appearance of the light feels right for you, in each of these applications.

You may have already begun using light in your healing work in Chios® Level II, where you may have visualized the light while channeling energy into the chakras during the normal sequence of treatment hand positions. When you treat the chakras with the light, visualize, sense and become a cloud composed of the brilliant light surrounding your hands. Do not see the light as coming from your hands, but just surrounding them—as a *cloud of brilliant light around your hands and a layer of brilliant light below them, the light penetrating into your patient's chakra.* Always remember to visualize the light effortlessly—it is with less effort that you will achieve maximum results. It is a *calm, effortless and persistent visualization.* Visualizing the light in this way allows you to channel the healing power into your patient's chakra even more intensely than you did before, during simple energy channeling.

You may have also begun using the light in Chios® Level II to lend greater power to the specific energy healing techniques you use to correct energetic defects in the energy field of your patient. The light can be used when sealing leaks or tears, when clearing blocked chakras or when correcting disturbances in energy flow, and with several additional techniques. Visualizing, sensing and becoming the brilliant light as it seals leaks and tears, unblocks chakras, corrects energy flows or performs any other technique allows you to focus the healing power you are channeling in a more intense way—focusing it in the exact way needed in each of these techniques. The light can be used in any healing technique that uses the energy, in fact, because they are one—energy and light are one—and to visualize the light just adds power and specificity to whatever healing technique you are using. It is a more powerful and advanced way of using the healing energies that you channel through your hands.

Another important way you will use light in your healing work is in the treatment of physical illness in the body. In treatment of disease, you will use your other Chios® techniques to heal energetic defects in the chakras and aura layers of your patient, but will also need to direct the healing power to treat certain specific areas of the physical body that harbor disease. You will visualize the light treating specific areas in the body, with specific visualizations to direct the light (and energy) in a powerful and specific manner. This is not done by visualizing the light as coming from your hands and traveling to the diseased organ or area, but by visualizing the brilliant light as surrounding and suffusing the organ or area you are treating, so that it follows the form of the body or anatomical region requiring healing. When treating a diseased organ, for example, the light is visualized as a brilliant cloud of light, a layer of light surrounding the organ like a second skin. This directs and focuses the healing energy powerfully onto that organ. Remember, once again, to always visualize the light effortlessly. We will discuss the use of light in the treatment of disease much more in Chapter 4 -Treatment Procedures for Serious Illness.

Finally, light visualization is the ideal tool for performing distance healing. When the person you wish to treat is at a distance and not present with you, it is nowhere near as powerful to send energy alone. Light, however, can easily be directed any distance and retains much more power when used for distance healing. In distance healing you will be sending the light, but without use of your hands. As with disease treatment, you will use light during distance healing not by visualizing the light as coming from your hands and traveling to your patient, but simply by visualizing the brilliant light surrounding and suffusing the chakra or other area of your patient which you are treating. Do not visualize sending the light, but merely "see" the light at the desired destination. The light does not have a path in space-time; it is visualized at the location desired, surrounding the object of treatment. To send healing power to the entire body of a remote patient, for example, you will visualize the brilliant light surrounding the entire body as a layer or cloud of light. This serves to direct healing energy to that person, even if he or she is a great distance away. You can visualize the brilliant light surrounding a specific chakra, to powerfully treat that chakra at a distance. This is effective treatment, yet not quite as effective as when your patient is in front of you with your hands on your patient's body. Nevertheless, distance healing using light visualization can be a powerful technique, especially when you visualize the light healing specific areas—it will be more powerful healing than just sending the light to the overall body of your patient.

When you use the light for all these particular purposes it is essential that you strive for transparency in your treatment technique. You must not be self-conscious, but must maintain openness: you must be aware of and become one with your patient and his or her energy field, an open channel for the light. At the same time, you must visualize in the proper way: visualizing, sensing and becoming the color or light, and not just seeing it as if with your physical eyes. There has been a progression from Chios® Level I where you simply opened yourself to the energy, to Chios® Level II where you began to visualize the light around your hands, to now, where you will learn to direct and focus the light in specific ways through visualization. It is important that you be sure to maintain the transparency, the openness, as you direct the light/energy in these more focused ways. You should practice focusing and directing the light with this openness and without effort—it is an effortless visualization—so that your whole being participates in the healing being performed. This is what makes you a pure channel for the light, as it emanates from the field of pure consciousness to perform healing.

Energetic Defects of the Seven Layers of Aura

Now that you have learned how to visualize and channel color and light, we will discuss the nature of the seven layers of aura, with special emphasis on the energetic impurities you will find in them. As in Chios® Level II, where we discussed some simple energetic defects in your patient's energy field and then learned how to sense them, we will now learn more about the energetic defects that can occur in all seven layers of aura and you will then learn how to sense (and see) these layers, with their defects. We will then do the same for the chakra system—we will discuss all the energetic defects that can occur in chakras, and you will learn to sense (and perhaps view) these, as well. Finally, during the remainder of Chios® Level III, you will learn the Chios® Master techniques—a series of very powerful and effective techniques to heal all these energetic defects that occur in the entire aura and chakra system.

Let's begin by familiarizing ourselves with the seven aura levels. The seven layers of aura interpenetrate (occupy the same area of space in and around the physical body), but each layer extends a little further beyond the body surface than the layer before (at increments of approximately four to five inches). It's important to remember that these layers of aura are not defined by physical location (distances progressively further above the level of the physical body) but by the fact that they are successively higher vibrational levels. The chakras exist at each of the seven layers of aura: just as there are points on the physical body where chakras exist, so are there points or areas on all the higher layers of aura that are also part of the chakra (see Figure 29).

Each layer of aura is a realm of being and consciousness—with its own appearance, characteristics and specific way that energetic defects typically appear within it. As with the chakras, we will not give a complex description of the nature of these aura layers, but only describe them using a few simple concepts, so you have a basic idea of their nature. As we do so, note the similarity between the nature of each aura layer and that of its corresponding chakra (as we have previously described it). You will learn to sense the real, spiritual nature of the chakras and these aura layers for yourself, later in this Chios® level. For now, we briefly describe these layers, not to tell you what you should see but only so that you will recognize and have a basic understanding of what you see. It is especially important for you to learn to recognize energetic defects in each of these layers, so you can plan and implement proper treatment. After we discuss these layers, and these energetic defects you will find on them, you will proceed to learning to see them. We will not give any system for interpretation of the *meaning* of the energies and energetic defects you will see in these layers—you will also learn how to do that for yourself.

In Chios® Level II, you learned how to sense and see four simple energetic defects in the aura: energetic impurities in the aura, leaks and tears in the aura layers, energy depletion in the aura and disturbance of energy flow in the body energy. We will now talk much more about energetic impurities in the aura. You learned to sense and treat these energetic

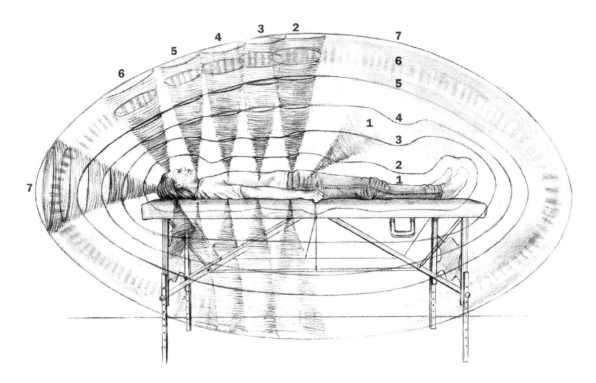

Figure 29: The Chakra System and Seven Layers of Aura

impurities in a simple way, in Chios® Level II. You will now learn much more about them, and learn to sense and see them in detail, throughout the aura. You will still use the aura clearing technique you learned in Chios® Level II, to remove them near the body surface, yet will learn several Chios® Master techniques that also remove them from the higher layers. You will also still employ the other Chios® Level II techniques you learned, to treat the other energetic defects in the aura (leaks and tears in the aura layers, energy depletion in the aura and disturbance of energy flow in the body energy), and so will now have a complete treatment repertoire for healing defects in the aura.

The 1st Layer

The 1st layer of aura (or etheric body) usually appears as a light blue or colorless layer, surrounding the surface of the body at a maximum distance of one or two inches or so, which may deepen to a medium blue after some practice. You have almost certainly already seen this 1st layer already, during your practice of the basic technique for learning to view the aura given in Chios® Level II. It is not usually necessary to employ additional techniques to see this 1ˢᵗ layer. This etheric body is the energy pattern on the surface of and within the physical body—it is an energetic mirror of the structure of the physical body. Energetic impurities in this layer will appear as clumps, fuzzy areas or clouds of dark energy and are treated with the aura clearing technique you have already learned.

The 2nd Layer

The 2ⁿᵈ layer of aura (or emotional body) is composed of energies that appear as multicolored clouds or areas of color—usually indefinable shapes of variable color and size. This layer has a shell-like shape, similar to the shape of the body yet less-defined up to a maximum of four to five inches above the surface of the body. These multicolored clouds within it are usually in a condition of constant flow, change and movement.

The nature of the 2ⁿᵈ layer relates to emotions and feelings. The moving colors usually correlate with emotions and feelings in the psychological state of your patient, which will vary with the feelings and activities in which he or she is engaged. These emotions stored in the emotional body are not just conscious feelings, however, but also include unconscious (often repressed) negative emotions. These negative core emotions often contain great energy and have great influence on your patient, yet your patient may not be fully aware of them. Energetic impurities in this layer (which correspond to these negative emotions) generally appear as discolored, muddied, smeared or streaked colors or patterns which are unhealthy-looking. The 2ⁿᵈ layer will be clearly visible, in your mind's eye, and is usually not very difficult to see with your physical eyes.

Generally speaking, colored energies appearing in any layer of aura that are bright, clear and that have a sense of "health" to them represent healthy aspects of the operation of the energy field—aspects related to the character, personality and activity of the individual that are positive and not detrimental to energetic functioning. Healthy colors will be appealing and appear vibrant and radiant. Harmful or unhealthy energies (containing energetic impurities) will have a discolored, muddied, smeared or streaked appearance, and the color will be unappealing—they will look and feel unhealthy. These unhealthy energies can be energies generated by your patient's own body, emotions, mind and spirit (in combination), and often have spread from other aura layers, from chakras or from outside your patient's energy field altogether (e.g. from other people). Note how the same general criteria we used previously in Chios® Level II, to differentiate the appearance of healthy vs. unhealthy energies in the chakras, apply in the very same way to healthy and unhealthy energies in the aura layers.

When your patient has disease or such unhealthy energy impurities in an aura layer or a chakra, you will see colors that contain *black*, or, if the black influence is less pronounced, a *dirty gray* or *dirty silver* color. The unhealthy energies may also have colors that contain *dark brown* or *brownish red* or, if the brown influence is less pronounced, a *very dusty yellow*. These unhealthy-looking colors will infuse into healthy colors—making them appear unwell—and will streak, smear or discolor these regions. The intensity with which these unhealthy and unappealing colors appear is an indicator of the degree of sickness of the individual, in body, emotions, mind or spirit—the more intense and easily noticeable the ill-appearing colors are, the more detrimental the energies have become to your patient's energetic health.

The 3rd Layer

The 3rd layer of aura (or mental body) primarily appears yellow in color. In actuality, it is not composed of yellow light but has a radiance which makes it appear light yellow or golden. This layer does not have clouds of color, like the 2nd layer, but has fine, light colors within this yellow radiance. This layer has a shell-like shape, similar to the shape of the body yet less-defined, which exists up to a maximum of about eight to ten inches from the body surface. Like the 1st layer, it also exists as an energy pattern which exists on and in the physical body, and which mirrors it.

The nature of the 3rd layer is thought. These colors usually correlate well to thinking and specific thoughtforms in the mind of your patient, some static but many others dynamic and changing, which will (as in the 2nd layer) vary with the thinking of your patient or the activity in which he or she is engaged. These thoughts in the mental body are not just conscious ones, however, but also include unconscious (often repressed) negative thoughtforms, self-limiting beliefs and judgments (regarding self and others). These thoughtforms can have great influence on your patient, but (as with the 2nd layer) your patient may not be fully aware of them. Energetic impurities in this layer are indicated by the same sort of darkened, discolored, smeared or streaked colors which have been described above, but these colors are very light and fine—they are barely noticeable in the light yellow-gold radiance of this layer (which shines through all, and makes the colors and their impurities more difficult to see). You will see these impurities in your mind's eye, but perhaps not with your physical eyes (even if you are able to gain some vision of the layer itself).

The 4ᵗʰ Layer

The 4ᵗʰ layer of aura (or astral body) is similar to the 2ⁿᵈ layer, in that it is composed of multicolored clouds. The colors in these areas or clouds are finer, paler and lighter, however—they are dimmer and harder to see—and they exist in an area up to a maximum of approximately 12 to 15 inches above the surface of the body. These multicolored clouds, like those of the 2ⁿᵈ layer, are always in motion.

The nature of the 4ᵗʰ layer has to do with universal love, and the ability to give and receive love. Energies in this layer may relate to healthy aspects of this important part of life, or may be unhealthy energies that relate to fundamental deficits and issues in the ability to love and be loved. Energetic impurities in this layer present themselves as unhealthy-looking discolored, muddied, smeared or streaked colors or patterns, as have been described above. Because this layer and its colors are lighter, however, impurities will generally appear lighter and finer to the eye. You will often see these light colors (and impurities) in your mind's eye, and may also learn to see them with your physical eyes (but this is harder than learning to see the colors of the 2ⁿᵈ layer).

The 5ᵗʰ Layer

The 5ᵗʰ layer of aura (or etheric template body) primarily appears as a deep blue radiance to the eye, a radiance that is not as bright, however as the yellow radiance of the 3rd layer. It has an overall shape that is like an eggshell, although it is not as large nor wide an eggshell shape as the 7ᵗʰ layer, existing at a maximum level of perhaps 16 to 20 inches above the body. This layer also, like the 1ˢᵗ and 3ʳᵈ layers, exists as a pattern that mirrors the surface and inner structure of the physical body. This layer is a *vibrational mirror* and transition layer, for levels above and below—its eggshell shape mirrors the vibrational structure of the 7ᵗʰ layer above it, and its body-like structure exists as a higher vibrational template for the etheric body and physical body below (hence the name "etheric template").

The nature of the 5ᵗʰ layer relates to expression. It takes the spiritual powers from above (the 7ᵗʰ layer)—particularly as they relate to expression, power and will—and shapes and directs them down and outwardly into physical life. This includes communication and creativity. Energies in this layer can be indicative of healthy or unhealthy functioning in this process. Impurities in this layer exist, however, *not* as darkened or sullied colors, but as *disturbances of vibration*. You will therefore perceive these impurities differently than the colored impurities we have just discussed. These *energetic disturbances* are not sensed as variations in color hues therein (as in the 2ⁿᵈ, 3ʳᵈ and 4ᵗʰ layers), nor are they textural changes in the quality of light (as in the 7ᵗʰ layer, described below), but are vibrational energetic disturbances particular to this layer which you will sense in a manner analogous to a sound or feeling that is disharmonious and is expressed as a disturbance in the pitch of vibration.

The 6ᵗʰ Layer

The 6ᵗʰ layer of aura (or cosmic or celestial body) appears as multicolored softly flowing streams and soft streaks of light emanating from the center of the body, in all directions, to 20 to 25 inches above it (and often beyond). This layer has no clouds of color, nor eggshell or bodily shapes, but only consists of these streams and gentle streaks alone.

The nature of the 6ᵗʰ layer pertains to intuition and insight. It is not a vehicle for outward expression—like the 5ᵗʰ layer—but takes the spiritual power from above for an inward receptivity of intuition, insight, understanding and knowledge (which manifest in the individual consciousness). As with all the layers below, energies on this layer can be healthy or unhealthy. Energetic impurities in this layer are indicated by *discolored, muddied, smeared or streaked regions or infused unhealthy colors within these multicolored streams*, but such impurities are very difficult to see—they are usually quite dim and not always visible. You will often see these very dim colors in your mind's eye, but usually not with your physical eyes (although this is possible).

The 7ᵗʰ Layer

The 7ᵗʰ layer of aura (or ketheric body) appears as a fine, transparent eggshell, with a soft glowing light that may appear bright or golden to your psychic sight and your eyes, although it is actually composed of a light that contains all the colors. This layer is a maximum of approximately 24 to 30 inches (sometimes nearly three feet) above the body surface at its widest point above the midriff.

The nature of the 7ᵗʰ layer is spiritual wisdom, keen spiritual awareness and the spiritual totality of the individual. This layer is also exceedingly important, to the energy healer, because it is the past life layer: it contains within it energies that store the fundamental issues and existential biases from past lives, which can potentially filter down and affect all lower layers. It is very common for unresolved issues and biases, from past lives, to be recapitulated into your patient's present life circumstances. This layer is perhaps the most influential "part" of the entire energy field, and its energies can be either healthy or unhealthy. Energetic defects in this layer manifest as energetic impurities, but ones that are not detected on the basis of unhealthy color. Impurities on this layer manifest as spots, zones or areas which display a *change in texture—not* any significant change in the color or intensity of the light of the shell, but a *roughness and a change in the quality of the light* of the golden eggshell. You will commonly see these impurities in the 7th layer with your mind's eye, and may learn to see them with your physical eyes, as well (the 7th layer is easier to see than the 5th and 6th layers). The 7th layer of aura is a vitally important layer, and there is a special Chios® technique you will use to treat it when these impurities are present.

Learning to View All Seven Layers of Aura

It's time to learn to see these aura layers! In Chios® Level II you were introduced to the practice of learning to view the aura. You began by viewing the 1st layer, the one that is closest to the surface of the body, and then opening yourself to the 2nd layer, with its colors. The full aura is composed of seven layers (or higher bodies), which become more difficult to see as you proceed from the lower to the higher, more refined layers. As you began learning to view the aura, you employed the technique for doing an intuitive reading, with its alternation between active and receptive principles, as a learning tool to allow impressions to first form in your mind's eye. You then attempted to confirm with your physical eyes whatever appeared first to your mind's eye. This was effective at helping you to learn to see, because the aura is seen first with the mind's eye, and then with the physical eyes. It is true, however, that ultimately there is a unity between intuitive and physical vision of the aura, and that the aura is actually seen with the physical eyes in conjunction with the mind's eye. The two are really the same.

In Chios® Level III you will use the same basic technique for employing an intuitive reading to learn to see the aura, but now with some important additions and refinements. You will now use a Chios® symbol in color, from the basic progression, to "be in" that color, and this will enable you to become more attuned to the corresponding layer of aura you are attempting to see. You will use an orange Circle, for example, to make it easier to focus in on and see the 2nd layer (the emotional body, a yellow Circle to make it easier to see the 3rd layer (mental body, a green Trine to make it easier to see the 4th layer (astral body), and so on. You will, during the active phase of your practice, visualize the symbol in color and at the same time focus on the area around your subject's body where the particular aura layer you are attempting to view would be. You will then glance away and release into the receptive phase, allowing an impression of that aura layer to form in your mind's eye. After gaining some impression of the aura layer, in your mind's eye, you will then look back with your physical eyes to attempt to confirm with them what you saw in your mind's eye.

Another refinement to the basic intuitive reading technique that you will use when learning to view the higher layers of aura will be to practice the active principle phase of the intuitive reading technique in a more effortless way. In your practice of this technique during Chios® Level II, you may have used some effort in the active principle phase of the technique, when concentrating upon the area around the body, before glancing away to allow impressions to form in your mind. This was necessary to begin to train your mind to stay on one object or area of awareness—to fix your gaze on the area around the body, for example. By this time, however, you should have become very familiar with this basic technique. Less effort should be necessary for you to focus on the area around the body. In its true meaning, "concentration" does not actually imply any kind of effort, but merely a *localization of awareness*. You are simply allowing one thing—and one thing only—to occupy your awareness. In using this new, expanded Chios® technique to view a specific layer of aura, you should be able with little or no effort to localize your awareness for a brief instant on the area around your subject's body that the aura layer occupies, while at the same time effortlessly visualizing the necessary symbol in color from the basic progression, before glancing away and releasing into the receptive phase. It is still an "active phase," as we have described it, but one in which the mind is focused effortlessly.

Contrary to what you might assume, it is with *less effort* that the greatest power of the intuitive reading technique is released. This refinement is a step towards complete proficiency in this technique, when you will no longer need to consciously go through the steps when using it. The entire technique is a learning tool—you will, with practice, acquire the ability to effortlessly and instinctively "see" the aura in your mind's eye and then with your physical eyes. You will effortlessly receive the intuitive information that this technique—and every variation of it that you will use in healing—provides. The description of this technique, in terms of active and receptive phases, has simply been a description and training aid; as your ability develops you will no longer need to think of it in these terms. This is the product of practice, however, and much practice will be needed until you are able to master it and gain some vision of all seven layers. Invest time in this practice and you will learn to see everything you expect to see.

We should mention again the critical importance of openness. Open yourself to the higher layers and allow a vision of them, and the phenomena within them, to come into your awareness. When learning to see the colors of the 2nd or 4th layers, for example, you may glance away, while practicing the technique, and your mind may suddenly be drawn to a specific area of that layer, and impulsively think "blue!" *Do not doubt*. Release the need to doubt these impressions that will come. If you do this, you will eventually grow into seeing the colors and other phenomena in the aura layers. You will see energies that have a color, form and movement. *Trust your perceptions*—the impressions will take shape in your mind's eye first, if you allow them, and then with your physical vision. After some practice, you will begin to understand that you have often seen more than you realized, that on a deeper level of your being you are already seeing these layers and are now just learning to bring out this ability you already possess inside yourself.

Viewing the Higher Layers

Learning to view the higher layers of aura is a step-by-step process, one layer to the next. Each layer will usually be more difficult to see than the ones below it. When beginning to learn to see the higher layers, observe all the basic considerations for learning to view the aura that we previously discussed in Chios® Level II (re-read them, if necessary). It is once again particularly important to choose an environment where the lighting is neither too bright nor too dim, and to have a neutral-colored cover for your healing table and the entire background area behind it. Remember to relax your eyes, quiet your mind and release yourself from all expectations of what you might see. Complete release and openness is the key to sensing and seeing the higher layers: *you must be as one floating on water*. Here is the Chios® technique for viewing the higher layers, using the 2nd layer as an example and place to begin:

Exercise 3-C: Intuitive Reading: Viewing All Seven Layers of Aura

1. With your eyes open, and your patient lying down in front of you on your treatment table, visualize, sense and become the Chios® symbol in color, from the basic progression, that corresponds to the layer you wish to view. For the 2nd layer (emotional body), this will be an orange Circle.

2. *At the same time*, localize your awareness (effortlessly "concentrate") on the area around your patient's body where the layer you wish to view is located. Do not include the physical body itself, as you localize your awareness on this area, but on the entire region that the layer occupies. You will still see the body, yet negate it, as you focus just on the entire area around the body in which the layer should appear. For the 2nd layer, this is an area shaped somewhat like the shape of the body, yet larger than the body, extending to

approximately four to five inches beyond the body surface. During this active phase visualize, sense and become the Chios® symbol in color and localize your awareness on this area as effortlessly as possible, for a brief moment.

3. Now release yourself into the receptive phase, glancing away and averting your eyes (still open) to an area of empty space off to the side. Completely release and let go, suspending all thinking.

4. Allow yourself to become aware of what your mind's eye perceives. As you know from your previous practice of this technique, your mind's eye can "see" even while your physical eyes are open and looking upon something entirely different. What do you see in your mind's eye? Give yourself a brief moment for an impression to form. (See Figure 30).

5. Repeat this cycle: perform the active phase again, exactly as described above, and then glance away, releasing yourself into the receptive phase and whatever your mind's eye may perceive. Repeat these rounds of alternation between active and receptive phases several times.

6. What impressions are you getting—what are you "seeing," in your mind's eye? Is your awareness drawn to certain areas around your patient's body, perhaps with some subtle impression of color? It will be *subtle* impressions that first form.

7. When you do get some impression of colors or patterns, in your mind's eye, start bringing your physical sight (still in receptive, "soft" phase) back to your patient's body, to see if your physical eyes will begin to register anything of the impression your mind's eye received. Gaze at the area around your patient's body, the open space surrounding the area near the body surface (where the particular layer of aura should be) with a de-focused and very diffuse gaze. Can you see any hint of what your mind's eye perceived?

8. Begin this technique with the 2nd layer. After you have gained a good impression in your mind's eye of the 2nd layer, and have perhaps even begun to see it with your physical eyes, it is time to try to view the next layer up. Proceed to attempting to view the 3rd layer (mental body). When you practice the active phase of the technique, you must make two important modifications. In step 1, you must visualize a yellow Circle (the Chios® symbol in color that corresponds to this 3rd layer). In step 2 you must localize your awareness to a somewhat larger area: to a shell-shaped area again somewhat like the shape of the body, yet larger than the body and extending to approximately eight to ten inches beyond the body surface (the region that the 3rd layer occupies). Other than these changes, perform the technique exactly as before, in steps 1 to 7 above.

9. After gaining good impressions of this 3rd layer, proceed successively to the 4th, 5th, 6th and finally 7th layer. Each layer will extend to a level of

approximately four to five inches above the maximum extent of the previous one (although this will vary, especially with the 4th layer and above). You will therefore need to further modify the active phase of the technique. For the 4th layer (astral body) you will visualize a green Trine and also localize your awareness to a shell-shaped area again somewhat like the shape of the body, yet larger than the body and extending to approximately 12 to 15 inches beyond the body surface. For the 5th layer (etheric template body) you will visualize a blue Trine and also localize your awareness to a eggshell-shaped area extending to a maximum of approximately 16 to 20 inches beyond the body surface at the midriff (yet somewhat closer to the body above the head and feet). For the 6th layer (cosmic body) you will visualize an indigo Trine and also localize your awareness to a large area with no specific shape yet extending to a maximum of approximately 20 to 25 inches beyond the body surface. For the 7th layer (ketheric template body) you will visualize a violet Star and also localize your awareness to a eggshell-shaped area extending to a maximum of approximately 24 to 30 inches beyond the body surface at the midriff (yet again somewhat closer to the body above the head and feet).

10. As you proceed to the higher layers, you will also need to employ a progressively more softened and de-focused gaze with your physical eyes when you bring your eyes back to the area around your patient's body to try to confirm impressions you have seen in your mind's eye. This is especially important for the 4th layer and above. You will also have to stand progressively further back from the body of your subject, up to six feet or more for the 4th layer to perhaps as much as ten feet for the 7th layer. Other than these changes, perform the technique exactly as described in steps 1 to 7 above.

As you proceed to the higher layers, remember that these layers interpenetrate—they occupy the same physical space. That is, the phenomena you see in the astral body, for example, will show as phenomena at the body surface and then all the way out to a foot or so from the surface of the body and actually occupy the same area in space as phenomena at lower layers. Once again, it is not physical distance from the body alone that defines the layers, but differences in the vibratory rates. Each layer corresponds to a different realm of the being and consciousness of your subject—a realm that has its own characteristic level of vibration and unique nature.

This technique works because proper visualization of the colors using the symbols raises your vibratory rate so that the corresponding body—the corresponding layer—will come into view. When your vibratory rate is thus increased, you are able to sense energy on that level. You are "in" that color and able to sense that layer of aura because you have raised your vibratory level to a point where you are able to perceive phenomena at this higher level. This technique will not only increase your ability to view that layer, but will also highlight that layer to your vision so that its contents may be seen more clearly, like a filter, although other layers may be seen at the same time. When practicing this effective technique for

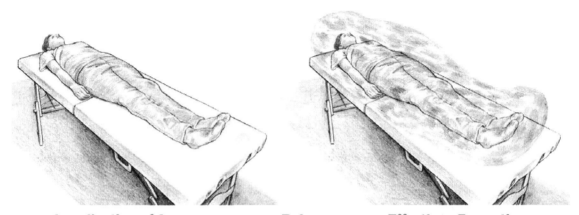

Localization of Awareness .... Release .... Effortless Reception
(Using the 4th Aura Layer as an Example)

Figure 30: Viewing the Higher Layers of Aura

viewing the higher layers, however, do not think of it as a process of "raising your vibratory rate," simply visualize the symbol in color and the area that the layer occupies, and do not attach any mental interpretation to the process—to do so will inhibit and limit the effectiveness of this technique.

Work your way up, from one layer to the next, to bring all the layers into view, while placing special emphasis on learning to sense and see the impurities that appear on each of the layers. You should be able to gain a good intuitive impression of all the layers in your mind's eye, with just a little practice using this technique for viewing these higher layers. This is actually not difficult at all. More practice will strengthen this intuitive information that you receive. This technique merely makes you a clear channel for knowledge coming from a higher level of reality. This intuitive vision of all seven layers will be vital information that you will use in every healing treatment—it is the information you will use to understand your patient's condition, at least in the beginning. It will take longer to see the higher layers with your physical eyes, however, and you may never see all of them. At first, it is normal to begin to see only the first few layers with your physical eyes. You will probably be able to see the 4th layer after some practice, but the 5th and 6th layers are quite difficult to see and may be elusive to your physical sight. Fortunately, the 7th layer is a little easier to eventually see with your eyes. It may take years of practice to gain a physical view of most or all of the seven layers.

Reading your patient's aura will be of central importance to you as you work. In your healing treatments, you may perform your viewing of the aura using this new technique immediately after the intuitive reading technique you learned in Chios® Level II, or instead of it, depending on what is best for you. If you perform both techniques, remember that they are not really separate techniques, but that you are proceeding through a continuous method of learning to obtain progressively refining information regarding the energy field of your patient. It is good to eventually acquire the ability to see the aura and its levels directly with your physical eyes. You should practice viewing the higher layers of aura not only during scheduled healing treatments, but also throughout the day, as well, using the technique above. Often practice at random intervals throughout the day, instead of a disciplined regimen, is the most effective approach of all at learning to see the higher layers, and is highly recommended. It is also wise to employ these tools for sensing and viewing the aura, in all its layers, at various places during your treatment. This may be done all over the body, or you may focus on certain regions of interest. As an aid to learning, it is wise to attempt to view with your physical eyes everything that you see in your mind's eye.

It's important to note that, when you are viewing the aura layers of small adults or children, you should employ increments of three to four inches instead—as their physical bodies are smaller the spacing between the aura layers is proportionately reduced.

Interpreting the Meaning of Energetic Impurities, Colors and Phenomena in the Higher Layers of Aura

When gaining information on your patient's layers of aura prior to treatment, using the new technique you just learned above, you will also find it helpful to ask for information on the meaning of the phenomena that you sense and see in the layers; that is, to do an intuitive reading requesting further information on them. This is especially important when you sense unhealthy energies—energetic impurities or energetic disturbances—in the various layers, but you can do it to learn the true meaning of normal, healthy colors, as well. To do this, perform an intuitive reading using the general technique you have learned, now modified for this specific purpose:

**Exercise 3-D: Intuitive Reading: Energetic Impurities,
Colors and Phenomena in the Aura**

1. With your eyes open, localize your awareness (effortlessly "concentrate") on the energetic impurity, energetic disturbance, color or other phenomenon you see in an aura layer of your patient. If you have not yet acquired the ability to see on the layer with your physical eyes, but have seen the energetic impurity, energetic disturbance, color or other phenomenon in your mind's eye, localize your awareness on that vision in your mind's eye. For a brief moment, during this active phase, effortlessly focus on just it alone, asking for more information about it.

2. Now release into the receptive phase, glancing away and averting your eyes (still open) to another area of empty space off to the side. Completely release, let go and suspend all thinking.

3. Allow yourself to simply receive whatever intuitive information comes, regarding the energetic impurity, color or phenomenon. Images may appear to you, in your mind's eye, giving you a great deal of information on what the phenomenon is and why it is there. Sounds may come, as the color (whether a colored energetic impurity or a healthy color) speaks to you, giving you information about it. Feelings may spontaneously come to you, giving you information or adding to the other information you are receiving. Simple "inner knowings" of the meaning of the energetic impurity, color or phenomenon may emerge in your whole being.

   The energies in the aura layers are intelligent energy and consciousness: some that you will encounter are even like beings, or people—you can talk to them. Memories of your patient's entire life experience (including traumatic memories) are stored in different parts of the layers, and these may be revealed to you (sometimes like a story or a movie—even one that you absorb almost instantaneously). In one or more of these ways, you will get information on the meaning of the phenomenon you are focusing on, and how it may relate to present or past life experiences of your patient (including traumas), core psychological issues in your patient, phenomena in your patient's chakras or other aura layers, and disease conditions in your patient's body.

4. As you proceed to higher layers of aura, the 4th and beyond, it may be more difficult to completely "understand," with words or ideas, the information you are receiving. When you sense or see phenomena on the 2nd, 3rd or 4th layers of aura, for example, you may get easily-understood images, sounds or feelings, as we just described in step 3 above. When you read the meaning of

130

phenomena you see the 5th, 6th or 7th layers, however, you may not be able to immediately "put a finger on" the meaning of whatever comes (see below).

As you work to perceive the meaning of phenomena within the 5th layer, and above, you will receive information in a more "felt sense" way. As an analogy: you often hear sounds at lower frequencies that you can easily hear and understand, but as the frequency is raised to near and somewhat beyond the perceptual range of the human ear the sound is actually "felt" slightly, instead of heard as sound in the normal way. So will your perception become more delicate and refined as the higher levels are sensed. The vibration shifts to a progressively higher level, as one ascends to the higher bodies, and becomes finer and less discernible to living human beings—it becomes a finer vibration, with finer perceptions. Perception, understanding and treatment of phenomena on the lower layers of aura deal with grosser distortions of energy in the auric field layers, but perception and understanding of energies on the higher layers involves a finer and more delicate perception and understanding—one that takes place in the higher awareness. It is important to understand, however, that these delicate energetic phenomena on the higher layers are vitally important, and have an all-pervasive meaning and influence on your patient and upon all lower layers of the energy field. Unconditional openness—and practice—are your keys to sensing and gaining some deep understanding of them. If you maintain openness, you will just know what you need to ask for additional information on, as you proceed through the healing treatment. This information, which will come to you in the form of pictures, sounds, feelings, a "felt sense," or in other forms of information, will greatly increase your knowledge of your patient's condition and how to proceed.

Much has been written about color in the aura, that is, the supposed meaning of certain colors as they appear. While it is true that *sometimes* certain colors in the aura mean certain things, in practice there is no set and reliable system of interpretation for these colors, as they appear on different layers and in different locations—they often mean different things. When certain colors appear within aura layers that you sense are important, however (whether the unhealthy colors of energetic impurities, or normal healthy colors), you can ask for more information about them, using the intuitive reading technique as we just described above. Information, in the form of pictures, sounds, feelings, a "felt sense" or in other ways, will often inform you of the meaning of certain colors, as you observe them, and will also provide details regarding the source of the colors. Usually it is not the color itself, but the purity, tone, hue and brightness of the various colors which appear that holds more fundamental importance. This is a much more accurate and complete way to learn the meaning of the energetic impurities, colors and phenomena you see in your patient's aura than to use any fixed system of interpretation.

Persistence of Visualization and the Principle of Healing

In learning to see the higher layers of aura, you first "see," in your mind's eye these layers and the energetic impurities and disturbances within them. You eventually usually progress to seeing most of them with your physical eyes. These are not two different mechanisms of perception, however, but merely stages of a process that begins—and is always fundamentally—a process of deeper awareness. The aura levels and the phenomena within them are "seen" first and foremost with your deeper awareness and whole being. Seeing them in your mind's eye ("psychic sight") is the next stage of this process, and seeing them with your physical eyes the final stage. The mere act of attempting to see certain levels of the aura establishes some deep awareness of conditions upon them, even if this information does not immediately become available in your mind's eye or is not immediately confirmed with your physical eyes.

One central purpose of the healing treatment that you will perform after viewing your patient's higher layers (with either your mind's eye or your physical eyes) will be to heal the energetic impurities and disturbances which you have sensed within them. You will do this through the use of specific Chios® healing techniques that you are about to learn, but it is not these tools that heal—it is the healing power of pure consciousness that heals, through your conscious, transparent use of these tools. When you view the higher layers of your patient's aura, prior to treatment, you do so for the purpose of acquiring a deep and complete sense of the contents of the layers, in your whole being, prior to treatment. This deep sense of the state of your patient, in your whole being, is then employed through the tools to heal.

As you view the layers, allow a sense of each layer to emerge in your whole being and take special note which layers possess energetic impurities which require removal or energetic disturbances that need correcting. Each time you see a layer that needs healing, note these conditions and also *visualize, intend and sense the layer restored to health*—see, in your mind's eye, the impurities removed and disturbances corrected. This is actually a single process, where you note the impurities and disturbances that exist in the layer and also visualize restoration and correctness—all of which you perform with your whole being as you view the layer and its impurities. This process establishes a link between you and your patient; it establishes a unity of healer and patient and a visualization of energetic health which is then effected as you later employ specific healing techniques to heal the layer. When you later treat this layer of aura using a particular technique, you will have a remnant awareness of unhealthy conditions to be corrected—a *persistence of visualization* of the conditions existing on the layer and those conditions returning to a state of health, while you perform the technique.

You may, for example, examine a patient who has impurities on the 4th layer, which consist of blackened yellow or reddish-yellow streaks that appear unwell. You may also have detected, on the 5th layer, disturbances in vibration in the structure. As you examine these layers, you will see these conditions and visualize these conditions correcting; you will "see" the blackened yellow or reddish-yellow streaks in the colors of the 4th layer healed, such that the impurities are removed and the colors return to a healthy hue. You will similarly "see" the vibrational disturbances on the 5th layer corrected to a healthy, harmonious state. You will then treat your patient, using techniques which have an effect on these layers (techniques you are about to learn). Your deep connection to your patient, with your whole being, and persistence of visualization, channels the healing power of pure consciousness to heal these layers, as you perform the specific techniques needed.

This fundamental approach to healing and ultimate source of the effectiveness of all true healing is not limited to the layers of aura. You will use this same basic process when you treat the chakras of your patient using other special techniques you are about to learn—when you learn to sense and see the energetic defects, in the chakras, you will similarly employ persistence of visualization and see them healed, as you view them. Healing the chakras relies upon this same basic principle, as does every other aspect of energy healing. Healing is the act of holistically sensing the condition of your patient's energy field, in all aspects, and visualizing the energy field healed and restored to health, even as you use all the specific healing tools. The healing passes from healer to patient at a deeper level—the healer heals and the patient receives healing, each with the whole being. This is the fundamental *principle of healing* that makes all true energy healing effective.

Energetic Defects of the Chakra System

Now that you have learned a powerful new technique for viewing the seven layers of aura and the energetic defects within them it is time to turn our attention toward the other main component of the energy field of your patient: the chakra system. Chios® Level III will also include a powerful new technique to sense and see your patient's chakras, but before learning this new technique it will benefit us to learn more about the chakras and the energetic defects that can occur in them.

In Chios® Level II, you learned how to sense and see one simple energetic defect in chakras: blocked chakras. We will now talk much more about the other energetic defects that can occur in chakras, which are: *undercharged chakras*, *unbalanced chakras*, and *chakras exhibiting structural energetic defects*. You will still use the unblocking chakras technique you learned in Chios® Level II, to treat blocked chakras, yet will now learn several very powerful Chios® Master techniques to treat these other energetic defects. You will then have a complete treatment repertoire for healing defects in the chakras.

Energetic and Radiant Characteristics of Chakras

Our first step in learning about energetic defects in chakras is to explore how chakras work. We have already discussed the fact that each chakra is an energy junction, and is always conducting energy in certain ways. This energy conduction is an *energetic characteristic* of each chakra; each chakra possesses a quality of energetic conduction. There are two aspects to this energy conduction. One is the upward flow of energy through each chakra, and through the chakra system as a whole. The energy comes up from the earth and into the 1st chakra, and then ascends through the central energy channel passing through each higher chakra in succession, all the way up to the 7th chakra. The lower chakras are simple in their functioning but the chakras grow progressively more complex and spiritual in their functioning, at each step upwards. As the energy ascends through each of the seven chakras, each chakra takes part of the energy and processes it according to its own particular nature. It transmutes the energy, according to its particular character (which we described in Chios® Level I), and then passes it upward to the next chakra in the system. Like locks on a river, each step takes (or transmutes) the energy to a higher level than the step before. In processing the energy, each chakra is like a small engine operating and running in accordance with its own particular nature, at each level. It is a blockage in this upward energy flow that is what you have already learned to treat with the technique referred to as unblocking chakras.

Although this upward flow of energy is the one that is of primary importance in energy healing work, it is interesting to know that there is also a small but constant stream of energy flowing back down through the chakra system—a form of higher spiritual energy that has been transmuted up through all of the chakras, up to and including the 7th, and then works back down through the system, through each chakra, to infuse the chakras and the energy moving upward. This downward flow of spiritual energy is not transmuted again on its way back down, but works to stimulate and infuse each chakra. Some spiritual systems envision this downward flow as being within a separate central energy channel—with an overall circular flow up through all the chakras, and then a downward flow back to the place of beginning. The chakras are linked by this upward (and downward) stream of energy.

The second aspect of the energy conduction through each chakra is the manner in which each chakra takes in energy from all around and passes the energy through itself and then distributes it throughout the body and energy field. The energy is passed to the other chakras, all the layers of aura and the organs and tissues of the physical body. It is vital to the health of the entire energy field that each chakra conduct the energy in a pure and healthy way, as the energy moves up the chakra system and also as it moves into and through each chakra to be distributed to the entire system. If the chakra's state of health is less than ideal, the energy flow is disturbed, negatively affecting not just the energy processing at that particular chakra but also the entire energy field.

In addition to their energetic characteristic (their function as energy junctions for conduction of the energy in these two ways), each chakra has a second important characteristic to its functioning. As each chakra takes some of the energy that nourishes it and transmutes it according to its own particular character, it also radiates energy outward from the body in a visual field. This *radiant characteristic* is a higher and more subtle manifestation of the chakra, beyond its function as an energy junction and energy conductor. It is not a primary movement of energy but a visible indicator of the performance, condition and state of the health of the chakra. It is the visual appearance of the chakra, from which the condition of the chakra (and therefore its energetic influence on the rest of the energy field) can be inferred. This visual field has as its dominant color the true color of the chakra (although other colors are often present), and it is this visual field of color that you began to learn to sense, as it reflects on the back of your hands, in Chios® Level II.

This radiant characteristic of each of the chakras can be understood through an analogy. Consider the chakra system as a stem with flowers upon it, seven flowers at different levels up and down the stem, from red at the bottom to violet at the top. Energy from the earth ascends through the stem and nourishes each flower, in succession, each flower taking some energy for the purpose of nourishing itself and producing its petals, the energy also continuing upwards to the remaining flowers above. Each flower is also nourished from sunlight streaming down from above and all around, a higher energy and light which stimulates and nourishes each chakra (and makes all life possible). Each flower does not radiate energy, like chakras do, but each flower does absorb energy from all that surrounds it and processes it according to its nature, and has a visible appearance which is an indicator of its health as it does so. Each flower radiates a visual appearance which is an indicator of its "energetic" health and well-being.

It is the radiant characteristic of each chakra—the visual indicator of the state of health of the chakra—that you will now learn to sense more completely. When this radiant characteristic informs you that a chakra is unhealthy, you will heal the chakra using special Chios® color channeling techniques. There will be two basic conditions that you will evaluate and treat with color: 1) chakras that are undercharged, that are inadequate or that are impure in their native energetic operation; and 2) chakras that are unbalanced, that are over- or under-activated in their operation, in comparison with the other chakras in the chakra system. To refer again to the analogy above, some flowers may show a diseased or weak color or hue to their petals—they may not be gaining enough energy from the energy ascending through the stem to ensure good health, and have therefore become subject to disease. These may be likened to undercharged chakras. Other flowers may show too much or too little growth, as seen in the size of their petals—they process somewhat more or somewhat less of their share of the energy and are therefore too active or too timid in their growth, compared to the other flowers. These may be likened to unbalanced chakras in the chakra system. These conditions are explained in more detail in the following sections.

Undercharged Chakras

Each chakra in the chakra system has a dominant true color, from red to violet. Consider the chakra system as a rainbow spectrum with seven steps, consisting of seven separate cells (from red at the 1st chakra to violet at the 7th). Each chakra resides in a cell at a certain location along the spectrum, but is also connected to the others and is part of the whole spectrum, which is ultimately one being (like the colors that appear separately when sunlight is passed through a prism, but that together comprise sunlight). Each chakra, in its cell, has an affinity for the specific true color there. This true color corresponds to the native energy of the chakra at that location (the specific vibrational level), which denotes its domain of activity and its realm of being. This native true color of a chakra will often be rich, strong and pure—its own color only—yet the presence of other pure colors is not an indication of lack of health, but a sign of activity. A pure orange chakra, for example, is not healthier than an orange chakra with bright flecks or sparks of blue and green; these other colors indicate normal, healthy operation of the chakra in conjunction with other healthy energies in the chakra system and energy field.

An orange chakra that is faded or lacks brightness in its color and radiant appearance, however, is an undercharged chakra—a chakra that is weak, depressed or inadequate in its native energetic functioning and indicates this unhealthy state by not radiating its dominant true color in a strong and pure way. It is a chakra that will be susceptible to energetic impurities as a result of this weakened condition. An undercharged chakra will appear diffused, muddied, watery, or smeared with color, or streaked with colored impurities (black, gray, silver, brown, brownish-red or dusty yellow—just as in the aura layers). The dominant true color of the chakra, and usually any other colors which appear within it, will look unhealthy as a result of these energetic impurities. Such unhealthy energetic impurities have invaded the chakra as a result of its weakened or inadequate energy (just as energetic impurities invade the aura layers). Whether simply weak and deficient in the content of its native energy or whether additionally sullied with energetic impurities, an undercharged chakra is a weakened chakra, a chakra that has squandered energy or has improperly processed the energy available to it in such a way that it is not properly maintaining itself—it is a chakra in a depleted condition and vulnerable to impurity. Its "engine" is out of tune and running rough. It is diseased and in need of treatment; it needs its native energy restored to a strong, healthy state, and any impurities which may be present in it removed.

Undercharged chakras do not make the healthy energetic contribution that they normally make to the overall operation of the energy field of your patient. The unhealthy-looking radiant characteristic is indicative of an unhealthy state of energy conduction. Each chakra makes a unique and necessary contribution to the entire energy field. An undercharged chakra does not contribute a proper vitality of its native energy to the overall operation of the energy field, and if impurities are present also introduces an element of energetic impurity to the influence it exerts. An undercharged chakra potentially depresses and may even introduce impurities into the normal energetic functioning of any or all of the other chakras and any or all the aura layers. The chakras in the chakra system share energy, through the central energy channel and generally throughout the energy field. Each chakra also bears a strong relationship to its corresponding aura layer—energy impurities in the chakra often directly relate to energetic impurities in that layer. But, there is more: the chakras exist at each of the seven layers of aura. Just as there are points on the physical body where chakras exist, so are there points or areas on all the higher layers of aura that are also part of the chakra. The operation of each chakra is therefore related to all layers of aura, and all the chakras share energetic influence through the aura layers they all exist upon. When a chakra is undercharged, the energetic functioning of not only the corresponding aura level is affected, but many related functions in the entire energy field. As we've discussed before, the energy field is a holistic entity—every part influences every other part.

When the 3rd chakra is undercharged, for example, it can affect the healthy operation of related organs in the physical body, related operations in the emotional body (as they relate to the 3rd chakra), operations in the mental body (the corresponding aura layer), and in the remaining aura layers and chakras. All operations in the energy field related to the operation of the undercharged chakra are affected. You may or may not be able to interpret this influence in the terms of the native character of that chakra ("perception and projection of self"), but its native and impure energy will affect these other energies in a complex way that inhibits the totality of the health of all. Not just that function will be negatively affected, but every other aspect of your patient's being will be affected in some way as well. Such a condition will often correlate to the psychological issues and life experience of your patient and will affect nearly every aspect of your patient's life to one degree or another. An undercharged 3rd chakra, for example, might correlate to a perception and projection of self that has weakened and deviated from a normal, healthy state. Unhealthy energies in this chakra might correlate to dysfunctional thoughtforms in your patient's self-image, but the effects are felt in many other areas.

It is quite common to find undercharged 3rd, 4th and 5th chakras in patients, and charging these chakras will often provide a vital and noticeable benefit to their physical, emotional, mental and spiritual health. The 1st and 2nd chakras need charging a little less frequently, and when an undercharged condition occurs in these it is perhaps less serious, although they should still be charged back to health. The 6th and 7th chakras similarly require charging somewhat less frequently, but when an undercharged condition is present in these higher chakras it is quite serious. The higher the chakra the greater the unhealthy effect of an undercharged chakra, because it will more completely affect the operation of the energy field on all levels. Charging of the 6th and 7th chakras, when required, is therefore highly necessary and highly beneficial to your patient in many ways.

The lower chakras have a self-healing aspect; that is, when in an undercharged state they have the tendency to charge and heal themselves back to health. This is particularly true with the 1st and 2nd chakras. As one proceeds to the higher chakras, however, this self-healing property of the chakras diminishes—the higher chakras cannot recharge and heal themselves—and so, unless charged by you the healer, these undercharged conditions will remain, sometimes indefinitely. This is another reason why restoring undercharged higher chakras is so important and so beneficial to your patient.

Unbalanced Chakras

Each chakra in the chakra system plays a particular part in the overall health and harmony of the entire energy field and potentially affects all the other elements in it, as we have just described. Chakras that are fully charged with their native energy, and free of impurity, are a requirement for the complete energetic health of your patient. There are other possible energetic defects in chakras which must be avoided, however, to ensure that the chakras make a healthy contribution to the functioning of the entire system.

Each chakra also has an activity level: it transmutes a certain quantity of the energy it takes in for its energetic operation, in accordance with its unique character and realm of being. It exerts its influence and contributes—according to its native energy and particular character—in the overall health of the energy field in a degree that corresponds to this activity level. This activity level is also indicated by the radiant characteristic of the chakra, not by the color of its radiant field (as in undercharged chakras) but by its size. For the energy field to function properly there must be an overall balance in the activity level of the chakras—each chakra taking and transmuting a balanced amount of the energy available and therefore working in a balanced and harmonious manner with the others, as they all project their influence to the entire energy field. A chakra that is either overactive or underactive, however, is transmuting too much or too little of the energy and hence is too high or too low in its activity level; it is unbalanced. It is exerting too much or too little influence in the overall being of your patient; the contribution it makes to the overall operation of the energy field (its "force") is either over- or under-represented, making the entire energy field and state of being of your patient unbalanced. Its "engine" is running too fast or too slow. This incorrect level of activation must be raised or lowered to bring it into balance with the other chakras in the chakra system.

An overactive 2nd chakra, for example, can correlate to the emotional aspect (especially as pertaining to desire or sexuality) that has become too forceful and too dominating in its influence on the energy field and overall state of being of your patient. Such a condition will influence the operation of all other aspects of the energy field, to one degree or another, as the over- or under-active influence of that chakra casts the entire system out of balance. The functions that correlate to the native character of the chakra (emotions, desire and sexuality) may be over-represented, in the life of your patient, but this unbalance will negatively affect many other aspects of the body, psychology and life experience of your patient as well. Although an unbalanced chakra, by itself, may not initiate an illness or affliction, it is often present as an important contributing factor. Unbalanced chakras, in any case, prevent a balanced physical, emotional, mental and spiritual life. Should any chakras be over or under-active in their activity level, they must be rebalanced by raising or lowering their activity level to match the others, so that a level balance in the entire system—from 1st chakra to 7th chakra—is achieved. For example, a 2nd chakra may be radiating a healthy orange hue, but too powerfully. This chakra is not in need of charging, but needs rebalancing so that its activity level is lowered to balance with the other chakras in the system so that they may all be equally active, restoring your patient's being to an overall balance.

It is interesting to note that an undercharged and an underactive chakra can be somewhat similar, at least in their effect. A chakra that is undercharged may have a weakness to its energy, but may nevertheless have a proper activity level. An underactive chakra may still have an adequate content and purity to its energetic functioning—may be charged and functioning—yet have an activity level below that which is required for it to be of proper influence in its operation. Both such chakras will depress the normal energetic functioning of the entire energy field: the normal healthy, strong contribution that chakra would make is weakened. Although the effect is nearly the same (although not quite, for the undercharged chakra may also contribute energetic impurity) the cause is different. The inability of each chakra to perform in a fully healthy way is similar in its effect but different in the underlying cause. The effect is similar, but the treatment required to heal the condition is different.

In the chakra system there are not chakras which are more or less likely to be unbalanced. There will therefore be no chakras in your patients more likely to need rebalancing, yet there will be *patterns of balancing* that you will find in each individual patient. In each patient, the balance of the chakra system will show some pattern of deviation from an ideally balanced state, such that there will be an overall pattern of imbalance instead of just single chakras being out of balance or dramatic shifts taking place in the activity levels of adjoining chakras. You will seldom find only one chakra out of balance in a patient, nor will you often find a very overactive chakra next to a very underactive one, but it will always be that there is an overall pattern or curve to the level of activation of the chakras in the chakra system such that there is a pattern of deviation from the equal, level degree of activation you would find when the system is in a perfectly balanced state.

This deviation from ideal balance in the chakra system is often a chronic structural condition in particular patients. It is a semi-permanent or permanent condition that will remain unless you work to rebalance your patient's chakra system to its proper state. You may, for example, have a patient who shows a fairly level balance in the lower chakras, yet the higher chakras show progressively lower levels of activation, such that the 5th, 6th, and 7th chakras require progressively greater degrees of rebalancing upwards. You will often find such chronic patterns of imbalance, in your individual patients. Repeated treatment will be required, to bring each patient's chakra system back into balance and maintain that balance. Patterns of imbalance in individual patients tend to be more chronic and pattern-specific than the occurrence of undercharged chakras in patients. It is nevertheless possible to heal unbalanced conditions in the chakra system with repeated treatments, which will progressively correct this condition.

Chakras with Structural Energetic Defects

We have thus far discussed undercharged chakras and unbalanced chakras—two energetic defects in chakras that are sensed from the radiant characteristic of the chakra and that inhibit the health of the entire energy field. There is a third energetic defect that may be present in chakras: one that is not sensed using the radiant appearance of the chakra but that nevertheless will make a very unhealthy contribution to the entire energy field if not corrected.

We've mentioned briefly how each chakra in the chakra system can be thought of as an energetic conductor into which energy is received, processed and sent forth to the rest of the energy field, in accordance with that chakra's particular character. In this processing of energy, each chakra has a fundamental energetic "structure" that facilitates this energetic conduction. While not like the structure of a physical object (chakras are not physical objects, but patterns of energy), this energetic structure is the energy conduction pattern of the chakra. It is the fundamental manner in which energy is processed through the chakra and then sent to the rest of the energy field. Chakras have been described as "whirlpools" of energy: this is the overall "macro" shape and largest appearance and structure of a chakra's energetic conduction pattern. There are smaller vortices, within this whirlpool shape, and yet smaller details, down to the finest "micro" elements of a chakra's energetic structure. If the energetic structure—at all these levels—is of the normal, healthy form, and conducts energy in a clean and clear way, the chakra will process and conduct energy in the pure way that the overall health of the energy field requires.

Chakras may, however, contain structural energetic defects, which are defects in the very structure and pattern of the chakra that detrimentally affect its ability to conduct energy. This sort of defect is not a lack of quantity or lack of purity in the basic native energy of the chakra (as in an undercharged chakra), nor is it a basic over- or under-activity of the chakra (as in an unbalanced chakra), but is a lack and failing in the very energetic structure of the chakra which limits its very ability to process energy and conduct it through itself and to the rest of the system, in a pure and healthy way. Chakras that exhibit structural energetic defects are unable to fulfill their portion of the energetic health of the overall energy field. All portions of the energy field that would otherwise interact and receive beneficial influence from the proper operation of the chakra are instead subject to a distorted, incomplete and improper functioning of the energy, which would normally flow through and be processed by the chakra. The result is a serious fundamental incompleteness and distortion of the energetic influence the chakra has upon the entire energy field, potentially including other chakras and all the layers of aura. All operations in the energy field related to the operation of the defective chakra are rendered distorted or incomplete in their operation, to one degree or another.

Structural energetic defects in chakras can occur at the "macro" or "micro" level. At the "macro" level, the chakra's overall whirlpool shape can be disfigured or damaged, as can the smaller vortices within the whirlpool. These defects in the overall energy conduction pattern of the chakra are indicative of a restricted and distorted energy flow, through it. Part or all of the energy is no longer conducted through the chakra in a clear and complete way—the structural energetic defect allows only a certain portion of the energy through, or places a "spin" or distortion onto part or all of the energy as it is conducted through the chakra.

At the "micro" level, the finest energetic elements of the chakras structure can become occluded and clogged. This way in which these structural energetic defects can result in an incomplete and distorted flow of energy through the chakra can be described through an analogy. Consider the flow of energy through the chakra as a flow through a screen in which tiny holes are present. The screen is a "filter" which is normally clean and clear, allowing for a pure, clear flow through it. If some of the tiny holes in the screen become blocked, however (through which the overall flow of energy cannot proceed), and other holes become partially occluded (in which the flow of energy goes forth a short way but is then blocked or diverted), the effect is an overall restriction and distortion of what should be a clear, smooth and complete flow of the energy.

The occurrence of structural energetic defects can correlate to fundamental ways in which the psychology and life experience of your patient have become distorted. A structural energetic defect in the 4th chakra, for example, may indicate a fundamental and profound distortion in your patient's ability to give and receive love, often as the result of traumatic experiences. This will, of course, also affect all other parts of the energy field, as the distorted energy conducted by the chakra affects the aura layers and chakras. It will, once again, ultimately affect every aspect of your patient's being. Structural energetic defects are the most serious condition of all that may be found in chakras—they often eventually result in serious physical disease or in conditions of chronic emotional, mental or spiritual limitation, affliction or illness. These defects do not heal themselves. Left untreated they will remain and will exert a very unhealthy influence on the entire life process of your patient. These serious defects in chakras may be corrected, however, and it is vital to do so whenever they are present.

It is quite common to find structural energetic defects in the 4th, 5th, 6th and 7th chakras; these are serious conditions that require treatment. Structural energetic defects of the 1st, 2nd and 3rd chakras, although somewhat less commonly found and somewhat less serious, nevertheless should always be treated, as well. All types of structural energetic defects in chakras are healed using the same basic technique.

It is important to note that these three energetic defects that we have just described—undercharged chakras, unbalanced chakras and chakras with structural energetic defects—often occur together. Very often you will find one or more ill, diseased chakras in your patient that exhibit two or even all three of these defects we've just discussed: a chakra that is undercharged may also be unbalanced and/or exhibit structural energetic defects, for example. Such chakras may additionally have auric energy impurities, in the layer(s) of aura directly above. Often your patient will have a chronically weak chakra or chakras which require treatment with multiple healing techniques. You will find quite often this will be the case with the higher chakras—the 4th, 5th, 6th and 7th. These chakras, having a more sophisticated spiritual functioning, have more that can "go wrong." They will often display several defects at once and will require multiple healing techniques and much of your time and attention to heal. And yet, because of the profound importance and overall influence of these higher chakras, your treatment of them will bring profound and lasting benefit to your patient.

Sensing the Condition of the Chakra System

Now that we have discussed the energetic defects that may be present in chakras, it's time to learn to sense these defects. You will use four main perceptual tools to sense the condition of your patient's chakras: 1) a new modification of the intuitive reading technique that you will use to obtain intuitive information to identify undercharged and unbalanced chakras; 2) viewing the reflection of chakra color on the back of your hand, which you will use as a second tool to confirm undercharged chakras (you have already learned this technique in Chios® Level II); 3) your "felt sense," or *empathic sense* of chakra condition, to sense chakras with structural energetic defects, and 4) the subtle sensations in your hands, during the passing of hands (which you have likewise practiced before in Chios® Levels I and II). We will first introduce the new modification of the intuitive technique that you will use to obtain intuitive information regarding the state of your patient's chakra system. We'll then add the procedure for empathic sensing of chakra condition. Finally we will discuss how to combine the information that you receive from all these sources to get an integrated assessment of treatment needs for your patient's chakra system.

Sensing the Condition of the Chakra System Through The Reception of Intuitive Information

In Chios® Level II you learned the basic intuitive reading technique, with its alternation between active and receptive principles. You have used this basic technique (with modifications) for some very important purposes: 1) to learn to sense the condition of your patient's aura and chakras in a simple manner: to detect blocked chakras, leaks and tears, auric energy impurities, etc; 2) to begin to view the 1st layer of aura, with the glancing technique; 3) to begin to see the chakra colors on the back of your hand; 4) to learn to view the higher layers of aura, and 5) to interpret the meaning of the impurities and colors which you see on the aura layers. We will now modify the basic intuitive reading technique again, so we may this time use it to detect undercharged and unbalanced chakras in your patient's chakra system. This information will be of central importance in your treatment of your patient.

This new technique—like all the variations of the basic intuitive reading technique we have used—is an effective way to learn to obtain intuitive information. The information you obtain ultimately comes from the field of pure consciousness—the realm that you the healer open yourself to and cultivate a connection with. Obtaining this intuitive information is an effective way of gaining knowledge of the condition of your patient, and learning to perform an intuitive reading of the chakra system is another powerful and effective perceptual tool. When preparing to practice this technique, observe all the considerations for the proper performance of intuitive readings that we have discussed previously. Once again quiet your mind and release yourself from all expectations of what you might sense and see. As before, complete release and openness is the key to effective practice. Here is the Chios® technique for sensing the condition of your patient's chakra system and identifying chakras that are undercharged and unbalanced:

Exercise 3-E: Intuitive Reading: Sensing the Condition of the Chakra System

1. With your eyes closed, and your patient lying down in front of you on your treatment table, visualize an outline of a body profile of your patient: the outline of your patient's body as it would appear to you with your patient lying on his or her back facing upwards, as seen from the side.

2. Now imagine a rainbow shell of color, a gently curved rainbow traveling from above the hips of your patient's body outline (the area of the 1st chakra, where the rainbow is red), to the top of your patient's head (the area of the 7th chakra, where the rainbow is violet). See, in your mind's eye, seven segments of this rainbow shell, separated by boundaries between adjacent colors, yet with the top of the shell in a gentle, even curve. You do not need to visualize the chakra in each colored segment, but will of course know that a chakra of the corresponding true color occupies each. Briefly and effortlessly localize your awareness on this complete image, in the active phase, knowing that you will shortly be getting information on which of your patient's chakras are in need of charging or rebalancing.

3. Release into the receptive phase, keeping your eyes closed. Completely release, let go and suspend all thinking and allow any change to the image you created (your patient's body outline with the rainbow shell of color above it) to occur. (See Figure 31).

4. Notice any changes in the overall shape of the rainbow shell, or in the colors exhibited in the seven colored segments (the seven chakra fields). Does the shape now appear different, with the apparent level—the height—of any of the seven colored segments now deviating from a gentle, even curve they possessed before, as you now view the curve? If so, this may be indicative of chakras that are over- or underactive—a pattern of imbalance in the chakra system. "Bumps" upward indicate chakras where the activity level is too high, with the larger size of the chakra field denoting overactivity. "Dips" downward indicate chakras where the activity level is too low, with the smaller size of the chakra field indicating underactivity. Take careful mental note of which chakras are underactive or overactive, for future treatment.

5. Now examine the color of each of the seven colored segments, from red to violet. You can do this by looking at all together, or begin at the red end and proceed upwards looking at each colored segment in succession. Which colors still look strong and pure? Are there any colors that now appear faded, weak, diffused, muddied, watery, or smeared with color, or streaked with colored impurities, as we've described them? If so, these chakras may be undercharged. Fairly often a chakra will be both undercharged and out of balance, yet it will also be often that a chakra will be only one or the other.

Some chakras will be neither; they will show the same healthy hue and same color field size as before, indicating that their state of charge and balance requires no correction. Take careful mental note of which chakras are undercharged, for future treatment.

6. You may repeat the active/receptive cycle again, performing several rounds, if that assists you in gaining a full image of the chakra system, with all this information. You may find that, as when viewing the aura layers, several cycles of the technique will bring more and more detail to the image you develop in your mind's eye.

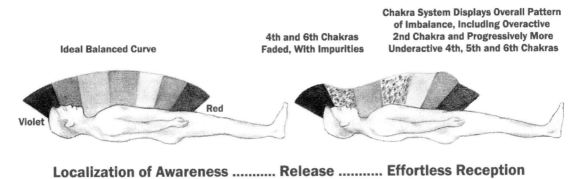

Figure 31: Sensing the Condition of the Chakra System

After you are satisfied with the information you have received, you should employ persistence of visualization in the same way that was recommended when viewing the higher layers of aura. For each chakra that you have noted as undercharged visualize, intend and sense the chakra color restored to a strong, healthy hue. See any energetic impurities in the undercharged chakra removed. For all chakras that you have seen as being over- or underactive, visualize, intend and sense those chakras lowered or raised in their activity level, such that the gentle, even curve of the rainbow shell is restored. This is again a single process, where you obtain an image in your mind's eye of both undercharged and unbalanced chakras and also visualize restoration and correctness—all of which you perform with your whole being as you perform this new technique. Once again, you employ a visualization of energetic health which will later be effected as you employ specific healing techniques to heal the chakras that require it.

While you are examining your patient's undercharged chakras, you can also ask for more information on the energetic impurities you see within them (as you did with energetic impurities in the higher layers of aura). To do this, again perform an intuitive reading: focus on the impurities in the chakra color, during the active phase, and then release into receptive phase to get intuitive information (which will come as pictures, sounds, a "felt sense" or in other ways). Perform this intuitive reading, just as we described it in Exercise 3-D: Intuitive Reading: Energetic Impurities, Colors and Phenomena in the Aura, yet now focusing on the phenomena you see in the chakras. You may receive important information regarding how these impurities in the chakra relate to energetic impurities you've seen in the aura layers, psychological issues in your patient which correlate to the impurities, related life experience or physical disease which might be present. As with the layers of aura, in which you could also ask for and obtain information on any of the colors in the layers (including healthy colors), you can ask for more information on clear flecks of color in the chakra (other than the dominant true color of the chakra). Although this may not correlate to disease, it may nevertheless contribute to your understanding of the current state of your patient's psychology and life experience.

After a short period of practice using this technique, you may find that you no longer need to consciously follow the steps—that a visualization of the state of your patient's chakra system will simply appear in your mind's eye. Information regarding the meaning of what you see may also just simply come to you. As with all the other techniques we have derived from the basic intuitive reading technique, regular practice will soon make the technique automatic. You will find that you will automatically get all the intuitive information you need, with just a brief moment of intention.

You will probably want to learn this technique while keeping your eyes closed, both in the active phase and receptive phase of the technique. It is not necessary to glance back with your physical eyes open to attempt to view the colored chakra fields above the body of your patient. Most healers, in fact, never fully see the chakras with their physical eyes. We will talk soon about how to attempt to see the chakras, but your intuitive information is potentially a very accurate source of information on chakra charge and balance. Your practice of this technique creates an awareness, deep in your being, of the condition of your patient's chakras. Your mind's eye will see everything it needs to see, and this information can be used on its own to plan and effectively implement the needed treatment. If physical vision of the chakras eventually manifests, so much the better, but this is not necessary at all.

Empathic Perception of Chakras With Structural Energetic Defects

The new modification to the basic intuitive reading technique that we have just described employs a visual sense of the chakras in the chakra system to detect undercharged and unbalanced chakras. The third type of energetic defect that may be found in chakras—structural energetic defects—is usually not sensed visually, however. Like undercharged and unbalanced chakras, chakras with structural energetic defects are commonly present in patients, but they must be detected in a different way: through your intuitive and empathic sense, as you the healer treat these chakras.

We have discussed the practice of openness in energy healing work: how you lose your individual identity and instead move towards a state of unity with your patient, your patient's energy field and whatever healing technique you are employing. As you advance in this process of openness, your intuitive sense of your patient and his or her condition (in which you still have some sense of your individual self) progresses to an empathic sense (where you become your patient and his or her energy field). You progress from knowing the condition of your patient using your intuition to sensing his or her actual condition, as if in yourself. Your body, emotions or mind may therefore mirror that of your patient, and you may sense in yourself various conditions which require treatment. One important example of this phenomenon that we must discuss now is your sensing—in your own chakras—chakras in your patient that have structural energetic defects.

You will usually detect structural energetic defects in your patient's chakras as you channel energy into them during the normal sequence of treatment hand positions, with your hands on the chakra. In Chios® Level II, we discussed the manner in which you can become more aware of the energy during energy channeling: you learned to become aware of delicate sensations in your hands as you channeled the energy and that any energy irregularities that you sensed could be indicative of a chakra that was ill and in need of treatment. To this basic awareness, you will now add an empathic sense of the condition of your patient's chakra—in yourself—to detect structural energetic defects. To do this, use the following process:

Exercise 3-F: Sensing Chakras With Structural Energetic Defects

1. As you channel energy into each chakra, during the normal sequence of treatment hand positions, do you sense, intuitively, almost a *pain in the chakra*, as you channel energy into it—a pain that seems to also extend into the body of your patient and may even seem to extend and radiate outward through the layers of your patient's aura?

2. Most importantly, however, do you sense this pain, empathically in your own corresponding chakra, or in your body or your own aura, in the area around that chakra? You might, while treating the 4th (heart) chakra of your patient, feel a distinct sense of pain in and around your own 4th chakra, for

example, or in your own body in the region of your heart, or in your own aura above it. It is important to understand that this may not be a strictly physical pain (although a physical sense of pain may certainly be present) but is a larger "felt sense" of a pain that you sense with your whole being. You are relying on your own intuitive sense—and in the more advanced state your sense of empathic identity with your patient—to detect this sense of pain in a chakra, which indicates a chakra with structural energetic defects.

3. Take careful mental note of each chakra for which you sense this pain. Each chakra for which you sense this pain is likely to be a chakra with structural energetic defects—a chakra that is damaged and disfigured, perhaps even a chakra in crisis—and requires treatment.

While you are sensing a chakra with structural energetic defects in this way, you can also ask for more information about it (as you did with energetic impurities in the higher layers of aura and energetic impurities in undercharged chakras). To do this, again perform an intuitive reading as you did in Exercise 3-D: Intuitive Reading: Energetic Impurities, Colors and Phenomena in the Aura, yet now for the chakra and the sense of pain: focus effortlessly on the chakra and the "felt sense" of pain, during the active phase, and then release into receptive phase to get intuitive information regarding the state of the chakra (which will come as pictures, sounds, a "felt sense" or in other ways). You may receive important information regarding phenomena in other parts of your patient's energy field and how the structural energetic defects in the chakra relate to them, psychological issues in your patient which correlate to the defects, related present or past life experience, or physical disease which might be present in the body of your patient. You may even see, in your mind's eye, some detail of the disfigurement. It is also important to ask for and sense how the structural energetic defects in the chakra might have affected your patient's layers of aura. We have discussed how energetic defects (of whatever kind) can affect the entire energy field of your patient. While structural energetic defects are not indicated by colored impurities in the chakra (as with undercharged chakras), it is important to know that energetic impurities and energy disturbances on one or more higher layers of aura will often be related.

Integrating an Interpretation of Treatment Needs for the Chakra System

Now that you have learned all the techniques that you will use to sense the condition of the chakra system of your patient, it's time to learn how to integrate the information you will obtain on energetic defects in your patient's chakras, and plan treatment. The specific energetic defects you've identified, the additional information you may have obtained about the energetic defects, and the way these "separate" phenomena in the energy field relate to one another is integrated and used together, to obtain a complete and overall understanding of your patient's condition.

Undercharged chakras will often be first sensed as such when you use your new intuitive reading technique to sense the condition of the chakra system, although you may also first notice them when viewing the reflection of the color of that chakra on the back of your hand, during the normal sequence of treatment hand positions. Whichever of these two ways you first notice a chakra's undercharged state, use the other to attempt to confirm it. The chakra will appear faded, watery or lacking in brightness, in its color and radiant appearance. If energetic impurities are additionally present (as they will often be, yet not always) you will also see muddied, smeared or streaked areas with the unhealthy colors we've discussed. The chakra's color and appearance will clearly look unhealthy—the hue will not be robust and the color will not be appealing. Remember, you may also see colors other than the dominant true color of the chakra, yet if these other colors are pure they do not indicate an unhealthy, undercharged chakra but merely activity within it. You can also use the passing of hands to confirm what you sense: when you pass your hands over an undercharged chakra you will sense a weakness and unhealthiness to the chakra, in your whole being. An undercharged chakra will perceived not only by your sight, but by your "felt sense" as being sullied, impure and unhealthy in its energy functioning. As we have mentioned before, undercharged 3rd, 4th and 5th chakras are quite common, while undercharged 1st and 2nd chakras are somewhat less so, and undercharged 6th and 7th chakras are a little less common still. All chakras in your patient that you have detected as being undercharged, however, will need to be charged back to their normal, healthy hue using the Chios® technique known as *Chakra Charging*.

Unbalanced chakras will usually also be first sensed as such when you use your new intuitive reading technique to sense the condition of the chakra system. They will be denoted by colored segments, within the seven-step rainbow shell (or curve) of color, whose height extends either above or below the gentle, even curve. "Bumps" upward indicate overactive chakras. "Dips" downward indicate underactive chakras. An examination of this curve—noting at which chakra points the curve bumps or dips—will indicate to you chakras that need to thus be raised or lowered in their activity level (rebalanced upwards or downwards) to bring overall balance back to the chakra system. You will not be able to notice, or confirm, unbalanced chakras by viewing the reflection of chakra color on the back of your hand because this is not a reliable way to sense the size (and hence level of activity) of the chakra field. You can again use the passing of hands, however, to confirm what you sense. An overactive chakra will not merely be indicated by a "bump" in the profile during your intuitive reading of the chakra system, but you will additionally feel an overexcited, unsteady, even jagged-feeling quality to its energy—in your whole being—as you pass your hands over that chakra. An underactive chakra will not merely appear as a "dip" in the profile, but also will be felt—in your whole being—as having a weakness or timidity in its energy. Note that you might perceive an undercharged chakra and an underactive chakra as having this weakness or timidity, when passing your hands over them, yet the undercharged chakra will also usually have an unhealthy, impure feel as well. As we discussed before, there are not particular chakras that are more or less susceptible to being unbalanced, but there will almost always be a pattern of imbalance. You will then proceed to rebalance those chakras which require it, thereby bring the entire chakra system back into balance, through use of the Chios® technique called *Chakra System Rebalancing*.

Chakras with structural energetic defects will primarily be sensed through your empathic sense of chakra condition as you channel energy into them during the normal sequence of treatment hand positions. You will sense, either intuitively or empathically, a pain in the chakra that may also extend into the body and/or radiate outward through the aura layers. You will sense this pain—ideally in an empathic way in your own corresponding chakra—that is not merely a physical pain but a pain that you sense with your whole being. Chakras with structural energetic defects are common, in patients, so you must remain fully aware and open to this empathic phenomenon, as you treat each chakra in your patient. Although this empathic sense is the primary way that you will sense a chakra with structural energetic defects, you may also get intuitive information that indicates that this condition exists in one or more of your patient's chakras. This may happen at any time during a healing treatment, but most often will occur as you employ intuitive reading techniques (either the simpler version you learned in Chios® Level II, or the new technique for reading the chakra system that you learned in this level). You may receive information (in the form of pictures, sounds or just a deep knowing) that indicates that a certain chakra or chakras in your patient have this damage, perhaps including further information of the damage itself or its correlating conditions and/or cause in the psychology and life experience of your patient. Even when you receive such information that one or more chakras have structural energetic defects, however, it is important to attempt to confirm it with your empathic sense of the chakra(s) in question. As we have mentioned before, you will detect this condition most often in the upper chakras—in the 4th, 5th, 6th and 7th. It will also sometimes appear in the 1st, 2nd and 3rd, however, and whenever such chakras with structural energetic defects are found they must be treated with a Chios® technique known as *Radiatory Healing* to restore healthy, proper form to their energetic structure.

Before we move on, we shall mention yet again the importance of openness, as you practice all these techniques for sensing undercharged chakras, unbalanced chakras and chakras with structural energetic defects, and integrating the information you receive. It is always important to remain open and allow a complete understanding of your patient's condition to unfold, in your whole being. While we have discussed at length the process of sensing these conditions and interpreting them, to assist you in learning the techniques, but once again this is ultimately not an analytical process. When you place these perceptual healing tools into use, they are there to facilitate a process of conscious knowing—an accumulation of impressions that coalesce and form a knowing felt in your whole being. This process, and every tool that you the healer use, begins and ends with openness.

Integrating Conditions in the Chakras With Conditions In the Aura Layers: How Energetic Defects Spread and How They Are Healed

Now that you have learned all the basics of sensing the condition of your patient's chakra system and integrating them into an interpretation of treatment needs for the chakras, we should discuss how to integrate this with conditions you have seen in your patient's aura layers. All parts of your patient's energy field work together.

We have recommended asking for more information regarding the energetic impurities and disturbances you see in your patient's layers of aura. We have also suggested asking for more information regarding the meaning of energetic impurities you see in undercharged chakras and of chakras with structural energetic defects (and how these energetic defects in chakras may relate to energetic impurities or disturbances on one or more aura layers). Energetic defects in chakras and energetic impurities and disturbances in layers of aura are often related.

This relationship begins with the close relationship between a chakra and its corresponding layer of aura. The chakras do not project the layers of aura (the higher bodies), in terms of cause and effect, yet the chakras and their corresponding higher bodies are *existences that mirror each other*: if energetic defects are present in a chakra, energetic defects will almost always be present in its corresponding aura layer, and vice versa. Energetic defects in one will have a definite relationship to energetic defects in the other. For undercharged chakras, for example, the colors of whatever energetic impurities may be found in the chakra may not necessarily be the same as the colors of whatever energetic impurities are found in its corresponding aura layer, but intuitive information you receive will often indicate the relationship and its meaning. For chakras with structural energetic defects, you will likewise often find that the corresponding aura layer will exhibit energetic impurities and/or disturbances, and you can get information on the meaning of the structural energetic defect and its relationship to these unhealthy energies in the corresponding aura layer. We should mention that unbalanced chakras do not normally, by themselves, directly relate to energetic impurities and disturbances in the aura layers, but are often present as an important contributing factor to ill conditions in the aura layers and in the entire energy field. They must be sensed, evaluated and treated just the same.

This relationship between energetic defects in chakras and energetic impurities and disturbances in its corresponding aura layer is not the only way that energetic defects in one part of the energy field are transmitted to other parts, unfortunately. Energetic defects in chakras often spread to nearby chakras, affecting them, and the newly-affected chakra's corresponding layer of aura will then be affected, as well. Energetic impurities in any layer of aura will often spread, filtering through the aura and becoming lodged in whichever of the other layers may be susceptible. Very often, energetic impurities or disturbances in a higher layer filter down and affect lower layers, for example—it is easy for these higher-vibrational phenomena to spread this way, and affect lower-vibrational layers. Energetic defects in any chakra or any layer of aura can therefore potentially spread, and result in energetic defects, in almost any other chakra or aura layer that may be susceptible. In general, unhealthy conditions in any part of the energy field will often transmit themselves to many other parts. This is because the energy field is a holistic entity: every part affects every other part.

Whenever you get intuitive information on energetic impurities and disturbances in a layer of aura, or on energetic defects in a chakra, be open to receiving more information on how these energetic defects have spread—what relationship they have to unhealthy energies in other parts of your patient's energy field. Be open to sensing the entire pattern of energetic defects in your patient's field, and how the entire pattern occurred. You may also get information on your patient's psychological issues, present or past life experience and any physical disease which may have resulted. As we've discussed before, this is the value of being completely open as you sense the condition of your patient: as you examine energetic defects in any one part of his or her energy field, you will be open to, and sense, the connection to other defects in other parts. This process will give you a great deal of information on the condition of your patient, in every aspect. Whenever you use an intuitive reading to sense the condition of your patient's chakras, or sense or see your patient's aura layers, be open to this expanding, complete vision of the condition of your patient's energy field and how it relates to all aspects of his or her body, emotions, mind and spirit.

There is another reason that we have discussed the relationship between energetic defects you will sense in chakras and energetic impurities and disturbances you will find in the various layers of aura. Because unhealthy conditions in the chakras and unhealthy conditions in the aura often occur together and are related, in your healing work you will treat all chakras and all layers of aura that have become affected. In Chios®, we do that in a way that takes into account, and makes use of, the way these energies spread, in the energy field.

First of all, because energetic defects occur in chakras and their corresponding aura layers, when we treat undercharged chakras or chakras with structural energetic defects *we treat the chakra and its corresponding layer of aura together*. When we do this, we focus on the chakra but treat it using techniques that treat the chakra but that also work in its corresponding aura layer. Secondly, however, we do this by using techniques that *also treat all layers of aura lower than the corresponding aura layer, as they relate to that layer and may have been affected by energetic defects filtering down to them*. This makes possible the most efficient and complete healing of the entire condition that exists—it heals the energetic defects in the chakra, and removes the energetic impurities and disturbances in the layers of aura that have become affected.

Chios® is a *chakra-based* energy healing art, because *it is easier to focus on the chakras in treating the energy field of your patient, than the layers of aura*. And yet, while treating a chakra with the Chios® techniques you will often be treating both a chakra and the affected layers of aura together. You can see how practical this approach is: however high a level of the energy field has been affected with energetic defects, it will show in that chakra and its corresponding aura layer. Treating each chakra showing energetic defects, by focusing on the chakra, yet in a way that also treats the corresponding layer and the layers below, will treat that layer and all affected lower layers of aura. We have a special technique to treat the highest (7th) layer of aura, however (which is often the ultimate source of energetic defects that filter down to the layers below). This approach provides complete healing to the entire energy field. You will experience the beauty and power of this approach soon enough, in the very effective Chios® Master techniques you are about to learn. Learning to view the aura layers is important, because *it is easier to focus on the aura layers, in sensing the condition of the energy field of your patient, than the chakras*. An additional important reason for learning to view these aura layers is so you will, using your persistence of visualization, bring effective and complete healing to these layers (as you treat the chakras and the aura layers together)— this is a critical part of sensing (and thus being able to heal) the whole being of your patient.

Learning to View the Chakras

There is one final advanced and optional step for gaining information on the condition of your patient's chakra system that we will mention now, before moving on to the exciting series of Chios® Master techniques you will use to heal the many energetic defects we have discussed. That is the manner in which you may attempt to learn to view the chakras directly.

As we have said before, to view the chakras directly with your physical eyes is quite difficult. Many very experienced and capable energy healers never learn to see the chakras in this way, but instead (very successfully) rely on intuitive information appearing in their mind's eye to sense the condition of the chakras. And yet, if you wish to try to learn to see the chakras directly you may modify the intuitive reading technique for sensing the condition of the chakra system, to attempt to confirm with your physical eyes the information seen in your mind's eye. This is similar to the progression you made when you first learned to do an intuitive reading using a body outline, to sense simple energetic defects in the aura and chakras (in your mind's eye), to here in Chios® Level III where you learned the technique to view all seven higher layers of aura (with your physical eyes). To attempt to view the chakras with your physical eyes, proceed as follows:

Exercise 3-G: Learning to View the Chakras

1. Perform steps 1 to 6 of Exercise 3-E: Intuitive Reading: Sensing the Condition of the Chakra System, just as you have learned.

7. After gaining a sense of your patient's chakras in your mind's eye, using the visualization of the body profile, open your eyes and glance back with your physical eyes—in a *very non-focused, relaxed receptive condition*—at the area above the body of your patient where the rainbow shell of color would be, from the same side-on perspective.

8. Can you see very faint colored fields or bands where the chakras should be? Viewing the chakras from the side of your patient, you may see that the colors of the chakras are not completely separate—they merge above the body, as if in a faint mist or cloud of moving energy. They appear as in a rainbow, and the colors merge into a continuous band, so that it is difficult to say where one color becomes another—where indigo becomes violet, for example. They appear much as the spectrum we have described.

9. If you are fortunate enough to gain some glimpse of the chakra colors with your physical eyes, you may additionally begin to see phenomena in

them, such as color impurities indicative of undercharged states, brightness or dimness or larger or smaller apparent size of the fields that are indicative of over or under-activity, or even structural energetic defects in the chakra "whirlpools."

To see the chakras, however, is very difficult. They are difficult to see and will be the last part of the energy field to become visible to your physical eyes. They can be felt with the passing of hands, and a sense of their color can be gained in your mind's eye, yet they will begin to appear to your physical vision perhaps only as indefinable shapes, like clouds, even after much practice. This is why most energy healers rely upon intuitive information instead to gain the information needed to treat them. Even with much practice it will be some time before their complete structure can be seen in toto. As with learning to see anything this way, there is really a unity of intuitive and physical sight, and you are always really seeing with your entire awareness, not moving from one sight to another, but combining all. It is interesting to know that it is very difficult to see the aura levels and the chakras at the same time. One can view the layers of aura, or one can see the colors of the chakras as we've just described, but it is very difficult to do both at once. It is something like the popular drawing where one can either see a vase, or two faces facing each other, but not both at the same time.

Chakra Charging

You are about to embark on the most exciting stage of your energy healing journey: your exploration of the extraordinarily powerful Chios® Master techniques that you will use to heal the fundamental energetic defects of the chakras and layers of aura. Before proceeding, however, we will mention, once again, the importance of maintaining openness and transparency whenever you employ a treatment technique that uses your hands. Whenever you use any healing technique you are always actually treating your patient with your whole being, through your hands. Be aware and open to the entire act, with your whole being, and do not consider that it is just your hands alone that are working on some small part of your patient's energy field. This is especially important with the techniques we are about to discuss, so you will be able to employ them with their full power and effectiveness. Remember: you are acting with your whole being on your patient's whole being. This principle of healing is essential for proper practice of the techniques you are about to learn.

After gaining complete information on the state of your patient's chakra system and aura layers, the first Chios® Master technique you should employ in healing the energetic defects you've sensed is to treat any undercharged chakras you have detected, using the Chios® Chakra Charging technique. Undercharged chakras are in need of having the strength and purity of their native energetic functioning restored—they are in need of charging. Chakras are charged by *adding their own true color to them*, using color channeling as we have described it. You may wish to review the section on Learning to Channel Color and Light, near the beginning of this Chios® level, to ensure maximum effectiveness as you learn this chakra charging technique, and the chakra rebalancing technique that follows. In contrast with simply adding energy to the chakras, as is done during regular energy channeling, adding a chakra's own true color to it specifically restores its native energetic content and returns it to pure functioning. It also eliminates any energetic impurities present. The chakra is strong and pure again, and protected against further intrusion of unhealthy energies.

When you charge a chakra, you will also treat its corresponding aura layer (as your primary focus) but also all lower layers of aura, as they relate to and may have become affected by energetic impurities in the chakra and corresponding aura layer. You are providing complete healing of the energetic impurities as they exist at that level and also as they may have filtered down to lower levels.

As the chakra is charged, its true color is restored to its pure, vibrant and healthy hue. Charging chakras back into a normal, healthy state such that they no longer contain any energetic impurities, while also clearing the affected aura layers, is vital for the energetic health of your patient's entire energy field, and serves as an excellent foundation upon which further advanced healing work may then be done.

To charge the chakras in your patient that require it, you may begin at the highest or lowest chakra in need, as you prefer. Often you may choose to begin at the lowest chakra in need of treatment, and this is often the best chakra to charge first, but to begin at a higher one (especially if you receive intuitive information suggesting doing so) is not wrong, and your individual preference or varying needs and conditions within your patient may make this preferable in some cases. To charge a chakra in need, use the following technique:

Exercise 3-H: Chakra Charging

1. With your eyes open or closed, and your patient lying down in front of you on your treatment table, place your hands at the location of the first chakra you wish to charge. For the 2nd, 3rd, 4th, 5th and 6th chakras this will be with your hands lightly on the body surface of your patient, with your right palm

centered over the chakra and your left hand gently overlapping your right hand (the "hands overlapping" hand position). Note that, for the 5th and 6th chakras, this is *not* the same hand position as you used for energy channeling (the normal sequence of treatment hand positions), because with this technique you treat only the front component of the chakras. For the 7th chakra lightly place your hands on the top sides of your patient's head with a gap of two to three inches between them (the same hand position as during the normal sequence of treatment hand positions). (For the 1st chakra, see the special instructions near the end of this section).

2. Now visualize, sense and become the Chios® symbol in color, from the basic progression, that corresponds to that chakra (see Figure 28).

3. *At the same time* visualize, sense and become a cloud of the same color surrounding your hands (as a cloud of color around your hands, and a layer of color below them penetrating into the chakra). You are not yourself, nor merely your hands working, but are the entire act of visualizing, sensing and becoming the Chios® symbol in color and the cloud of color around your hands and layer of color below them, channeling the color into the chakra. When beginning to charge the 3rd chakra, for example, you will use a yellow Circle, with your hands channeling yellow and positioned as shown in Figure 32.

   As you do this, be aware that you have within you the remnant persistence of visualization of the chakra condition—you are at a deep level intending and sensing the chakra being restored to its pure color. Seek to restore the color to its pure hue: you may note the chakra color on the back of your hand, using the technique you have learned, as it changes. Be a completely open and transparent channel for the color. Channel the color into the chakra in this way for several moments, or until you sense you have adequately supplemented the chakra with color.

   (Optional: If you have trouble visualizing both things at once—the Chios® symbol in color, and the cloud of color around your hands and layer of color below them—try making the cloud of color around your hands and the layer of color below them your primary visualization, yet with an awareness that you are also using the symbol in color. This may make it easier to learn this technique).

4. After treating the chakra at the body surface, in this way, raise your hands to about five or six inches above the body surface (the level of the 2nd layer of aura), and move your hands apart slightly, so that instead of overlapping with the thumbs and index fingers, they are only overlapping slightly (for the 7th chakra your hands will be a little further apart than before, about three to four inches). Now again visualize, sense and become the same Chios®

symbol in color, from the basic progression, that corresponds to that chakra, and at the same time visualize, sense and become a cloud of the same color surrounding your hands (as a cloud of color around your hands, and a layer of color below them penetrating into the chakra) yet now with two important additions: 1) see the color also dispersing laterally from your hands and into the layers of aura at this level, and 2) allow your hands to move, in small semicircular movements of two or three inches in diameter, to help diffuse the color into the aura layers. Note that you are channeling color into the chakra and also into the aura layers: *you are treating both the chakra and the layers of aura (especially the corresponding layer, but also all lower layers), at this level, at the same time.* When charging the 3rd chakra, for example, you will continue to use a yellow Circle, with your hands channeling yellow but now positioned as shown in Figure 33.

You will find that your intuitive sense will inform you how to move your hands, when making the semicircular movements. With just a little practice you may find that your hands move almost automatically as you perform this technique. You will almost always feel a desire and drive to move your hands in this way, but if not, do whatever you feel is best. Perhaps you will not feel driven to do so, and there will be times when this seems best, due to the condition and needs of each particular patient. You may possibly feel guided to have only the idea of movement, in your awareness, as your etheric hands alone move in this way (with your physical hands stationary). It will be the usual case, however, for your physical hands to want to move, as we have described.

You will again be aware that you again have within you a remnant persistence of visualization of the aura layers also being cleared of any energetic defects—you are at a deep level intending and sensing both the chakra and the aura layers being restored and healed. As you channel color into the chakra and aura layers, again be a completely open and transparent channel for the color. Channel the color into the chakra and aura layers for several moments, or until you sense you have adequately supplemented the chakra and aura layers with color.

5. After treating the chakra (and aura layers) at this 2nd level, raise your hands an additional five to six inches, so that they are now 10 to 12 inches above the body surface (the level of the 3rd layer of aura). Spread your hands apart a little more, so that they are perhaps 1 inch apart (for the 7th chakra your hands will be yet further apart, about four to five inches). Now perform this charging technique exactly as you just did for the level immediately below. Once again visualize, sense and become both the Chios® symbol in color, from the basic progression and the cloud of color around your hands (as a

cloud of color around your hands, and a layer of color below them penetrating into the chakra), with your hands dispersing the color laterally into the aura layers and moving in the small semicircular movements to help it in doing so, as you just did on the layer immediately below. When charging the 3rd chakra, for example, you will continue to use a yellow Circle, with your hands channeling yellow but now positioned as shown in Figure 34.

Be aware of your remnant persistence of visualization, as you again intend and sense both the chakra and the layers of aura being restored and healed, as before. Channel the color into the chakra at this 3rd level for several moments, or until you sense you have adequately supplemented the chakra and aura layers with color.

6. Continue charging the chakra and aura layers in this same way, at successively higher levels, until you reach the level of the corresponding aura layer of the chakra you are charging, which is the final level you will usually treat using this technique. Use a five to six inch increment as you move up each additional level, as required. As you move up each level, you must also spread your hands apart a little further (perhaps 1 to 1 ½ inches further apart) as you move up to the next higher level. This is because the field of the chakra grows wider, like a funnel.

When charging the 2nd chakra, you will use the complete technique described above, but treat up to the level of the 2nd layer (your hands five to six inches above the body), using an orange Circle and channeling the color orange at all levels—so you will stop after step 4 above.

When charging the 3rd chakra (the example we just used), you will use the complete technique described above, but treat up to the level of the 3rd layer (your hands 10 to 12 inches above the body), using a yellow Circle and channeling the color yellow at all levels—so you will stop just after step 5 just above.

When charging the 4th chakra, you will use the complete technique described above, but treat up to the level of the 4th layer (your hands 15 to 18 inches above the body), using a green Trine and channeling the color green at all the levels.

When charging the 5th chakra, you will use the complete technique described above, but treat up to the level of the 5th layer (your hands 20 to 24 inches above the body), using a blue Trine and channeling the color blue at all the levels.

When charging the 6th chakra, you will use the complete technique described above, but treat up to the level of the 6th layer (your hands 25 to

30 inches above the body), using an indigo Trine and channeling the color indigo at all the levels.

When charging the 7th chakra, you will use the complete technique described above, but treat up to the level of the 7th layer (your hands 30 to 36 inches above the body), using a violet Star and channeling the color violet at all the levels.

7. There will be times—with certain chakras on certain patients—when you will feel guided to continue charging certain chakras to levels beyond that of the corresponding aura layer. You may be treating a 4th (heart) chakra, for example, and sense that you must actually charge this chakra for two extra levels above the body, and so you will additionally treat that chakra at the 5th and 6th levels, as well. Whenever you feel so intuitively guided, be sure to perform the chakra charging healing technique at these higher levels. It may be for one or two levels beyond the level of the corresponding layer of aura, or up to and including the highest (7th) level. This will not usually be required—it is not common—but there will be times you will feel guided to do so.

8. Treat each chakra that requires chakra charging, using this same technique as given in steps 1 to 7 above.

You may have noticed that these five or six inch increments do not exactly correspond to the four to five inch increments of the aura layers, as we described them when you were learning to view the aura. They are the increments where you can optimally charge the aura layers, however, because your hands are most effective channeling color when just above the outer limit of any particular aura layer. In reality, there are various accounts and ways of defining the size of the aura levels, yet these five to six inch increments provide for the maximum effect when treating the aura levels. These increments also correspond to the approximate elevations of the chakra location on the higher bodies—the points on the higher layers of aura that are analogous to those points on the physical body where you place your hands to treat a chakra. When treating small adults or children, however, you should employ increments of four inches instead, because of their smaller physical bodies the spacing between aura layers is proportionately reduced.

When treating the lower chakras (the 1st and 2nd), treatment of most of the layers of aura will not usually be required. You may note that in treating a 2nd chakra, for example, it is only necessary to go to the 2nd level (five to six inches above the body), yet you may proceed out an additional layer or two, on occasion, if you feel it is needed or you feel guided to, with these lower chakras. This is not always necessary, however, nor will it usually be

Charging a Chakra
(Using an Undercharged 3rd Chakra as Example)

Begin charging the chakra by placing your hands on the chakra at *body level* and visualizing the Chios® symbol in color, from the basic progression, that corresponds to the chakra. *At the same time* visualize a cloud of the same color around your hands, and a layer of color below them, with the color penetrating into the chakra.

For the 3rd chakra, you are visualizing a yellow Circle while channeling yellow through your hands and into the chakra. (See text for complete instructions).

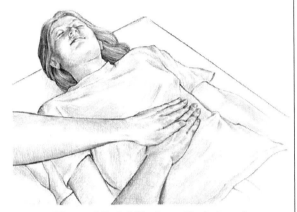

Figure 32: 3rd Chakra - Body Level

Then, charge the chakra and the aura layers at the *2nd level*, by placing your hands five to six inches above the body surface and visualizing the Chios® symbol in color, from the basic progression, that corresponds to the chakra. *At the same time* visualize a cloud of the same color around your hands and a layer of color below them, the color penetrating into the chakra *and* dispersing laterally into the aura layers, at this level. Your hands are making small semicircular movements, to help disperse the color.

For the 3rd chakra, you are still visualizing a yellow Circle while channeling yellow.

Hands 5"-6" Above Body

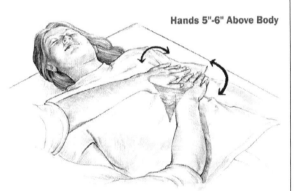

Figure 33: 3rd Chakra – 2nd Level

Finally, charge the chakra and the aura layers at the *3rd level*, by placing your hands 10 to 12 inches above the body surface and visualizing the Chios® symbol in color, from the basic progression, that corresponds to the chakra. *At the same time* visualize a cloud of color around your hands and a layer of color below them, the color penetrating into the chakra and dispersing laterally into the aura layers, at this level. Your hands are making small semicircular movements, to help disperse the color.

For the 3rd chakra, you are still visualizing a yellow Circle while channeling yellow.

Hands 10"-12" Above Body

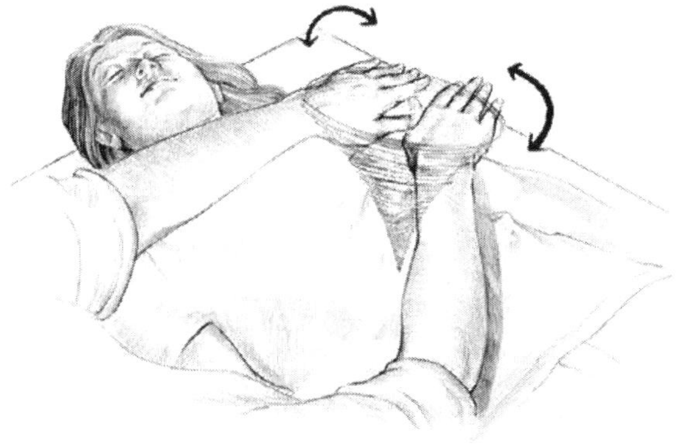

Figure 34: 3rd Chakra – 3rd Level

required. The 1ˢᵗ chakra will not commonly require charging, yet if it does you may charge it as follows:

Exercise 3-I: Charging the 1ˢᵗ Chakra

1. Place your hands side-by-side and about ten inches diagonally out from the body surface of your patient, from the area of the body closest to the 1ˢᵗ chakra (genital region), so your palms are perpendicular to the axis of the 1ˢᵗ chakra as it extends out diagonally (your hands will therefore be slanted instead of level, palms facing diagonally down to the genital region). (See Figure 35).

2. Charge the chakra, at this one level, by visualizing, sensing and becoming a red Circle, and *at the same time* visualizing, sensing and becoming a cloud of red surrounding your hands (as a cloud of color around your hands, and a layer of color below them penetrating into the 1ˢᵗ chakra). You need not visualize the color red dispersing into an aura layer, as before, but move your hands in the semicircular movements if you feel driven to. Employ a persistence of visualization, as before, seeing the red color of this chakra restored, and continue until you sense the charging is complete.

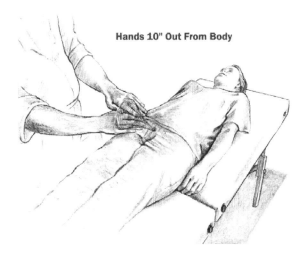

Hands 10" Out From Body

Figure 35: Charging the 1ˢᵗ Chakra

This modified procedure is done as a courtesy to your patient, as your hands are never placed on or near the genital region.

As you charge all the chakras in your patient in need of charging, you may find that sometimes, as you treat an individual chakra to restore its color, there will be a sullying of the energy surrounding the chakra that may extend as well to the neighboring chakras, requiring that they (and their layers of aura) also be treated. You will therefore need to strive to be continuously aware of not only the chakra you are treating, but nearby chakras as well. You will need to maintain your openness and holistic awareness of your patient's chakra system and layers of aura, and the effect your treatment is having on them. Note that only the front of the body—the front component of each chakra and the front portion of the aura layers—is treated during chakra charging.

Chakra System Rebalancing

After charging all of the chakras in your patient's chakra system that require it, you should next proceed to treat any unbalanced chakras that you have identified. Unbalanced chakras are in need of having their activity level either lowered or raised so that their activity level becomes equal to, and balanced with, that of the other chakras in the chakra system. You will use the Chios® Chakra System Rebalancing technique for this purpose.

Once chakras are in an adequately charged state, with their native energy strong and pure, their activity level can be changed by *adding colors to them that are either lower or higher than their own native true color*. The seven colors of the chakra system are akin to seven energy levels—from red to violet—and each color has the nature of a successively higher level of vibration. Adding a color to a chakra that is lower than the chakra's own true color—a color with a lower rate of vibration—quiets the activity level of the chakra, thus lowering it. Adding a color to a chakra that is higher than the chakra's own true color—a color with a higher rate of vibration—stimulates the activity level of the chakra, thus raising it. By rebalancing whichever chakras are contributing to a pattern of imbalance, the chakra system is returned to a level and balanced condition. Rebalancing a chakra works with the chakra only—it does not directly affect the layers of aura nor will you treat the aura layers at the same time you treat the chakra, as you did with chakra charging. A balanced chakra system, however, has a far healthier and more harmonious influence on the higher aura layers and the entire energy field and life of your patient than does one with a significant pattern of imbalance.

To rebalance the chakras in your patient that require it, you may again begin at the highest or lowest chakra in need. Often the lowest chakra in need is the best chakra to rebalance first, but to begin at a higher one (especially if you receive intuitive information suggesting doing so) is not wrong, and your individual preference or varying needs and conditions within your patient may make this preferable in some cases. To rebalance a chakra in need, use the following technique:

Exercise 3-J: Chakra System Rebalancing

1. With your eyes open or closed, and your patient lying down in front of you on your treatment table, place your hands at the location of the first chakra you wish to rebalance. For the 2nd, 3rd, 4th, 5th and 6th chakras this will be with your hands lightly on the body surface of your patient, with your right palm centered over the chakra and your left hand gently overlapping your right hand (the "hands overlapping" hand position). Note that, for the 5th and 6th chakras, this is *not* the same hand position as you used for energy channeling (the normal sequence of treatment hand positions), because with this technique you treat only the front component of the chakras. For the 7th chakra lightly place your hands on the top sides of your patient's head with a gap of two to three inches between them (the same hand position as during the normal sequence of treatment hand positions). (For the 1st chakra see the special instructions near the end of this section).

2. Now visualize, sense and become the Chios® symbol that is associated with the chakra (see Figure 22) in the *next lower or higher color* to the chakra's native true color, depending on whether the activity level of the chakra needs to be lowered or raised. Use the next higher true color, if the chakra needs its activity level raised, and use the next lower true color if the chakra needs its activity level lowered. Note that you are *not* using a Chios® symbol in color from the basic progression. In rebalancing, unlike charging, you always use the symbol related to the chakra, and not changing the symbol as you vary the color.

3. *At the same time*, visualize, sense and become a cloud of the same color surrounding your hands (as a cloud of color around your hands, and a layer of color below them penetrating into the chakra). You are not yourself, nor merely your hands working, but are the entire act of visualizing, sensing and becoming the Chios® symbol in color and the cloud of color around your hands and a layer of color below them, as you channel color into the chakra. When rebalancing the 4th chakra upwards, for example, you will use a blue Trine, with your hands channeling blue and positioned as shown in Figure 36.

   As you do this, be aware that you have within you a remnant persistence of visualization—you are at a deep level intending and sensing the chakra's activity level being raised or lowered, as needed. Be an open and transparent channel for the color. Channel the color into the chakra in this way for several moments

(Optional: If you have trouble visualizing both things at once—the Chios® symbol in color, and the cloud of color around your hands and layer of color below them—try making the cloud of color around your hands and layer of color below them your primary visualization, yet with an awareness that you are also using the symbol in color. This may make it easier to learn this technique.)

4. After seeking to lower or raise the activity level of the chakra by using the next lower or next higher color in this way for a few moments, briefly check your progress through the use of an intuitive reading (through visualization of a body profile) to determine whether or not the activity level of the chakra has moved closer to a level that is in balance with the other chakras in the chakra system. Is there still a dip or bump in the shape of the colored segment of the rainbow shell that corresponds to the chakra you are rebalancing? If so, you must then use a stronger influence—a color *two steps* removed from that chakra's native true color—so that the even lower (or higher) energy level of this new color will work to affect the chakra's level of activation in a stronger way.

5. If the activity level of the chakra needs to be further altered, treat the chakra in the exact same way as in steps 1 to 3 above, visualizing, sensing and becoming the same Chios® symbol in color, yet using a *new* color that is *two steps lower (or higher)* than the native true color of the chakra, depending on whether the activity level of the chakra needs to be further lowered or raised, and at the same time visualize, sense and become a cloud of the same *new* color surrounding your hands and penetrating into the chakra. Do this for a few moments more. Note that, unlike chakra charging, your hands will remain on your patient's body in the exact same position as before, as you do this—you do *not* treat the layers of aura, at levels above body level, but just the chakra itself. When rebalancing the 4th chakra upwards, for example, you will now use an indigo Trine, with your hands channeling indigo, yet still positioned on the body as shown in Figure 37.

Be aware of your remnant persistence of visualization—you are at a deep level again intending and sensing the chakra's activity level being raised or lowered, as needed. Be an open and transparent channel for the color, as before. Channel this new color for an additional few moments, until you get a sense of completeness.

6. Once again check your progress using an intuitive reading of the body profile, just as you did in step 4 above. If a dip or bump is still present and

the chakra has not yet been brought into balance, you will now need to use a color *three steps* removed from the chakra's native true color.

7. If the activity level of the chakra needs to be altered further still, treat the chakra in the exact same way as in steps 1 to 3 above, visualizing, sensing and becoming the same Chios® symbol in color, yet using a *new* color that is *three steps lower (or higher)* than the native color of the chakra, depending on whether the activity level of the chakra needs to be further lowered or raised, as you visualize, sense and become a cloud of the same *new* color surrounding your hands and penetrating into the chakra. When rebalancing the 4th chakra upwards, for example, you will now use a violet Trine, with your hands channeling violet yet still positioned on the body as shown in Figure 38.

   Be aware of your remnant persistence of visualization—you are at a deep level again intending and sensing the chakra's activity level being raised or lowered, as needed. Channel this new color for an additional few moments, until you get a sense of completeness.

8. Continue until your intuitive reading shows the activity level of the chakra balanced and level, in comparison to the other chakras in the spectrum. Sometimes chakras will only require the application of one lower or higher color to bring them into line. Most times a chakra will require at least two steps upwards or downwards in color, to raise or lower its activity level, respectively. Sometimes a chakra will require three steps upwards or downwards in color, and this is usually the maximum number of steps you will use. It will be rare that you will need to use a color more than three steps removed from the chakra's true color, and you should not do so except in rare occasions when absolutely necessary.

9. Treat each chakra that requires rebalancing, using this same technique as given in steps 1 to 8 above.

When treating low chakras that are overactive or high chakras that are underactive, you will only have a limited number of color steps available. In these cases, it is not usually difficult to use what lower or higher colors are available to rebalance the chakra, yet it may sometimes require a longer application. Always start, however, with the next-higher or next-lower color to that chakras own native color—do not "jump" two or more steps at a time—because it is far gentler on the chakra system and your patient to gradually increase or decrease the energy level applied to affect the activity level of the chakra. Increase or decrease the color applied one color step at a time, until whatever color difference is necessary to correct the activity level has been reached. To begin with adjacent colors and move one color step at a time is a gentle and effective method. Schemes of color balancing that immediately

Rebalancing a Chakra
(Using an Underactive 4th Chakra as Example)

Begin rebalancing the chakra by using a color *one* step lower or higher on the spectrum (lower if the activity level of the chakra needs to be lowered, or higher if the activity level needs to be raised). Place your hands on the chakra, at body level, and visualize the Chios® symbol related to the chakra, in that color, and *at the same time* visualize a cloud of the same color around your hands, and a layer of color below them, the color penetrating into the chakra.

When rebalancing an underactive 4th chakra, you are visualizing a blue Trine while channeling blue through your hands and into the chakra. (See text for complete instructions).

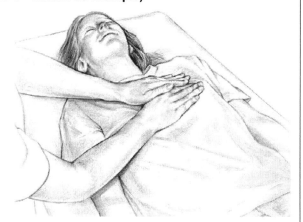

Figure 36: Rebalancing the 4th Chakra – Step 1

Then, check your progress by doing an intuitive reading to sense the condition of the chakra system. If the chakra is still over- or underactive, you must then use a color *two* steps lower or higher on the spectrum. Leaving your hands on the body, visualize the Chios® symbol related to the chakra, in the new color, and *at the same time* visualize a cloud of the new color around your hands, and a layer of color below them, the color penetrating into the chakra.

For an underactive 4th chakra, you are now visualizing an indigo Trine while channeling indigo.

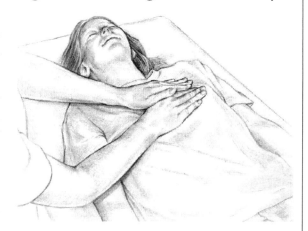

Figure 37: Rebalancing the 4th Chakra – Step 2

Check your progress again, by doing an intuitive reading. If the chakra is still over- or underactive, you must now use a color *three* steps lower or higher. Leaving your hands on the body, visualize the Chios® symbol related to the chakra, in the new color, and *at the same time* visualize a cloud of the new color around your hands, and a layer of color below them, the color penetrating into the chakra.

For an underactive 4th chakra, you are now visualizing a violet Trine while channeling violet.

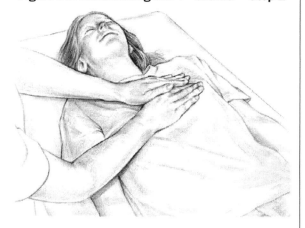

Figure 38: Rebalancing the 4th Chakra – Step 3

employ a much higher or lower color (such as a color opposite) are much harsher, and are often ineffective, too.

Rebalance each chakra that requires it—working either from lower to higher chakras or from higher to lower. When you have finished rebalancing the chakras, they should all radiate with equal strength—no one chakra will possess more force than another. They will appear as an even rainbow shell of color with a gradual, even curve, from red to violet. Note again that you do not treat the higher levels of aura when rebalancing chakras—your hands remain on the body surface at the location of the chakra being treated. Note also that, as with chakra charging, only the front of the body is treated.

The 1st chakra is as likely to require rebalancing as any of the other chakras. If it requires rebalancing upwards, you can proceed as follows:

Exercise 3-K: Rebalancing Underactivity of the 1st Chakra

1. Place your hands side-by-side and about ten inches diagonally out from the body surface of your patient, from the area of the body closest to the 1st chakra (genital region), so your palms are perpendicular to the axis of the 1st chakra as it extends out diagonally (your hands will therefore be slanted instead of level, palms facing diagonally down to the genital region). (See Figure 39).

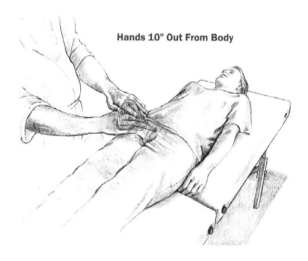

Figure 39: Rebalancing Underactivity of the 1st Chakra

2. Rebalance the chakra by visualizing, sensing and becoming an orange Circle, and *at the same time* visualizing, sensing and becoming a cloud of orange surrounding your hands (as a cloud of color around your hands, and a layer of color below them gently penetrating into the 1st chakra), performing the technique just as given in steps 2 to 8 of Exercise 3-J, above. Check your progress using an intuitive reading (through visualization of the body profile), and proceed to using higher colors, as needed.

There are special considerations to be observed when rebalancing the 1st chakra downwards or 7th chakra upwards. Underactivity of the 7th chakra or overactivity of the 1st chakra cannot be treated using color, because there are no colors in our spectrum that are higher than violet or lower than red. Underactivity of the 7th chakra can be treated however, as follows:

Exercise 3-L: Rebalancing Underactivity of the 7th Chakra

1. Position your hands about 10 to 12 inches above the crown of your patient's head, as shown (see Figure 40).
2. Now visualize, sense and become the Star, *without color*.
3. *At the same time*, you must visualize, sense and become—using the power of your will—the activity of the 7th chakra increasing. Really visualize, intend and sense this increase in the activity level.
4. Check your progress by using an intuitive reading (through visualization of the body profile), and do this until the activity level of the 7th chakra has been raised to a state of balance. This may require between two and five minutes.

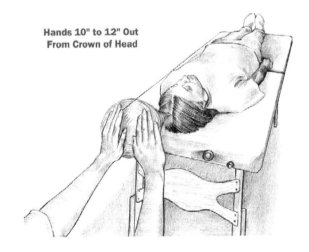

**Hands 10" to 12" Out
From Crown of Head**

Figure 40: Rebalancing Underactivity of the 7th Chakra

Overactivity of the 1st chakra can also be treated, as follows:

Exercise 3-M: Rebalancing Overactivity of the 1st Chakra

1. Place your hands side-by-side and about three inches diagonally out from the body surface of your patient, from the area of the body closest to the 1st chakra (genital region), so your palms are perpendicular to the axis of the 1st chakra as it extends out diagonally (your hands will therefore be slanted instead of level, palms facing diagonally down to the genital region). (See Figure 41).
2. Now visualize, sense and become the Circle, *without color*.
3. *At the same time*, you must visualize, sense and become—using the power of your will—the activity of the 1st chakra decreasing. Really visualize, intend and sense this decrease in the activity level.
4. Check your progress by using an intuitive reading (through visualization of the body profile), and do this until the activity level of the 1st chakra has been lowered to a state of balance. This may require between two and five minutes.

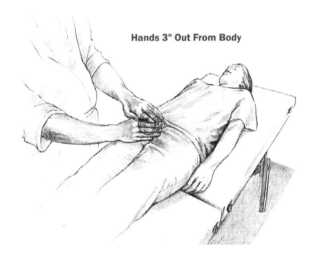

Hands 3" Out From Body

Figure 41: Rebalancing Overactivity of the 1st Chakra

Use the force of your will when performing these techniques—you will find that there is a strong bond between you and your patient when you do this.

Chakra rebalancing is done after chakra charging, and you may wonder whether the addition of colors other than the chakras own true color (as is done in this chakra rebalancing technique) can render a charged chakra weak or impure again. Charging and rebalancing, although both using color, are fundamentally different processes. The addition of the chakra's own color, during charging, is performed to correct an impure functioning of the native energy in the chakra—to strengthen and purify its native energetic functioning. Once the native energy of the chakra is pure and strong in its true color, the addition of higher and lower true colors during rebalancing has a different effect—a stimulating or quieting effect on the activity level of the chakra. Adding lower or higher true colors to a charged chakra does not introduce impurities; the addition of a pure color to a chakra cannot weaken or pollute it again.

Radiatory Healing of Chakras

Charging and rebalancing the chakras in your patient's chakra system that require these healing techniques has a great positive effect upon the operation of your patient's entire energy field, and yet to supplement and enhance the strength and purity of the native energetic functioning of the chakras (as done in chakra charging) and correct imbalances in the activity levels of the chakras (as is done in chakra rebalancing) is sometimes not enough. It is also possible for your patient's chakras to have structural energetic defects—defects in the structure, energy pattern and energy flow of the chakra. This is a very serious condition, one which often eventually results in illness in the physical body and chronic ill conditions in the emotions, the psychology and even the spiritual life of your patient. Structural energetic defects in chakra structure can be corrected, however, through the use of the Chios® Radiatory Healing technique. Treating all chakras that exhibit structural energetic defects, using this powerful technique, is your next important step in healing your patient's chakras.

We have discussed how you the healer become an open, transparent channel when performing energy healing work. You are open to intuitive and empathic sensing of your patient's condition, and are transparent to the energies and healing forces that you act as a channel for during the healing process. You are a vehicle for the knowledge and power of pure consciousness, which is the force that actually effects healing, and there is a unity between you, your patient and your patient's energy field as you work. In sensing and treating structural energetic defects in chakras you make full use of this profound role of the energy healer. You will sense structural energetic defects by making use of this unity (and knowledge): you will empathically sense the structural energetic defects that exist in your patient's chakras empathically, in your own chakras, with your whole being. You will then treat structural energetic defects by again making use of this unity (and power): you will *visualize, sense and become the chakra in need*, to be a perfect and unqualified channel for the healing power needed to heal this serious condition—with your whole being. Radiatory healing is a recapitulation of the entire role of the energy healer, and the purest form of healing there is.

When you use radiatory healing to heal a chakra with structural energetic defects, by visualizing, sensing and becoming the chakra in your patient that requires this treatment, you become a pure channel for the healing power of pure consciousness, which acts in the specific form of a sympathetic resonance between the chakra in your patient that requires radiatory healing and your own corresponding chakra (by virtue of their similar native energies and vibrational rates). This identity between you and your patient (you are one), and this specific identity between your corresponding chakras, radiates healing power into your patient's chakra in a very pure way. The act of merely visualizing, sensing and becoming your patient's chakra—without use of even a concept of energy, color or light— allows healing powers and energies to pass into the chakra so powerful we do not even use such concepts to understand them. These are energies beyond our healing vocabulary, which effect the powerful changes needed to heal chakras with these structural energetic defects. You will still use your hands, however, to assist in directing these energies.

Radiatory healing, when properly performed, is an act of self-transcendence on the part of you the healer. This pure visualizing, sensing and becoming of the chakra in need requires that you set your own self aside and become only the chakra. When you practice radiatory healing you are not your worldly self at all, but only a channel for these higher energies. It is the purest form of healing, where you move into a state where you, your patient and your patient's chakra meet and become transparent to this meeting—you become one. It is important to understand that while you are performing radiatory healing you are not in control of, and may not know the details of, the healing taking place. You simply surrender yourself to the healing power being directed through you.

Radiatory healing is similar to chakra charging, in practice, because you will not just treat the chakra at the body level but you will also be treating its corresponding aura layer (as your primary focus) but also all lower layers of aura, as they relate to and may have become affected by the structural energetic defect in the chakra and the defects in the corresponding aura layer. You will disperse energies laterally into the aura layers, at the same increment levels as you did with chakra charging. The energies infuse into and effect changes in the aura layers, to heal the unhealthy conditions that the structural energetic defect in the chakra may have potentiated and projected into the aura. You are providing complete healing of the structural energetic defect and also the defects in the corresponding aura level and also as they may have filtered down to lower levels.

To treat chakras exhibiting structural energetic defects with radiatory healing, you may once again begin at the lowest or highest chakra in need, as your judgment dictates. To perform radiatory healing on a chakra in need, use the following technique:

Exercise 3-N: Radiatory Healing of Chakras

1. With your eyes open or closed, and your patient lying down in front of you on your treatment table, place your hands at the location of the first chakra you wish to treat with the radiatory healing technique. For the 2nd, 3rd, 4th, 5th and 6th chakras this will be with your hands lightly on the body surface of your patient, with your right palm centered over the chakra and your left hand gently overlapping your right hand (the "hands overlapping" hand position). Note that, for the 5th and 6th chakras, this is not the same hand position as you used for energy channeling (the normal sequence of treatment hand positions), because with this technique you treat only the front component of the chakras. For the 7th chakra lightly place your hands on the top sides of your patient's head with a gap of two to three inches between them (the same hand position as during the normal sequence of treatment hand positions). (For the 1st chakra see the special instructions near the end of this section).

2. Now *visualize, sense and become your patient's chakra*: you must allow all else to drop away from your awareness and simply become one with the chakra of your patient. Do not visualize the chakra in a "visual" sense, as though you were seeing it. Do not visualize any particular shape or appearance, to the chakra and its energy, but perhaps sense it only as a source of radiant energy and then feeling "yourself" as this source of radiant energy. Set aside your own identity and become only the chakra you are healing, with your whole being. Do not "think about" the chakra or do anything else except become the chakra. You and your patient's chakra are *one*. Release yourself completely, without concern for any energies which may flow through you. When beginning to treat the 5th chakra, for example, your hands will be positioned as shown in Figure 42.

    You will not be consciously aware of the fact that you will have a remnant persistence of visualization of the chakra healing—you are visualizing, sensing and becoming just the chakra, while not thinking—yet at a deep level you are intending and sensing the chakra being healed. Be an open and transparent channel for the energies. Continue visualizing, sensing and becoming the chakra for several minutes, at this body level, until you get a sense of completeness (often intuitive information will inform you of this).

3. After treating the chakra at the body surface, in this way, raise your hands to about five or six inches above the body surface (the level of the 2nd layer of aura), and move your hands apart slightly, so that instead of overlapping with the thumbs and index fingers, they are only overlapping slightly (for the 7th chakra your hands will be a little further apart than before, about three to four inches). Now again visualize, sense and become the chakra, in exactly the same way as before. Do not visualize the chakra in any visual sense, nor think about it in any way, but merely sense and become it with your whole being. Release yourself again to whatever energies flow through you to this second level. There will be two important additions, however: 1) do not think about, yet you will nevertheless be aware of the fact, that healing energies are dispersing from your hands laterally into the layers of aura at this level, and 2) allow your hands to be driven to move, in small semicircular movements of two or three inches in diameter, to help diffuse the energies into the aura layers. Note that, as in chakra charging, you are channeling energies into the chakra and also into the aura layers: *you are treating both the chakra and the layers of aura (especially the corresponding layer, but also all lower layers), at this level, at the same time*. When treating the 5th chakra, for example, you will now have your hands positioned as shown in Figure 43.

    You will find that your hands will often move automatically, as you perform the small semicircular movements—all you need do is let go of yourself and allow them to be moved. Your hands will almost always be driven to move, yet if not simply allow this, as well. Even if your physical hands are not driven to move, you may receive an impression of movement, in your mind, and sense your etheric hands moving automatically.

    Once again, you will not be consciously aware of the fact that you have a remnant persistence of visualization, but will at a deep level be intending and sensing both the chakra and the aura layers being restored and healed. As you treat the chakra and aura layers, again be a completely open and transparent channel for the energies. Continue visualizing, sensing and becoming the chakra, and dispersing the healing energies into the aura layers for several moments, until you intuitively sense that your treatment of this level is complete.

4. After treating the chakra and aura layer at this 2nd level, raise your hands an additional five or six inches, so that they are now 10 to 12 inches out, at the level of the 3rd layer of aura. Spread your hands apart a little more, so that they are about 1 inch apart (for the 7th chakra your hands will be yet further apart, about four to five inches). Now perform the radiatory healing technique exactly as you just did for the level immediately below. Once again

just visualize, sense and become the chakra, while allowing your hands to disperse the energies laterally into the aura layers and moving in the small semicircular movements to help it in doing so, as you just did on the level immediately below. When treating the 5th chakra, for example, you will now have your hands positioned as shown in Figure 44.

As before, you will not be consciously aware of the fact that you have a remnant persistence of visualization, but will at a deep level be intending and sensing both the chakra and the aura layers being restored and healed. Continue visualizing, sensing and becoming the chakra, and dispersing the healing energies into the aura layers for several moments, until you receive intuitive information that your treatment of this level is complete.

5. Continue treating the chakra and aura layers in this same way, at successively higher levels, until you reach the level of the corresponding aura layer of the chakra you are treating, which is the final level you will usually treat with this technique. Use a five to six inch increment as you move up each additional level, as required. As you move up each level, you must also spread your hands apart a little further (perhaps 1 to 1 ½ inches further apart) as you move up to the next higher level. This is because the field of the chakra grows wider, like a funnel. At each level, it is vital that you focus your entire being on becoming one with the chakra you are treating, and remain totally open to whatever energies are flowing through you—a perfectly open and clear channel.

    When treating the 2nd chakra, you will use the complete technique described above, but treat up to the level of the 2nd layer of aura (your hands five to six inches above the body)—so you will stop after step 3 above.

    When treating the 3rd chakra, you will use the complete technique described above, but treat up to the level of the 3rd layer (your hands 10 to 12 inches above the body)—so you will stop just after step 4 above.

    When treating the 4th chakra, you will use the complete technique described above, but then treat up to the level of the 4th layer (your hands 15 to 18 inches above the body).

    When treating the 5th chakra (the example we just used), you will use the complete technique described above, but treat up to the level of the 5th layer (your hands 20 to 24 inches above the body). When you treat the 4th level your hands will be positioned as in Figure 45, and when you treat the 5th level they will be positioned as shown in Figure 46.

    When treating the 6th chakra, you will use the complete technique described above, but treat up to the level of the 6th layer (your hands 25 to 30 inches above the body).

When treating the 7th chakra, you will use the complete technique described above, but treat up to the level of the 7th layer (your hands 30 to 36 inches above the body).

6. There will be times—with certain chakras on certain patients—when you will feel guided to continue your radiatory healing of certain chakras to levels beyond that of the corresponding aura layer. You may be treating a 4th (heart) chakra, for example, and sense that you must actually treat this chakra up to and including the 7th level above the body, and so you will additionally treat that chakra at the 5th, 6th and 7th level, as well. Whenever you feel so intuitively guided, be sure to perform the radiatory healing technique at these higher levels. It may be for one or two levels beyond the level of the corresponding layer of aura, or up to and including the highest (7th) level. You are channeling energies that are repairing severe damage to the chakra, at all these levels. Treating the chakra at levels higher than that of the corresponding layer of aura will not always be required with radiatory healing, but is more common than during chakra charging.

7. Treat each chakra that requires radiatory healing, using this same technique as given in steps 1 to 6 above.

As with chakra charging, these five or six inch increments do not exactly correspond to the increments of the aura layers, but roughly so, and they are the increments where you can once again optimally treat the aura layers with the healing energies you will channel using this technique. When treating small adults or children, however, you should employ increments of four inches instead, because of their smaller physical bodies the spacing between aura layers is proportionately reduced.

Radiatory healing is a very powerful energy healing technique. While engaging in it, you may feel elevated in spirit, or have experiences related to the level of consciousness being worked on. It is also very possible that, as you sense and become the chakra, you will receive intuitive information regarding the life experiences that led to the damage, and correlating conditions in the psychology of your patient, as well as the influence the damage has had to the physical, emotional, mental and spiritual levels of your patient's being. As in charging and rebalancing, only the front of the body is treated using the radiatory healing technique.

Now that you've learned the radiatory healing technique, you may wonder if it supersedes the unblocking chakras technique that you learned in Chios® Level II, such that the unblocking chakras technique is no longer needed. The radiatory healing technique does more powerfully address the structural energetic defects that cause the energy blockage that you treated by using the unblocking chakras technique, but it does not render the

Radiatory Healing of a Chakra
(Using a 5th Chakra With Structural Energetic Defects as Example)

Begin radiatory healing of the chakra by placing your hands on the chakra at *body level* and just visualizing, sensing and becoming the chakra. Do not pretend to see the chakra, or think about it, merely sense and become it, with your whole being. Sense it as a source of radiant energy, and sense the chakra as "yourself." You and the chakra are one. Release yourself completely to whatever healing energies may flow through you. (See text for complete instructions).

Figure 42: 5th Chakra – Body Level

Then, perform radiatory healing of the chakra and the aura layers at the *2nd level*, by placing your hands five to six inches above the body surface and again just visualizing, sensing and becoming the chakra, exactly as described above.

Be aware of the fact that you are channeling healing energies that are penetrating down into the chakra *and* dispersing laterally into the aura layers, at this level. Your hands are making small semicircular movements, to help disperse the energies.

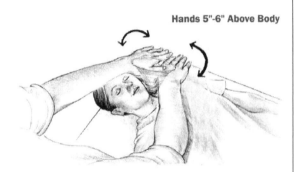

Hands 5"-6" Above Body

Figure 43: 5th Chakra – 2nd Level

Next, perform radiatory healing of the chakra and the aura layers at the *3rd level*, by placing your hands 10 to 12 inches above the body surface and again just visualizing, sensing and becoming the chakra, exactly as described above.

Be aware of the fact that you are channeling healing energies that are penetrating down into the chakra and dispersing laterally into the aura layers, at this level. Your hands are making small semicircular movements, to help disperse the energies.

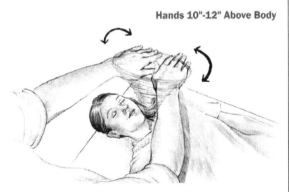

Hands 10"-12" Above Body

Figure 44: 5th Chakra – 3rd Level

Next, perform radiatory healing of the chakra and the aura layers at the *4th level*, by placing your hands 15 to 18 inches above the body surface and again just visualizing, sensing and becoming the chakra, exactly as described above.

Be aware of the fact that you are channeling healing energies that are penetrating down into the chakra and dispersing laterally into the aura layers, at this level. Your hands are making small semicircular movements, to help disperse the energies.

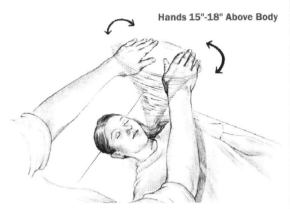

Hands 15"-18" Above Body

Figure 45: 5th Chakra – 4th Level

Finally, perform radiatory healing of the chakra and the aura layers at the *5th level* by placing your hands 20 to 24 inches above the body surface and again just visualizing, sensing and becoming the chakra, exactly as described above.

Be aware of the fact that you are channeling healing energies that are penetrating down into the chakra and dispersing laterally into the aura layers, at this level. Your hands are making small semicircular movements, to help disperse the energies.

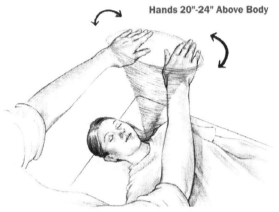

Hands 20"-24" Above Body

Figure 46: 5th Chakra – 5th Level

unblocking technique unnecessary. You will find stubborn chakras, in many patients, that will require that both techniques be performed, to fully clear them. You will also often find less seriously ill chakras that only require the unblocking technique to be rendered clear and do not require radiatory healing (and it is more efficient to just use the unblocking technique in those cases, so your time and attention can be directed to areas of your patient's energy field in greater need).

The 1st chakra will often not require radiatory healing, yet if it does you may treat it as follows:

Exercise 3-O: Radiatory Healing of the 1st Chakra

1. Place your hands side-by-side and about ten inches diagonally out from the body surface of your patient, from the area of the body closest to the 1st

chakra (genital region), so your palms are perpendicular to the axis of the 1st chakra as it extends out diagonally (your hands will therefore be slanted instead of level, palms facing diagonally down to the genital region). (See Figure 47).

2. Visualize, sense and become the chakra, in the exact same manner described in step 2 of Exercise 3-N, above. You will usually not sense the healing energies dispersing from your hands, nor will you usually feel your hands driven to move in the semicircular movements (yet allow them to, if they do). Proceed as before until you sense your treatment of this chakra is complete.

This is done as a courtesy to your patient, as the hands are never placed on or near the genital region.

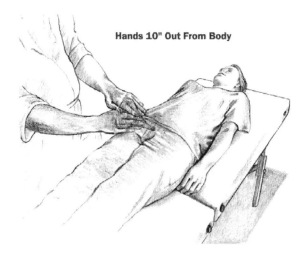

Hands 10" Out From Body

Figure 47: Radiatory Healing of the 1st Chakra

Experiencing the Ultimate Nature of the Chakras

The seven major chakras are of central importance in energy healing. Each chakra has its own unique nature—the 3rd chakra, for example, has a nature and function different from that of the 6th chakra. Much has been written regarding the nature and function of the chakras, and yet the truth is that this cannot be understood through the use of words and ideas. The chakras are entities beyond any mental understanding and must be experienced to be truly known. Mere descriptions employing generalities of various sorts may serve to give a rudimentary idea of each chakra's manner of functioning and realm of influence, but the full experience is much greater than any such verbal description.

The radiatory healing technique you have just learned, however, offers an excellent way to begin experiencing the ultimate nature and function of the chakras for yourself. When you simply visualize, sense and become a chakra, you merge with it and experience it in a pure way, with a wider awareness and with your whole being. You become one with that chakra and its realm of being and consciousness, experiencing it without the use of words or ideas. To visualize, sense and become the chakra makes possible this deeper learning, in which knowledge of the real, ultimate nature of the chakra becomes part of you at a fundamental level instead of merely being conveyed to you intellectually.

You can make use of this process, to gain more experience of the ultimate nature and function of the chakras. This is an important practice, for the true energy healer, and you may begin to experience this for yourself by proceeding as follows:

Exercise 3-P: Experiencing the Ultimate Nature of the Chakras

1. With your eyes closed, and your patient (or a willing subject) lying down in front of you on your treatment table, select a chakra, at random. Perform steps 1 and 2 of Exercise 3-N: Radiatory Healing of Chakras, just as you have learned, to visualize, sense and become the chakra. Really focus (yet effortlessly) to become only the chakra, letting all else (all potential distractions, inside or outside yourself) fall away and become unimportant.

2. During the entire time you visualize, sense and become the chakra, according to the instructions, have the sense that you will remain completely open and allow a wider awareness of it to take root in your being. Do not think about this, but just be aware that you are going to allow a deep sense of the chakra itself to emerge in your awareness, without qualifying it in verbal or mental terms. Just release, let go and (of course) suspend all thinking, while just being aware that this deep sense of the chakra is forming, in your whole being.

3. Do you gain some deep sense of the chakra's realm of being? This is like a form of meditation, in which knowledge simply comes to you at a deep level. It need not come as images, feelings, sounds or sensations, but as an unqualified, deep sense of being—a deeper knowledge and wider awareness inexpressible in any of these forms. Each chakra is a realm of being and consciousness—it is a unique state of consciousness. You are acquiring a deep awareness of this state of consciousness and the being and power of the chakra.

4. Continue visualizing, sensing and becoming the chakra for a few moments, and then stop and rest for a moment, with your eyes remaining closed.

5. Now select another chakra at random. You can open your eyes, for a brief moment, to place your hands on this new chakra, and then close them and repeat steps 1 to 4 above. Once again, allow a deep sense of the unique state consciousness of the chakra take root in you and form, in your whole being. Do you get any sense, deep in your being, of how this chakra differs from the previous one?

6. Repeat this exercise with each of the remaining chakras, at random, and with each seek to gain a feel of each chakra's being and power. Note that it is as if each chakra has its own identity, and that the sense you get from the 3rd chakra, for example, is different than that from the 6th. You need not do this in any particular order—select the chakras at random, yet include all.

As you perform the exercise with each chakra, remember not to differentiate between or sense any of the chakras on the basis of any particular mental notion—including ones you may have read in the descriptions given in books (including this one). The chakras are beyond all words and cannot be understood purely on the basis of these particular ideas but must be visualized and experienced in their essence, with your whole being. Become familiar with the true being and power of each. You must learn to know them and become them, and this is done by bringing out a knowledge of them that you actually already have inside yourself. You are cultivating a deeper understanding—an awareness that exists and grows in a larger realm, beyond mere mental descriptions.

It is interesting to know that, because each chakra mirrors its corresponding layer of aura, to visualize sense and become a chakra also serves to allow you to experience the ultimate nature of its corresponding aura layer. As you sense, deep in your being, the state of consciousness of a chakra, you are also sensing the state of consciousness of the corresponding aura layer. They are one. In practice it is much easier to use the chakra as a focus—it is easier to visualize, sense and become a chakra than it is to do the same for an entire layer of aura—but when you visualize a chakra but you are really experiencing both the chakra and its corresponding aura layer together.

You can also visualize, sense and become your own chakras, as a way to get in touch with their real, spiritual nature, and we give instructions for this as part of Exercise 6-B: Chakra Self-Healing, but it is very good to actually use several patients or willing subjects—especially to start. This will give you the experience and perspective most useful towards experiencing the chakras in an unbiased way. Your efforts will cultivate a deeper awareness of the real, ultimate nature and function of the chakras (and aura layers), and it will have another benefit as well: you will also become more sensitive to and able to perceive individual variations and characteristics of the chakras (and aura layers) in each of your patients. The chakra system and aura are not fixed, but vary from patient to patient just as human personalities vary from one individual to another. Each energy field has particular characteristics, and to learn more about the ultimate nature of the chakras (and aura layers) will also make you more sensitive to and able to perceive and grasp each individual variation. As with human beings in general, where a wide understanding of human nature brings more real understanding of each individual person.

Seventh Layer Focal Healing

Now that you have learned some very powerful and effective techniques to sense and heal fundamental energetic defects in your patient's chakra system and aura layers, it is time to bring special attention to a particularly important part of the energy field: the 7th layer of aura. The 7th layer contains within it energies that store the fundamental issues and existential biases from past lives. The issues, experiences and spiritual lessons in your patient's present life (present incarnation) are often a recapitulation of those in past lives (previous incarnations).

The 7th layer exerts a powerful influence upon your patient's entire energy field and life experience. This highest layer of aura contains the most refined and most permanent energetic characteristics in the aura layers—characteristics with the ability to filter down affect the energetic operations in all lower layers of aura and correspondingly affect the entire life experience and state of being of your patient. Therefore, unresolved past-life experiences impressed in this 7th layer (which often include related experiences in the present life) will have a major impact on your patient's present life. When this layer of aura has damaged regions, which often correlate to unresolved experiences, issues and traumas, it can seriously reduce the potential of your patient to achieve the most spiritually aware, affliction-free and fulfilling life possible. This damage to the 7th layer places serious limitations upon your patient's ability to cope with and grow from the challenges and opportunities available in the present life. It will often also eventually foster emotional or psychological afflictions, or even physical disease. It is therefore crucial to heal this layer when it possesses such damaged regions.

This 7th layer of aura often needs significant healing; direct and specifically focused healing is sometimes required to correct the conditions upon it that can have such negative effect on your patient. Because of the special importance of this layer of aura, and because healing of this layer can have such a profound benefit to your patient, a special technique for this layer alone is included here, and it is known as Chios® *Seventh Layer Focal Healing*. This technique is potentially very powerful, because to heal the 7th layer of aura potentially affects all of the lower layers and every aspect of your patient's being—physical, emotional, mental and spiritual. Although it will not be all patients who require the 7th layer healed using this technique—only a fraction will exhibit damage to the 7th layer that requires correction—healing the 7th layer gives your patient the opportunity to avoid many forms of illness and affliction, advance spiritually and, especially, to simply live a more fulfilling existence. Often it provides a healing effect that is profound and simply cannot be obtained any other way. To employ this technique, follow these steps:

Exercise 3-Q: Seventh Layer Focal Healing

1. With your eyes open and your patient lying down on your treatment table, first perform an in-depth and careful examination of your patient's 7th layer of aura. During your regular treatment of your patient you will probably have employed the Chios® technique for viewing the higher layers of aura, and may have seen, either in your mind's eye or your physical eyes, damage to the 7th layer. You may have received some intuitive information that indicated to you that treatment of the 7th layer was required. Before treating this layer, however, it is necessary to take some additional time to again view this 7th layer and carefully study the conditions upon it. Perform the Chios® technique for viewing this higher layer of aura (using steps 1 to 7 of Exercise 3-C: Intuitive Reading: Viewing All Seven Layers of Aura), employing the violet Star, and localizing your awareness to an eggshell-shaped area 30 to 36 inches above your patient's body. In the receptive phase, examine the 7th layer in your mind's eye and perform another round or two of the active/receptive cycle, if necessary. Allow yourself some time, to glance back with your physical eyes, to gain some physical vision of this layer. It is very desirable to have progressed in your practice to the point where you are able to see this layer, with your eyes, but if you are very confident of the accuracy of your vision of it in your mind's eye you can also proceed with this technique.

2. Quietly observe this outermost and finest layer of your patient's energy field. After some observation, over several minutes, you will see it as if it were a fine, transparent eggshell, with a very subtle soft glowing light that may appear bright or golden, to your physical eyes, or in your mind's eye. This layer is approximately three feet above the body surface, at its maximum over the midriff area. Study this 7th layer of aura carefully, over several minutes,

noting imperfections in the eggshell, particularly in the quality or constancy of its light.

Areas of damage in this layer will appear as spots, zones or areas of the eggshell that display a *change in the texture of the light*—not any significant change in the color or intensity of the light of the shell, but a roughness and a change in the quality of the light of the eggshell. The light of the shell will appear as a light would appear that has reflected from a different textured surface. These damaged spots, zones or areas can be of any shape or size— there is not one shape or size that they are more likely to be, although they do not usually grow to be extremely large. They are more frequently found on the top half of the shell—the portion around the upper half of the body— although they may occur anywhere. There may be one of these damaged spots, zones or areas, or there may be several. Make careful note of each. This is a process of careful observation.

3. Before you proceed to treat these areas with the seventh layer focal healing technique you should first add, to your observation of these damaged spots, zones or areas, a visualization of them being healed. Visualize each of these areas of the eggshell being healed: visualize, sense and become each damaged spot, zone or area of the 7th layer and see it being repaired and restored. Do this, for a brief moment, with each area. You are again creating a link between you, your patient and the parts of your patient's energy field that require healing, and your remnant persistence of visualization will add to the effectiveness of the technique you are about to perform.

4. As you visualize, sense and become these damaged spots, zones or areas in the 7th layer that require repair, you may find yourself receiving intuitive information regarding the meaning of these areas. When you learned the Chios® technique for viewing the higher layers, you learned to focus upon impurities or other phenomena you saw in aura layers, to get intuitive information on present or past life experiences, psychological issues or disease conditions relating to them. You can ask for that same information here, while viewing the layer and visualizing the damaged spots, zones or areas, by using this same technique that you learned in Exercise 3-D: Intuitive Reading: Energetic Impurities, Colors and Phenomena in the Aura. You may also get information on how each area of damage might relate to unhealthy energetic conditions on the lower layers of aura—defects in the 5th layer which mirror defects in the 7th layer shell, for example—as well as more information on how these areas may relate to the physical, emotional, mental and spiritual health of your patient.

5. You are now ready to treat your patient's 7th layer, using the seventh layer focal healing technique. Treat the first damaged spot, zone or area on the 7th

layer you wish to heal, by placing your right hand at a point between the center of your patient's body and the damaged area on the 7th layer, such that your hand is approximately ten inches above the body surface and with your palm open and facing directly toward the center of the body. The plane of your open hand will be roughly parallel to the surface of the eggshell at the damaged area to be treated, and therefore not necessarily level (if you are treating an area towards the side or top of the eggshell it may be slanted or nearly vertical).

6. Now, visualize, sense and become a stream of light flowing from the area near the center of your patient's body, through your hand, and outwards through the aura layers to the damaged region of the 7th layer. The light is drawn from the middle portion of your patient's body, in the area immediately under your hand. Your hand draws the light to itself, passing it through itself as if it were a concave lens, and then diverges and diffuses the light beam so that it spreads out and travels to the damaged region of the 7th layer eggshell, where it illuminates an area perhaps a foot in diameter (more or less) and where it then repairs, corrects and strengthens the eggshell and heals the damage that has occurred upon it. The light is concentrated, before it passes through the "concave lens" of your hand, and is then diffused as it is directed towards the region in need. You are not yourself, not your hand, but this entire act of visualizing, sensing and becoming this stream of light. (See Figure 48).

   You will also be aware that have within you a remnant persistence of visualization of the damaged spots, zones or area of the 7th layer being repaired and restored—you are at a deep level intending and sensing the area being restored and healed.

7. Continue visualizing, sensing and becoming the light in this way, repairing and restoring the damaged spot, zone or area for several moments, until you gain a sense of completeness or receive intuitive information that treatment of this area is complete. If you are able to view the 7th layer you may also use this to judge when your treatment of the area is complete.

8. Treat each damaged spot, zone or area of the 7th layer that requires it, using this same technique as given in steps 5 to 7 above. With each damaged area you may use either hand, but you will probably find your right hand easiest to use while learning. Use only one hand at a time to treat one damaged area at a time, however, and perform the technique clearly and accurately, until you ascertain that your treatment of that area is complete.

9. After completing treatment of all damaged regions on the front half of the eggshell, ask your patient turn over and lie on his or her stomach, and repeat the entire process of careful observation, preliminary visualization, and

treatment with the seventh layer focal healing technique, using the exact procedure given in steps 1 to 8 above. It is less likely to find damaged spots, zones or areas on the back half of the eggshell than on the front, but they will sometimes be found there, as well. As on the front side of the eggshell, damaged spots, zones or areas which are found on the back side are more frequently found on the upper half of the eggshell.

10. After you have fully treated every spot, zone or area of your patient's 7th layer with this technique that requires it, perform a passing of hands above the entire body surface of your patient, using the passing of hands technique just as you have learned it. As you do this, be open and sense with your whole being the harmony (or lack of it) in your patient's energy field. Does the energy feel harmonious, or do you detect any sense of disharmony in the energy? Hopefully, you will gain a tactile and intuitive sense of a harmonious and healthy overall energy flow in the field. This harmony indicates that the restoration attempted on the 7th layer has been effective. A well-healed 7th layer positively affects all lower layers of aura, and this effect can be noted during this regular passing of hands. In any case, take careful note of the harmony (or lack of harmony) in your patient's energy field. You are checking this to establish a reference sense of its harmonious flow after your 7th layer treatment, for future comparison.

11. Then, one to two weeks after you have treated this patient with the seventh layer focal healing technique, reassess this level of harmony in his or her energy field again, in the same manner. If you detected a lack of harmony in the 7th layer when you examined it immediately after performing the seventh layer focal healing technique, or if a lack of harmony has appeared in the one to two week period since, this may indicate an incorrect or incomplete 7th layer treatment. Perform the seventh layer focal healing technique again, with all the steps above, just as before.

It is important to know that, in order to safely employ this treatment, you must acquire a clear perception of the 7th layer, either with your physical eyes (preferably) or in your mind's eye, and work accurately and delicately as you direct the energy through your hand and out to damaged regions upon it. Although it is simple in nature, this technique is extremely powerful, and should be performed only with a clear perception of the areas on the 7th layer that require healing and an accurate performance of the technique. Otherwise it is possible for more harm than good to be done.

Figure 48: Seventh Layer Focal Healing

Delivering Intuitive Information to Your Patient

While performing step 4 of the seventh layer focal healing technique above, you may have received intuitive information giving you information regarding the psychological issues or present and past-life experience of your patient, or other information on his or her physical, emotional, mental and spiritual health. It is not uncommon to even receive specific information on present or past life traumas of a serious nature when viewing the 7th layer. You may also have received such information during other portions of your patient's healing treatment—when performing intuitive readings to discern the meaning of phenomena in the other aura layers or in the chakras, for example, or during your performance of radiatory healing on chakras. Whenever you focus upon, sense and become any aspect of your patient's energy field, this sort of information becomes available, as we've discussed.

This information is extremely useful to you the healer, for the purpose of coming to a full understanding of your patient's condition. You can use this information to assist your patient—under certain very important conditions—for your patient's learning, understanding and overall healing. A healing treatment is a very good time for personal growth on all levels, for the energy, color and light work you perform on your patient's energy field often catalytically potentiates and supports your patient's re-experiencing traumatic past experiences, consciously experiencing and coming to terms with repressed emotions, achieving a greater understanding of his or her condition, situation and problems, and acquiring a new and more beneficial spiritual relationship with him or herself. Delivery of intuitive information to your patient, for the purpose of complementing and enhancing your patient's overall experience of healing must be done only at the proper time and in the proper way, however, and only to the degree that is beneficial for your patient. You must carefully and consciously choose what portion, if any, of the information that has been received should be delivered to your patient, how it should be delivered, and when your patient has received enough. Otherwise, as in the seventh layer focal healing technique, it is entirely possible for you to do more harm than good.

The ideal way for you to incorporate the delivery of such information into a healing treatment is as a *gentle leading of your patient towards his or her own memory, understanding and release*, and as a confirmation of your patient's own experience in this process. That is, you do not "thrust" the information upon your patient in a way that is cold or insensitive, but in a way that instead encourages and assists your patient to discover and experience for him or herself whatever is important and needs to be looked at. While treating a seriously damaged heart chakra, for example, you may gently offer, to your patient, the observation that he or she holds a great deal of anger. Your patient will often acknowledge this, and you may then encourage your patient to explore this anger—to get in touch with this emotion and even go back to the time when this anger was felt strongly. You may gently assist by guiding your patient in doing so, being able to do so by virtue of having received information making you aware of the origin of your patient's trauma. Your patient may then begin to get in touch with this emotion and the experiences which have produced it. These may appear as memories, more emotions or even actual re-vivification of past traumatic experiences. This is often part of the healing process which energy healing work seeks to catalyze.

You may have seen this anger and its manifestations in the chakras and aura layers, may have seen the traumatic experiences in the present life of your patient that it correlates to, may even see various past life traumas of which the present-life experiences are a recapitulation, and may have a complete picture of the entire pattern of existential biases it has induced in your patient, but to deliver all this information (or even a part of it) to your patient, at once, is not in the best interest of your patient and can easily overwhelm or cause your patient to draw back, deny or reject further healing. You might be tempted to disclose to your patient, for example, such facts as "I see you may have been sexually molested as a child, and possibly also in a past life." *You must never impose such information on your patient.* It is far better to let out the information a little at a time, at the proper moments, as a process of leading your patient towards experiencing what is beneficial for him or her to experience during the healing, and assisting your patient in acknowledging and letting go of whatever comes up. It is important to understand, also, that *not every patient needs to recover an actual memory of past traumatic events*. Many patients will find healing and acquire a new understanding of themselves without re-vivification of past traumas. It is not up to you to choose what your patient should remember, but to only be a gentle and assisting guide as your patient and his or her higher self leads your patient to feel and experience that which is required for healing.

Instrumental in the judgment and timing required to be such a guide is your ability to follow your own intuitive sense. This intuitive sense will assist in directing the healing treatment to whatever faulty energetic conditions need treatment that day, to what past experiences and emotions need to come up and be understood and resolved, and to the best moment and the best way for this to happen. Complete healing is seldom accomplished in one healing session, and your patient's core issues and unresolved experiences can be revealed and resolved in a gradual, safe manner. Often you will get a real sense of when these moments can occur, and the way in which you can best serve your patient, in his or her healing process. The key is to remain open and clear in your awareness while retaining caution in what is released to your patient and how quickly your patient is led to deeper and deeper layers of experiences which contain the core issues and core emotions.

Healing of specific damaged areas in your patient's energy field will often occur at the same time that your patient gets in touch with, comes to an understanding of, and releases the experiences with which they correlate. Often this will occur during the most powerful Chios® techniques you have learned—chakra charging, radiatory healing and seventh layer focal healing—although it may occur at any time during treatment. Working to assist your patient during these times, in a sensitive, professional, caring and effective way, is a critically important service you perform for your patient.

Frisson Healing of Chakras and the Seventh Layer

Your study of Chios® healing is now nearly complete. As you employ the many healing techniques you have learned, you will find that with the large majority of your patients you are able to effect positive change to your patient's physical or psychological afflictions and facilitate for them a greater sense of health and well-being. The Chios® Master techniques that you have learned in this level—chakra charging, chakra system rebalancing, radiatory healing and seventh layer focal healing—are often especially effective. You will sooner or later encounter some patients who resist complete and lasting healing, however, despite your best efforts employing these powerful techniques. These patients can often be assisted with the final and most powerful technique in Chios®, however, beyond all these others you have learned: Chios® *Frisson Healing*.

The need for frisson healing is not indicated by the presence of any particular physical disease or psychological condition, or any combination of physical or mental symptoms in your patient. This is because the actual condition that exists produces physical and/or mental symptoms or diseases that will always vary, from patient to patient, and because of this variability no such specific symptoms may be used to diagnose it. The underlying condition is an energetic disease that is a *lingering disease and wasting illness of the being*. There is no name for this energetic disease in present healing vocabulary, but it nevertheless exists in some patients. Your patient may have come to you with specific physical diseases or ailments and/or a mental disorder—or any combination of recurrent physical and/or mental symptoms—and you may have attempted to treat these visible symptoms but without lasting success. This wasting illness of the being may affect the body, producing physical symptoms, physical pain or diseases of the body's organs, but not always. It likewise may produce psychological afflictions or disorders, but not always. The indicators that this condition *is* present and that frisson healing is required are: 1) a chronically failing chakra that resists healing; 2) one or more damaged areas of the 7th layer of aura that resist healing, and 3) intuitive information that you receive, that indicates that this condition is present.

A chronically failing chakra that resists healing is the primary indicator of this condition. As you have probably experienced, a particular healing patient will often have one (or sometimes more) chakras which are especially weak and in need of healing. In the patient requiring frisson healing, however, there is a difference: you will observe a chakra that you have charged and balanced (and probably used other healing techniques on as well) but that continues to be especially lacking in vitality and will frequently need recharging and/or rebalancing once more. You may perform these many times (even at frequent intervals), yet the chakra will nevertheless chronically relapse into a weak, impure and possibly also unbalanced state again. The more advanced the stage of failing weakness the more visible the indications will be, including a graying of the chakra color—a dullness, a lack of vitality and a clearly unhealthy appearance and feel that does not go away. This condition is more likely to be found in chakras as they are located closer to the heart: it is most common of all in the 4th chakra, it is found almost as often in the 3rd and 5th chakras, is still found somewhat often in the 2nd and 6th chakras, and is less likely to be found in the 1st or 7th chakras. Usually it is only one chakra that exhibits this condition, but on some rare occasions you may find two such chakras in a patient.

Damaged areas of the 7th layer of aura that are resistant to healing are the secondary indicator of this condition. One or more of these are almost always also present in addition to a chronically failing chakra, when your patient suffers from this condition. Your patient will have had one or more damaged areas on the 7th layer that you will probably have attempted to treat using seventh layer focal healing technique. If you have treated the 7th layer it will be in a greater state of health than otherwise, yet you will perceive areas that remain chronically resistant to full healing and are still not as they should be. You may find only one such area in the 7th layer that resists healing, but in the more advanced stage of this condition you may find two or possibly even more such areas. These areas are most likely to be on the upper front of the body—especially the upper torso and around the head—but can be found anywhere on the eggshell. These areas of the 7th layer that do not heal may be more subtle and difficult for you to discern than the chronically failing chakra that is the primary indicator of this condition, but will almost always also be present. These two indicators—one or more chronically failing chakras and defects in the 7th layer that resist healing—are signs of wasting through which this condition of wasting of the being manifests.

An intuitive sense that develops in you, indicating to you that your patient suffers from this wasting illness of the being, is a third indicator. You must take care, however, because this can be difficult to sense accurately. Often your patient will suffer from this condition yet subconsciously learn to feign health when it is present. Your patient does not do this consciously, nor to deceive either you or him or herself, but for the purpose of continuing to function and act in the world. The physical and mental symptoms your patient suffers—and that you at first attempt to treat with other techniques—can cloud your perception at first, such that you do not perceive this underlying energetic illness. And yet you may find that there develops in you a knowing that is felt by your whole being—an impression that emerges in your whole being—that your patient actually suffers from this wasting illness of the being that is actually producing the various more visible physical and mental symptoms. You will then know to look for the primary and secondary indicators discussed above, if you have not already noted them.

This wasting illness of the being is usually caused by a serious trauma in your patient's past that has not healed, due to either a lingering serious physical or mental illness or deep psychological or spiritual pain. The trauma may have occurred earlier in your patient's present life or (quite commonly) in a past life. The resulting condition is not merely a mental condition, but it is analogous to psychological depression. It is a depression of the being resulting from deep trauma. Your patient may not consciously know of the trauma, pain or illness that is the actual cause of the condition (especially if it is from early in the present life, or from past lives) but will rather know of the other illnesses, other pains, other struggles and complaints that have resulted. The underlying condition is a serious one—probably the most serious you will ever encounter in your energy healing work. The only really effective treatment is Chios® Frisson Healing.

The frisson healing technique should not be used to treat any specific chronic physical diseases or ailments and/or psychological disorders, but only when you have carefully ascertained the existence of this underlying lingering disease and wasting illness of the being, according to the diagnostic conditions given above. It should only be used after you have made certain it is necessary and not under any other circumstances. The word "Frisson" is a French word that, like the word "Chios," has no exact translation into English. The meaning of "Frisson" is akin to a sudden shiver, shudder or shock. Unlike all other techniques in Chios®, the frisson healing technique is a "shock treatment." It is *a shock treatment to restore the being*, to bring healing and vigor once more to the chakras and the areas of the 7th layer that have been affected.

Before employing the frisson healing technique on your patient, he or she must first be placed into the best possible state of energetic health. Your patient must have recently received complete healing treatment(s) including chakra charging, chakra system rebalancing and seventh layer focal healing. This healing work may have been performed by you or by another Chios® healer competent in the techniques. Note that seventh layer healing will have necessarily been included, as the patient requiring frisson healing will have had defects on the 7th layer which you (or another Chios® healer) will have attempted to correct. Your patient must have had this work done within the past three months (at a very maximum), or preferably within just a few weeks, so he or she is ready to receive the frisson treatment. This is required. You can then proceed with the frisson healing technique, which is done in two parts: 1) treatment of the chakra(s) in need, and 2) treatment of the area(s) of the 7th layer in need. Proceed as follows:

Exercise 3-R: Frisson Healing of Chakras and the Seventh Layer

1. With your eyes closed, and your patient lying down on your treatment table, first perform the Chios® technique for doing an intuitive reading to sense the condition of the chakra system (Exercise 3-E: Intuitive Reading: Sensing the Condition of the Chakra System), and confirm the chakra(s) in need. Most often, it will be one chakra only. You will have knowledge of the chronically failing chakra(s) from your previous experience giving treatments to your patient—this intuitive reading is not to discover new chakras needing frisson treatment, but to assess the current condition of chakra(s) known to be in need.

2. Now stand on your patient's right side, positioning yourself near the chakra, and call in the energy using visualization of the Chios® symbols, as you usually do at the beginning of a healing treatment. Open your eyes, and ask your patient to remain relaxed but perfectly still, during the entire procedure to follow.

3. When you are ready, place your hands held level but apart, palms-down, directly above the affected chakra in the corresponding layer of aura. If you are treating the 4th (heart) chakra, for example, you will have your hands not at the body surface (1st level), not at five to six inches above (2nd level), not 10 to 12 inches above (3rd level), but at about 15 to 18 inches above the body surface (the 4th incremental level). Note that you are using the same five to six inch increments you have used for chakra charging and radiatory healing. Your hands will not change levels, however, but will remain at this corresponding aura level while you treat the chakra with the frisson technique.

4. Your hands will also be in a new hand position unique to this frisson technique: the *Frame*. Hold your hands such that your wrists are not curved but so the hands are held flat, easily and relaxed, near each other but not touching. The thumb of each hand should be open and outstretched away from the fingers of its hand, such that the two thumbs are pointing towards each other yet not touching. The fingers of each hand should be held together but relaxed, and palms flat, but without the index finger of one hand touching the index finger of the other. The hands are also not held as far apart as when doing chakra charging or radiatory healing: there should be a gap, between the tip of the thumb on one hand and the tip of the thumb on the other hand (the thumbs are pointing towards each other) equal in inches to the number of the chakra (a four inch gap between thumbs for the 4th chakra, for

example). There should likewise be a gap between the tip of the index finger of one hand and the tip of the index finger of the other hand equal in inches to the gap between the thumbs (again, a four inch gap for the 4th chakra, for example). The hands are flat and level, palms down, and form a "triangle" shape (but with the specified gap between the thumbs and also the index fingers). Be aware that you will be channeling the energy downwards into the chakra from your hands, while they are in this position.

5. Now clear your mind—release all thoughts, release all business and concerns of the mind, release even any awareness of your patient. You will need to use great power of visualization when you employ the rest of this technique. Your eyes may be open or closed—whichever is more comfortable for you. Continue by visualizing, sensing and becoming the Chios® symbol in color, from the basic progression, standing on its edge vertically and facing you, in the middle of the frame you have made with your hands. You will use a green Trine for the 4th chakra, for example. The Chios® symbol should be approximately two inches high, regardless of which chakra is being treated and thus how wide the gap is between the hands. It is not flat, but as if it were a real object, perhaps ¼ inch deep, standing on its side facing you and floating between your hands. You must visualize the color of the symbol as especially vibrant—a very vibrant green Trine for the heart chakra, for example—even if there is some resistance to that vibrancy due to the weakness of the chakra or the illness of your patient.

6. And now you will now prepare to send a burst of brilliant light: the Frisson. You must see this intense burst of light coming from yourself—not from your head nor any other single part of your physical body, but from your whole being. It comes from *you*—from your core being perhaps somewhere near the center of your body—as a funnel of intense light which focuses down intensely and passes through the Chios® symbol and then to a pinpoint just behind the symbol. It is a very focused and intense pure white clear bright light—a powerful, extremely intense shock of light. It is not the duration of the flash that provides the power of this shock technique (it is very brief), but the incredible brilliance.

   Think of a brilliant flash of light from a brilliant burst of lightning in the sky, a very intense strobe, or even a nuclear explosion. It is not unusual to feel almost a shudder or shivering in yourself, as you send this brilliant flash of light. The burst of light passes through and illuminates the symbol, immediately before focusing to a pinpoint behind it, and as it illuminates the symbol it energizes, cleanses and purifies it, with the resulting energy burst transmitted downwards from your hands, not as light but as intensified and purified energy sent downwards into the chakra. Note that the burst of light does not go down into your patient's chakra, but just focuses into a pinpoint behind the symbol after it illuminates it. The light itself goes only to that point—not to your patient or directly to the chakra. Note also that you are not using your hands above the chakra to laterally disperse energy into the aura layer, as with chakra charging or radiatory healing, but to focus the light through the symbol and send the resulting energy downwards.

(Optional note: the brilliant burst of light can be thought of as not simply ending at the pinpoint, immediately behind the Chios® symbol, but as it enters this point also continuing to infinity within the point. If you have become familiar with Exercise 6-F: Advanced Meditation, and the point of pure being, this concept will make sense to you).

To perform the Frisson technique you must therefore, in your mind's eye and using your power of visualization, perform three things at once: 1) you are visualizing, sensing and becoming the Chios® symbol in vibrant color, floating in the middle of the frame; 2) you are visualizing, sensing and becoming the brilliant burst of light, from your core being, as a funnel focusing through the Chios® symbol to a pinpoint just behind it, and 3) you are sending the resulting burst of energy downwards, from your hands, into the chakra. You are not merely thinking about or pretending to see these things, but are releasing all other aspects of your awareness and visualizing, sensing and becoming these things, as one act. As with every powerful Chios® technique you have learned, you are acting with your whole being, through the use of this Frisson technique. This is the most powerful, focused technique in Chios®.

7. *Send the Frisson flash for a brief but extremely intense moment*, using the instructions just given above, and then withdraw the light, cease visualization of the Chios® symbol and drop your hands and rest for a minute or two. (See Figure 49).

8. Now repeat the entire exact technique once again. Stop and rest again for a few minutes and then repeat the technique one final time—a total of three Frissons, each sent just as described above. This completes treatment of the chakra.

9. If there is another chakra in need of frisson healing, you will need to repeat the entire procedure—steps 3 to 8 above.

10. After treating the chakra(s) in need, this way, briefly evaluate your patient using the passing of hands, to ensure that your patient has not become disturbed. As you did just after the seventh layer focal healing technique, perform a passing of hands above the entire body surface of your patient, sensing with your whole being the harmony (or lack of it) in your patient's energy field. You may detect a pulsing or throbbing from the chakra you have

just treated, but this is of no concern. If you detect a substantial lack of harmony or feeling of disturbance from the entire energy field of your patient, however, allow your patient to rest for a while, before continuing.

Figure 49: Frisson Healing - Chakra

11. You will then continue by treating the 7th layer of aura. Perform the Chios® technique for viewing this higher layer of aura (using steps 1 to 7 of Exercise 3-C: Intuitive Reading: Viewing All Seven Layers of Aura), employing the violet Star, and localizing your awareness to an eggshell-shaped area 30 to 36 inches above your patient's body. In the receptive phase, examine the 7th layer in your mind's eye and perform another round or two of the active/receptive cycle, if necessary. Allow yourself some time, to glance back with your physical eyes, to gain some physical vision of this layer. You will have knowledge of the damaged spots, zones or area(s) on the 7th layer, from your previous experience giving treatments to your patient—this intuitive reading is not to discover new damaged areas, but to assess the current condition of the area(s) known to be in need, and remind you of their precise location. Usually you will have knowledge of the area(s) with chronic defects, from your previous experience giving treatments to your patient.

12. Now stand on your patient's right or left side, as needed, positioning yourself near the first area of the 7th layer requiring treatment. Again ask your patient to remain relaxed but perfectly still, during the procedure. You will use the frisson technique again, as when you treated the chakras, but with some important changes.

13. When you are ready, position your hands again to form the frame, but this time with a gap of only two to three inches between the tips of the thumbs and the tips of the index fingers. The palms of your hands should now be about six to eight inches above the surface of the 7th layer, directly above the damaged spot, zone or area to be treated. The plane of your hands (as they form the frame) will be roughly parallel to the surface of the eggshell at the damaged area to be treated, and therefore not necessarily level (if you are treating an area towards the side or top of the eggshell they may be slanted or nearly vertical). Note that your hands will therefore be even further above the surface of the body than when treating the 7th layer of aura with the chakra charging or radiatory healing techniques (they will be up to a maximum of 3 ½ feet above the body surface, if the area is near the middle of the body). There are times when you may need a footstool or small ladder to position yourself correctly.

14. Now once again clear your mind. Release all thoughts, release all business and concerns of the mind, release even any awareness of your patient. Prepare again to use your power of visualization. You may again have your eyes open or closed, whichever is more comfortable for you. This time, however, you do *not* visualize a Chios® symbol inside the Frame. You will, however, send the Frisson by visualizing, sensing and becoming a brilliant burst of light, from the core of your being, as a funnel of intense light focusing into the entire Frame shape your hands make, and then *spilling out from there to pour over the affected area of the 7th layer.* As it spills, it is as if you are pouring the light through, and it runs and flows across the affected area of the 7th layer.

15. *Send the Frisson flash for a brief but extremely intense moment,* using the instructions given above, and then withdraw the light and drop your hands and rest for a minute or two. (See Figure 50). Then repeat the entire exact technique once again. Stop and rest again, for a few minutes, and then repeat the technique one final time—a total of three Frissons, each sent just as described above. This completes treatment of that chronically damaged spot, zone or area of the 7th layer.

16. If there is another spot, zone or area of the 7th layer in need of frisson healing, you will need to repeat the entire procedure—steps 12 to 15 above—for each damaged area of the 7th layer in need.

17. After you finish treating your patient with the frisson healing technique, ask your patient to relax and rest, for at least five minutes, on the healing table. It is *very* important that your patient then rest for the remainder of the day, and not engage in any busy activity of body or mind.

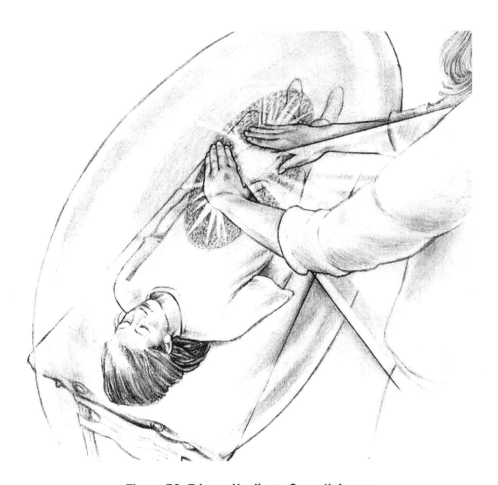

Figure 50: Frisson Healing – Seventh Layer

It is possible that your patient will require more than one frisson healing session—especially if the condition is in an advanced stage. The frisson healing technique should not be performed more than once, at the most, in a three month period, however. It should not be necessary to perform frisson healing more than a total of three times in any patient (and most patients will require that it be performed only once, or perhaps twice).

Distance Healing

You will usually treat your patients in person—in your physical presence—using your hands on and above your patient's body to channel energy, color and light as you practice the many Chios® techniques you have learned. It is desirable to give healing treatments in person whenever possible because you are able to more directly and completely examine the condition of the energy field of your patient and more directly and powerfully treat whatever energetic defects you find within it.

Your ability to sense the energy field of your patient and effectively treat many of the energetic defects in it is not limited by distance, however. Although an in-person treatment is usually somewhat more powerful and comprehensive, is possible for you to give a very effective and beneficial healing treatment to a patient in a remote location, even thousands of miles away. There will be times when it will necessary for you to treat a patient at a distance—with certain patients who are often at remote locations, for example, and cannot come for an in-person treatment. Patients with serious illnesses also often require distance treatment, for frequently the serious illnesses that they suffer from require treatment every day or every few days, and yet these patients will sometimes be unable to physically travel to you at these frequent intervals.

Most of the healing techniques that you have practiced with in-person healing treatments during your study of Chios® Levels II and III may also be employed at a distance. It is recommended, however, that you only perform distance healing on a patient that you have treated in person previously—a patient that you have, at least once, examined and treated "hands-on." This is because you will find it much easier to "tune in" to your patient's energy field and channel color and light to the parts of it requiring treatment if you have been in your patient's physical presence, and placed your hands upon his or her body, at least once before.

Distance healing treatments are conducted in a manner very similar to in-person treatments, but with some simple changes to the techniques—changes that are necessary because your hands cannot be used while performing them at a distance. It is important that you visualize whatever particular combination of Chios® symbols, color, light, or parts of your patient's energy field (e.g. chakras) that each technique requires with the same powerful technique of visualization you have previously used, however: you must visualize, sense and become each thing (or combination) with your whole being, performing the technique according to the instructions given for it previously, yet of course with the changes we mention that are necessary to adapt the technique for distance treatment without

200

use of your hands. Because we use color and light when healing at a distance, but not the energy (which is ineffective in distance healing), you may wish to review the section on Learning to Channel Color and Light, near the beginning of this Chios® level, to ensure maximum effectiveness. When using light, be sure to visualize, sense and become the brilliant pale white or bluish-white light in the same calm, effortless and persistent manner we've discussed previously.

It is also very important to practice your distance healing techniques with the same openness and sense of unity that we have discussed throughout your study of Chios®, remembering to always heal with your whole being. Distance healing treatments should be conducted in a state of quiet and complete openness. Do not limit your awareness to any one technique as you use it, but remain open to whatever intuitive information may come. Your patient is not in your physical presence, yet this openness will have the same benefit as before: you will be open to, and receive, information on every aspect of your patient's condition, even while engaging in specific healing techniques. You must also carefully maintain a state of unity between yourself, your patient and whatever healing tools and parts of your patient's energy field are involved as you perform distance healing—despite the fact you are not physically present with your patient. It can actually be even easier to maintain this state of unity (and the state of openness) when healing at a distance, because the potential distractions from your patient's physical presence and ego interactions between you do not intrude. Always remember that you are healing the whole being of your patient, with your whole being. This approach—to heal from your whole being, in a spirit of openness and with a sense of unity and oneness—is is even more vital than before, with distance healing, so that you may become a pure and clear channel for the healing power of pure consciousness to be projected at a distance, to your patient.

When planning a distance healing treatment, it is best to pre-arrange a treatment time with your patient when he or she will be alone and undisturbed and able to completely relax as the treatment is taking place. As the appointed time approaches, find a quiet, private location where you will not be disturbed and then seat yourself comfortably. You should usually perform distance healing with your eyes closed, as there is no advantage to having them open during a distance healing treatment and you will generally find it easier to focus on your patient and perform the healing techniques. Proceed as follows:

Exercise 3-S: Distance Healing

1. With your eyes closed, call in the energy using the Chios® symbols as you usually do before a treatment. Now begin to "tune in" to your patient. Let

all business, concerns of mind and thoughts drop away as you begin to become aware of only your patient.

2. Perform an intuitive reading to obtain intuitive information (using a body outline), for the purpose of checking your patient for 1) leaks and tears (including tears through multiple layers of aura); 2) blocked chakras, and 3) disturbances in energy flow (you will need to sense this with your "felt sense"). It is not necessary to look for auric energy impurities in your patient, for these cannot be treated at a distance—the aura clearing technique requires the use of the hands to be effective. Nor is it necessary to look for energy depletion, because aura charging similarly requires your physical presence to be done consistently and effectively.

3. After conducting this first intuitive reading, begin your treatment of your patient. As your first step, seal any leaks and tears you have detected by visualizing, sensing and becoming the brilliant pale white or bluish-white light fusing shut and sealing the breaks, like a surgeon using a laser. Do not imagine using your hands to perform this technique, however.

4. Treat each blocked chakra in your patient by visualizing, sensing and becoming the Chios® symbol that corresponds to the chakra, composed of the light, and *at the same time* visualizing, sensing and becoming the brilliant light flowing upwards through the chakra, the blockage in the chakra being removed, and the light flowing into the chakra from all around passing easily through it, with any blockage to that flow likewise being removed.

5. If you sense there are any other chakras in your patient that need distance healing, you can channel light to those chakras, also, but again do not imagine your hands on your patient nor a cloud of light around your hands or a layer of light below them. Instead, just visualize a cloud of the brilliant light surrounding each chakra, in succession. It is not always necessary to treat all the chakras in distance healing, however, and it is not necessarily desirable to do so either. It is better to focus only upon those chakras which you sense really need treatment.

6. Correct disturbances in energy flow by visualizing, sensing and becoming the Star, composed of the light, and *at the same time* visualize the brilliant light flowing smoothly and harmoniously through the body, removing energy irregularities. Should the disturbance in energy flow be in a local area, visualize the light in that area restoring the energy flow to its proper, smooth flow and correcting any disruption and diversion of the energy pathways. Do not imagine your hands upon the crown of your patient's head as you perform this technique, however.

7. Next, perform an intuitive reading to obtain intuitive information to sense the condition of your patient's chakra system (using a body profile). Which

chakras are undercharged? Which chakras are unbalanced? Take careful note, and briefly employ persistence of visualization by intending and sensing undercharged chakras strengthened to their strong, pure hue, with impurities removed, and unbalanced chakras raised or lowered in activity such that they return to a balanced state.

8. After this second intuitive reading, proceed to charge whichever chakras require it, by visualizing, sensing and becoming the appropriate Chios® symbol in color and a cloud of that color surrounding that chakra of your patient, but without imagining the use of your hands nor a cloud of color around your hands or a layer of color below them. See, in your mind's eye, the true color of the chakra being restored to its pure, healthy state, with any impurities removed. Note that since you are not using your hands, you will not be treating the aura layers, in successive increments above the chakra, as you would normally do during an in person treatment. Check your progress, during charging, by again doing another intuitive reading to sense the condition of the chakra system (using a body profile), to assess when your charging of each chakra is complete. It may require somewhat longer than when in person (up to five minutes, or more).

9. You should also rebalance whichever chakras require it, by visualizing the corresponding Chios® symbol for that chakra in either a higher or lower color, as required, and a cloud of that color surrounding the chakra of your patient, but again but without imagining the use of your hands nor a cloud of color around your hands or a layer of color below them. Proceed to use colors two or even three steps removed from the native color of the chakra, as needed. Check your progress, during rebalancing, by doing another intuitive reading to sense the condition of the chakra system (using a body profile), to assess when your rebalancing of each chakra is complete. It may again require somewhat longer than when in person (up to five minutes, or more).

10. After charging and rebalancing chakras in need, you should proceed to sensing chakras that may harbor structural energetic defects. Because you are not placing your hands on your patient's chakras in the normal sequence of hand positions, nor usually treating all the chakras during distance healing, you should instead perform a separate reading to specifically sense any chakras that may have structural energetic defects. You can do this reading by visualizing, sensing and becoming each of your patient's chakras for a few moments, in succession, while using your empathic sense of chakra condition. Do you empathically sense a pain in any of your own chakras, as you do this—not merely a physical pain but a pain that you sense with your whole being? If so, the corresponding chakra in your patient may harbor

these defects. It is also common to get intuitive information at various times, during a distance healing session, that indicates that this condition exists in one or more of your patient's chakras.

11. If you have identified chakras with structural energetic defects, treat them using the radiatory method, by visualizing, sensing and becoming the chakra with your entire being, in the same manner as you would in person, yet without imagining the use of your hands on the chakra. Note that, since you are not using your hands, you will not be treating the aura layers, in successive increments above the chakra, as you would normally do during an in person treatment. Continue radiatory healing treatment of the chakras that require it for as long as you feel it is necessary. It may be five minutes or more for some chakras.

12. As your final intuitive reading for your distance patient, perform the Chios® technique for viewing the higher layers of aura to read your patient's 7th layer of aura. Because you are not in your patient's physical presence, you must first see a body outline in your mind, yet negate the body outline itself and localize your awareness instead on the area around the body outline where the egg-shell shaped 7th layer of aura would be. Are there any damaged spots, zones or areas on the 7th layer? If so, you will be using a modification of the seventh layer focal healing technique to treat this layer at a distance. It is not necessary to use the technique to view the other layers, because you will not be able to treat them with your hands as you would do when performing the chakra charging and radiatory healing techniques during an in person treatment. If you have detected damaged areas on the 7th layer, however, briefly employ persistence of visualization by intending and sensing those damaged areas corrected and restored.

13. If you have detected damaged spots, zones or areas on your patient's 7th layer of aura, treat them with the seventh layer focal healing technique by visualizing the stream of light and using the same practice as has been detailed before, but instead of imagining the use of your hand, sense the place where you would normally place your hand instead as a focal point, the point where the light diffuses and then proceeds outward to the damaged spots, zones or areas of the 7th layer. This is not the same as visualizing or imagining your hand, but rather the "hand" you would normally place there is instead felt as a focal point and presence; this is a subtle yet important difference, yet one that is necessary to perform seventh layer focal healing correctly at a distance. Check your progress by again performing the technique for viewing the higher layers of aura to read the 7th layer, to assess when your treatment of each damaged area is complete. Once again, it may require somewhat longer than when in person (up to five minutes, or more).

14. Finally, treat any diseased areas or conditions which may be present in your patient. Usually you will give a distance treatment to a patient who you have seen before, and if an existing disease condition is present you will know this from your previous work with your patient. Should your patient have a serious illness, it is important to additionally incorporate whatever disease-specific energy, color and light procedures are recommended (see Chapter 4 – Treatment Procedures for Serious Physical Illnesses). Nearly all of these disease-specific procedures can also be performed at a distance, using the basic guidelines discussed above. Remember: you do not imagine using your hands on your patient's body. Rather, use the light, just as we've described it.

15. End treatment in the usual way with a quiet visualization of the Circle. This concludes your distance healing of your patient.

It is not possible to effectively perform the frisson healing technique at a distance. This powerful technique must be performed in person to be truly effective, and so should not be included in distance healing.

Although the general order of treatment given above is a good general framework, you may sometimes feel the need to "break free" from this order when giving a distance treatment, and instead employ these various tools in whichever order you sense is best. It is also important, when giving distance treatments, to concentrate on and treat only those aspects of your patient's energy field that really need it—distance treatments are somewhat less focused and powerful than treatments given in person. It will often take longer with each needed technique to produce the same effect as when you treat your patient with it in person, so it is good to be selective and use the time available to treat the most serious energetic defects present, thereby doing your patient the most good with the resources available.

When treating a patient with serious illness, it is beneficial to treat your patient often, twice or three times a week or more using distance healing, although physical visits should not be completely discontinued, if possible. Seriously ill patients, who might otherwise not be available two, three or more times a week, will often need and benefit from distance treatments.

Self-Healing Using the Chios® Techniques

An important part of being an effective healer is attending to your own personal healing process, and this is especially important for the master healer. The clearer your energy field, and hence your connection to the field of pure consciousness, the more genuine knowledge and power you have available to heal.

Most of the healing techniques you have learned, in this book, can be used not just to heal others—during in-person treatments and distance healing—but for your own *self-healing*, as well. You can employ the complete distance healing procedure above, with its modification of the powerful Chios® techniques for use in distance healing, to perform very effective healing on your own energy field. You are performing a "distance healing" on yourself, with you as the "patient." Simply follow the procedure above, with its series of intuitive readings (which you will perform on your own energy field), and the visualization of color and light (which you will visualize in the same manner as when treating a distance patient, yet now for your own aura and chakras). Do not use your hands—just follow the complete procedure given above, using the modified techniques as they are described. Employ persistence of visualization: with each intuitive reading that you perform on your own energy field, see the energetic defects in your own energy field healed. Be aware of this persistence of visualization as you employ the various Chios® techniques for your own self-healing.

For maximum benefit, it is wise to perform self-healing at regular intervals—every two weeks, or even every week. Many healers also find it very helpful to do self-healing before a day of healing work—it is especially beneficial to charge and balance your own chakras before doing healing work on your patients. While self-healing is a valuable tool for the healer, it does not entirely take the place of receiving healing treatments from another competent healer. Ideally, you should consider receiving energy healing treatments from another healer, as needed, and use self-healing practices to maintain and enhance your energetic health. When you use the powerful Chios® healing techniques for self-healing, as tools for your own energetic health, you are maximizing your effectiveness as a healer and also promoting your own personal growth. Do not underestimate the potential benefits of this self-healing work, to yourself and all those you heal.

For a more complete discussion of chakra self-healing using the Chios® chakra charging and chakra system rebalancing techniques, including reading your own chakras for your core issues and your entire physical, emotional, mental and spiritual state of being, see Exercise 6-B: Chakra Self-Healing.

Notes

Notes

Notes

4

Treatment Procedures For Serious Physical Illnesses

In your study of Chios® you have learned many techniques for sensing and healing energetic defects in the aura and chakra system. Many patients will come to you with physical, emotional or mental afflictions of a less-serious nature, seeking healing. Many other patients will arrive that have no such afflictions at all, but are simply interested in whatever benefits energy healing might provide towards enhancing body, mind and spirit in order to live a more fulfilling life and to better overcome the normal challenges therein. For all these patients you will heal the energetic defects you find in their aura and chakras, thereby often providing the benefits they seek. And yet there will also be times that patients will come to you with serious—even life threatening—physical illnesses. Such patients will not only have energetic defects in the aura and chakras that require treatment using the healing techniques you have learned thus far, but the defects will have precipitated serious disease in the physical body. You must treat these patients with additional measures and with extra effort to best serve their needs. This chapter is a supplement to Chios® Level III and will give you some additional healing techniques designed to assist your seriously ill patient.

Serious Illness is Treated in the Energy Field *and* Physical Body

In treating seriously ill patients, it is beneficial to understand how disease develops in the physical body and how a healer attempts to heal, that is remove, that disease. The health of the physical body is inextricably linked to the health of the energy field. It is the healthful flow of energy within the chakras and aura layers, in a balanced, harmonious and clear manner, that supports the physical body during life. Although the physical body eventually weakens and dies, the health of the energy field is the linchpin for the integrity of the physical body during life. It is a failure in this energetic underpinning that precedes physical illness and eventually allows it to manifest. It may be, for example, that a structural energetic defect in a certain chakra may precede by years the development of cancer in a related organ of the physical body.

Physical disease usually begins as one (or more) specific energetic defects in the chakras and aura layers that evolves into a pattern that affects several chakras and many layers of aura. Defects in a chakra and its corresponding aura layer usually occur together (as we have discussed). These defects then begin to spread. Energetic defects in the aura layer will filter through the aura and become lodged in other layers of aura that are susceptible to this energetic invasion—lower layers are particularly susceptible, but higher layers can also become affected. Energetic defects in chakras will affect neighboring chakras (and then other layers of aura). Each part of the energy field that is affected can potentially eventually affect any other susceptible part of the field. And so, one or two defects in a chakra or aura layer will become a pattern of energetic defects that includes much or even most of the energy field. These unhealthy energetic conditions in the chakras and aura layers eventually "filter down" into the physical body and render it susceptible to disease. A disease condition may then manifest in some part of the body, a part which no longer remains free and clear in its energetic functioning, as the ultimate result of these energetic defects in the higher energy field. The specific physical disease has a relationship to the energetic conditions within the energy field which produced it; the entire pattern of energetic defects in the chakras and aura layers, unresolved psychological issues and past traumas, and the physical disease itself, will all interrelate.

You will assist your seriously ill patient by first treating the higher cause of the disease— the energetic defects you find throughout the chakras and layers of aura. You must be thorough in doing so, however—you must thoroughly examine and treat all the chakras and aura layers, for there may be various subtle contributing higher causes to the illness that are present in various places in the energy field. Some energetic defects will be easy to identify. When physical disease is present in the body it often will be fairly easy to identify the energetic defects that will be present in the lower aura levels above the diseased location, for example. It will likewise be easy to identify the energetic defects in chakras that are related to, and near, the site of the disease. But you must go farther and diligently examine all remaining parts of the energy field and treat all unhealthy conditions you find. Do not neglect the upper layers of aura (the 4th and above), for there may be very important higher causes of the illness there that are not as apparent nor as easy to find as energetic defects in the lower aura layers, yet critical to treat. Often in the seriously ill patient you will find such energetic impurities and disturbances in these higher layers of aura. This complete healing of the chakras and higher aura layers is an important part of the overall healing process because it heals the higher cause of the illness. There is more that is needed, however. In a seriously ill patient, *you must additionally treat the disease in your patient's physical body* to maximize the chances of bringing back good health. The higher causes of the disease must be healed, but the physical disease existing in the body must also be treated and removed, if possible.

A patient with coronary artery disease, for example, will usually have a 4th (heart) chakra that is undercharged, unbalanced and contains structural energetic defects. You will also observe energetic impurities on the 4th layer of aura that have resulted, and probably on the 2nd and 3rd layers, as well. Other chakras will also harbor energetic defects, such as the 5th and 2nd for example. The colors in the aura around the heart will clearly show a great deal of held anger. If you are diligent, you will observe conditions on the higher layers (e.g. the 7th and/or 5th layer) that you will sense are ultimately involved, and probably many more phenomena in the energy field, too. The pattern of energetic defects will have ultimately "filtered down" and resulted in an isolation, weakness and suffocation of the energy flow through the heart—the cause of the heart attack that eventually resulted in the physical body. You will possibly receive intuitive information regarding relationship issues and past traumas that were the ultimate origin of all this. All this will create a complete picture of the condition of your patient and the cause of his or her illness, which you will use to plan effective treatment. You will treat all the energetic defects in the chakras and aura layers that you have identified with the healing techniques you have already learned, but you will *additionally* treat the energy flow in and around the heart with a procedure you will find later in this chapter that is specifically for patients with coronary artery disease.

Treatment of serious physical illness is accomplished by complementing treatment of the conditions in the chakras and higher aura layers that are the ultimate cause of the disease with additional disease-specific procedures designed to address the specific disease condition present in the physical body of your patient. You the healer, when treating a seriously ill patient, therefore treat your patient on all levels of his or her being—from any past life issues resident upon the 7th layer of aura, down to the disease in the physical body, and everything in between. You treat various interrelated energetic conditions throughout the energy field, all of which play a contributory and often complex role in whatever illnesses and afflictions are affecting your patient, including the physical manifestation of illness. And yet, as always, all these various parts of the energy field (and the physical body) are one—it is one being. As you perform each required healing technique for your patient—including those that address the disease in the physical body—remain open and always remember you are healing your patient's whole being.

Serious Illness is Treated by Battling Disease *and* Creating Health: Light Visualization and the Placement of Health

In the treatment of disease there is a polarity. On one hand, there is the wellness of your patient. Each patient, by virtue of his or her connection to pure consciousness and the true self of that person, has potentially unlimited health and wellness. On the other hand, there is the illness of the disease that is present, which is separate from the patient, like an invader.

Disease is an unnatural and unhealthy condition which is possible only when your patient's connection to the field of pure consciousness and his or her true self is disrupted. When the energy field of your patient contains energetic defects (of various sorts), it no longer provides a pure connection to the source of unlimited health and wellness that normally manifests as the natural state of ideal health of body, mind and spirit. Disease is a separate entity, an unhealthy energetic entity that injects itself into the energy field, interrupting health—it is an energetic entity to be eliminated. You the healer will therefore seek to eliminate disease, when present, but you must *also* seek to restore health and wellness to your patient. This is true healing, in both its aspects: you battle and eliminate illness but also create health. For the seriously ill patient, it is just as important for you to create health as to battle the illness.

You will battle the illness by treating both the energy field and the physical body, as we've discussed. You will treat the energy field with the Chios® healing techniques (especially the powerful Chios® Master techniques) to heal the energetic defects in it. You will treat the physical body using additional disease-specific procedures, which use light visualization to fight the specific form of disease present in the body. As you perform these disease-specific procedures using light, however, you will also—at the same time—*place health* in the diseased organs or tissues of your patient's body that you are treating with the light.

The disease-specific procedures you will use employ light visualization for specific purposes. You will use it to direct and focus the energy to diseased organs or areas of the body to treat them in a more directed and powerful way. You will use it to move energy through the body in certain ways necessary for healing the specific disease present—a calm flow of light, to quiet, or a bright burst of light to stimulate, for example. You may even perform light visualizations to convey a certain *quality* to the light you channel to diseased areas. As you perform whatever specific light visualizations are necessary to treat the specific disease present, however, you will at the same time visualize diseased areas coming back to a state of health. You will visualize, sense and become the diseased area surrounded and imbued by the light. You are drawing the disease into your "self" such that you are one with it. You are at the same time drawing the light, and the health inherent in it, into your "self" so you are also one with the health and light. *You become the disease and the light, correct the diseased condition, and substitute health for the disease, placing health in your patient, as one act.* You are not just a channel for the light used in treating the diseased area, but also a channel for the health and wellness that is placed in it. You are acting as a pure channel for the ideal health and wellness inherent in the state of pure consciousness to come in and restore health, in the diseased area. You become the disease, and then cure the disease in your "self." This is an intimate, eye-to-eye battle with disease, where you take the disease condition into yourself, heal it there, and thence in your patient, because you and your patient are one. This is the *placement of health*.

You will therefore not merely focus on battling the disease during treatment, but also on cultivating health and wellness. With a seriously ill patient, it is important not to place too much emphasis just on the disease, but to focus upon creating health. Your patient's body has potentially unlimited health available and so can become healed at any time through the application of the energies given in treatments. The body possesses the ability to heal itself, although a seriously ill patient is not able to command this ability by virtue of being limited by the illness. You the healer, by treating both the energy field and the disease present in the physical body (including placing health), stimulate your patient's own health process and sustain it. You work to remove the disease, reconnect your patient to the source of ideal health, and bring in health to replace the disease. The ultimate source of the health you bring is from your patient; you merely act as a pure channel to reconnect and re-establish the ideal health—already present in the consciousness and true self (higher self) of your patient—back into your patient's body. You facilitate your patient's own healing.

Practice of Meditation and Knowledge of Anatomy Are Useful Adjuncts

One highly recommended adjunct to learning to treat the seriously ill patient using the disease procedures given in this chapter is the practice of Chios® Meditation. Meditation fosters your visualization ability, and effective performance of the disease-specific treatment procedures is dependent upon your ability to use light visualization to treat diseased organs and tissues in the specific manner needed. You also employ your visualization ability when placing health in these diseased parts of the body: you visualize, sense and become the diseased organ or area surrounded by the light, and also place health, at the same time. Your ability to perform this fundamental process of light visualization and the placement of health is the key to effective treatment of serious illness. Chios® Meditation will greatly assist you in developing this ability, in addition to the other perceptual and intuitive abilities you use in healing.

It is also very beneficial for you to have a good working knowledge of anatomy, physiology, and human diseases. You will be able to employ light visualization and place health very effectively, having a good anatomical knowledge of the structure of the organs or tissues in which disease is present and that you will visualize during treatment. To understand the nature and manner of progression of the disease is also very beneficial as this is an important aspect of understanding the entire condition of your patient. You will also be able to comprehend whatever medical information your seriously ill patient may offer regarding the disease present. Many serious illnesses have a primary cause of disease, but also a number of interrelating conditions and complications, and you will be able to understand the entire illness and all its effects and address them in your treatments.

Two important additional points: first, with the seriously ill patient, perhaps more so than a patient who is not ill, you must rely first and foremost on your own judgment and intuitive sense, in determining the order and content of techniques employed in treating your patient. This may sometimes involve deleting treatment steps that are not needed, or spending a great deal of time on an area of particular concern, or even modifying techniques or engaging in new procedures as you feel guided to, as the situation demands. In treating the seriously ill patient, you must rely on your own judgment, perception and abilities rather than any set rules. Secondly, you will notice that we occasionally give procedures for diseases that have an ultimate cause that is ostensibly purely physical (e.g. a genetic cause). In these cases, we do not claim to be treating the ultimate cause of the disease with these energy healing techniques, but the procedures are given because they are a beneficial part of overarching treatment of your patient's whole being, and can sometimes even have unexpected physical benefits.

Color Therapy—Supplementing Disease Treatments With Color

One final tool you may use in your disease treatments is color therapy. Light visualization and the placement of health will usually be your primary tools, to treat disease in the physical body, but there may be times when you receive intuitive information to additionally employ color in your treatment of diseased areas or other specific areas of the body. Organs or tissues which have been subject to disease conditions, or to trauma of various kinds (wounds, broken bones, etc.) will sometimes benefit and be refreshed by use of an appropriate color, in addition to being treated with the light.

Various systems have been proposed that attribute certain colors with discrete properties or assign certain colors to treatment of specific conditions and diseases, but in reality the situation is too complex for any such system of rules to be practical. While *sometimes* such systems of color therapy will stipulate a color that actually will help a given disease or condition, it is more often that a recommended color will not actually be the best and most beneficial color to use, at all. You should instead perform an intuitive reading, to ask if using color is necessary, given your patient's specific situation, and if so which color to use in treating a specific area. Allow intuitive information to be your guide as to which color is really most appropriate. This is better than any system of set rules.

When channeling color to an organ or tissue you have sensed requires it, it is not necessary to use a Chios® symbol in color, merely to visualize, sense and become that color, seeing it as a cloud of color gently penetrating into the organ or tissue you are treating.

Diseases of the Heart and Circulatory System

The different kinds of heart disease correspond to differing maladjustments in the use of energy in the heart area of the body, and the precise energetic treatments differ, as detailed below. Common to all heart disease, however—especially serious heart disease—is a weakened, impure or structurally disfigured heart chakra. You may see an extensive damage to this chakra, which will almost always exhibit multiple energetic defects. For all heart patients, you will give a complete healing treatment but will *always treat the heart chakra last*—being sure to treat both the front and rear components. You will often need to perform unblocking, charging, rebalancing and/or radiatory healing on the heart chakra—sometimes all four. You will also almost always observe a darkening (almost a destruction) of the aura layers over and around the heart. You may need to perform the aura clearing technique over the heart, and diligently treat the higher layers over the heart during the charging and radiatory healing techniques. Do these things, and then add the specific treatments detailed below.

Coronary Artery Disease (aka Ischemic Heart Disease, Myocardial Infarction, Angina): Begin with complete healing treatments (including the special considerations given above for all heart patients). A series of treatments will be necessary to restore health to the heart. Coronary artery disease cannot be treated completely by only focusing on the heart; treatment must also draw from the energetic strength of the entire body. Therefore when beginning a course of treatment, the first step is to bring greater energetic health to the body by giving complete healing treatments (including the special considerations given above for all heart patients), on several occasions. Aura charging will probably be needed during treatments, and radiatory healing of the heart chakra is very important. The heart chakra, in degenerative heart disease, will almost always be underactive, and should be rebalanced upwards. After several treatments you will probably detect a positive change in the flow of the energy, a change towards health in your patient, a healthier feeling you may even notice in your patient's appearance. After detecting this, you can begin more specific treatment.

To begin specific treatment of coronary artery disease, first perform a standard treatment, again observing the special considerations above. While treating the heart chakra, use light and your power of visualization to visualize, sense and become the heart infused and invigorated with the light, strengthening it back to health, placing health in it. While conducting the energy, see the energy as a light surrounding the heart, at first, and then around the coronary arteries, invigorating them, clearing them and bringing health to them. Perhaps even specific blocked areas will come into view—treat these with the light as described, seeing the blockage shrinking away and the arteries clear, elastic and healthy as they conduct blood. After treating the heart chakra in this way, you must now perform the following specific procedure:

Exercise 4-A: Coronary Artery Disease

1. With your eyes open and your patient lying down on your treatment table, stand by the side of your patient with your hands on opposite sides of your patient's heart chakra. Place all ten of your fingertips lightly on the body surface over the heart, with fingers gently curved but without the palms on the body. The fingertips of one hand should be two to three inches away from the fingertips of the opposite hand, at the body surface.

2. You will now draw energy from the entire body of your patient and into the heart. Employ this specific light visualization: visualize, sense and become a brilliant, electrifying flow of the light, flowing powerfully from all parts of your patient's body simultaneously—from both arms, both legs, the entire torso and all the chakras—and collecting in a brilliant area all around your patient's heart. The purpose of this flow is to charge the heart and heart chakra electrically, to cleanse and strengthen them.

3. As you employ this light visualization, place health into the heart. Maintain this light visualization for two to three minutes.

4. Now simultaneously draw your fingertips and hands up above the heart and away from the body outward, as if the fingertips were tracing the lines of a funnel away, and at the same time visualize, sense and become the light coming forth in this way from the body—as a sign of the strength of the heart and a cleansing of the illness from it. Draw your hands at least three or four times in this way, at a moderate speed, taking perhaps three to five seconds to draw outward along a funnel 12 to 15 inches high. Your hands will begin with the fingertips of the opposite hands two to three inches apart, at the body surface, yet end with each hand at the opposite ends of the funnel shape, with the hands now approximately one foot apart.

5. This concludes the specific treatment. You should add this specific procedure to your regular treatment for the balance of the healing treatment regimen.

The nature of the energetic condition that corresponds to coronary artery disease is a suffocation in the energy, as if the energy is isolated and not able to freely circulate and complete a full circle from other points of the body through the heart. Energy is therefore drawn from all over the body and washed out. The patient with serious heart disease should be treated in this manner every two to three days.

Congestive Heart Failure (aka Heart Failure): Give your patient a standard treatment (including the special considerations given above for all heart patients). Then employ this specific procedure:

Exercise 4-B: Congestive Heart Failure

1. With your eyes open and your patient lying down on your treatment table, place your *left* palm directly over your patient's heart. Visualize, sense and become the Trine, composed of the light, and continue visualizing it for this entire procedure.

2. Reach now, with your right hand, to your patient's right hand, and place your fingertips lightly on this hand.

3. Visualize, sense and become a powerful burst of light from your own right hand: a strong, sharp, brilliant burst of light from your fingertips and through your patient's right hand and arm and directly to your patient's heart (which is under your left hand). This should take just a second. Maintain the energy that your patient's heart is receiving under your left

hand—see your patient's heart receiving and holding the large burst of brilliant light.

4. Now quickly remove the fingertips of your right hand and place them on your patient's right knee, and again send a similar burst of light between that knee and your patient's heart, in the exact same way as before. Maintain the energy that your patient's heart is receiving under your left hand—again see your patient's heart receiving and holding this large burst of brilliant light.

5. Repeat with your fingertips of your right hand on your patient's left knee, sending a similar burst of light from that knee to your patient's heart, in the exact same way as before. Maintain the energy that your patient's heart is receiving under your left hand—again see your patient's heart receiving and holding this large burst of brilliant light.

6. Repeat with your fingertips on your patient's left hand, sending a similar burst of light from that hand to your patient's heart, in the exact same way as before. Maintain the energy that your patient's heart is receiving under your left hand—again see your patient's heart receiving and holding this large burst of brilliant light.

7. Now remove your left palm from your patient's heart chakra and place your right palm there.

8. Place your left palm on your patient's 6th chakra and visualize, sense and become the light flowing down from the 6th chakra to the heart, sending the energy down to the heart, for about 10 to 15 seconds.

9. Finally, treat the heart chakra as usual, to again re-strengthen the heart, using light visualization and the placement of health.

The nature of the energetic condition corresponding to heart failure is a weakness, an inability to hold energy. This procedure energizes and strengthens the heart. The heart chakra may be underactive, and rebalancing upwards will also help your patient.

Cardiac Arrhythmias (Bradycardia, Tachycardias, Premature Depolarizations, Fibrillations, Heart Blocks): Begin with a complete healing treatment (including the special considerations given above for all heart patients). Treat the heart chakra in the normal way first, both the front and rear components, and then ask your patient to sit up. Now treat your patient with the following specific procedure:

Exercise 4-C: Cardiac Arrythmias

1. With your eyes open, ask your patient to sit up, if possible, and place your hands with your right palm over the front component of your patient's heart

chakra and your left palm over the rear component of the heart chakra (such that the heart is "sandwiched" between your hands).

2. Ask your patient to breathe freely and deeply, throughout this procedure.

3. Channel energy into the heart continuously, through both your hands, while performing the following steps. You need not visualize light but only feel the energy.

4. Now visualize, sense and become the Trine and at the same time bring your right hand directly out from the front of the heart slowly and steadily, taking perhaps five seconds to bring it to a total of a foot or so out, keeping the fingers gently together and palm flat. You are channeling energy continuously into the heart chakra, and visualizing the Trine symbol as you bring out your hand, but as you bring out your hand you must also visualize, sense and become the motion as it creates a balanced and steady pull of energy around the chakra and the heart, a pull of energy you will feel with your hand as you bring it away from the body. It is as though a band of energy from the rear hand to the front hand were being stretched out, and as the hand returns is drawn back to its proper shape, like a stretching rubber band.

5. Return your hand to the body surface and repeat this several times, for a total of four to five motions.

6. After completing the motions, ask your patient to lie down again, and again treat the heart chakra as usual, with light visualization and the placement of health.

The nature of the energetic condition corresponding to cardiac arrhythmias is a lack of or improper elasticity, a tightness or slackness in the energy flow in the areas around the heart. The motion creates a balanced and steady pull of energy around the heart which assists in removing irregularities. The heart chakra may also be underactive in cases where the heart rate is too low or overactive in cases where the heart rate is too high. Rebalance accordingly.

Arterial Hypertension: To always treat hypertension, when present, is essential to preventing future serious illness. Your patient's heart chakra *may* not need the special measures discussed above, but you can treat the hypertension as follows:

Exercise 4-D: Arterial Hypertension

1. With your eyes open and your patient lying down on your treatment table, give your patient a standard treatment, but incorporate in your treatment the

correction of energy flow technique (perform the technique thoroughly, using light, for up to five minutes).

2. Then, channel energy into your patient's arms, one at a time, by placing your right palm on the inside of your patient's elbow joint, and your left palm on the outside of the joint.

3. After treating both arms in this way, treat your patient's hands, one at a time, by sandwiching each hand between your palms (your palms inward, with your palm chakra directly on your patient's palm chakra, your patient's hand "sandwiched" between your hands) for a few moments. Hypertensive patients should be treated in this manner about twice a week, if possible.

Arterial hypertension corresponds to an improper flow of energy, energy that does not flow easily through the body, but that seeks irregular paths. The correction of energy flow technique is very important, in addressing this condition. While performing it, see the energy flow regularizing. The effect of the arms and hands is significant, and treatment of the arms and hands is especially effective and calms the hypertensive patient, as well.

Stroke (Cerebral Infarction, Cerebral Hemorrhage): The two kinds of stroke, cerebral infarction and cerebral hemorrhage, although different from a clinical medical viewpoint, are treated the same way. There is no regeneration for the tissue damaged by stroke, but prevention of stroke, or further stroke, is possible, and it is also possible to assist stroke victims in their work to regain use of affected parts of the body. Regular treatments are necessary for either endeavor. To treat for stroke:

Exercise 4-E: Stroke

1. With your eyes open and your patient lying down on your treatment table, give your patient a standard treatment, and then ask your patient to sit up. Place your hands on your patient's shoulders, in the shoulder position, with one hand on each shoulder.

2. Channel energy into your patient, in this position, for a minimum of five minutes or more, until you get a sense of completion. This may last up to ten minutes in some cases.

3. Stroke is often accompanied by hypertension, which is a common contributing cause of stroke. Treat the arms and hands of your patient next, as detailed under steps 1 to 3 of Exercise 4-D: Arterial Hypertension, above.

4. Aura charging is indicated on all patients who have suffered a stroke, even a small stroke, and especially for those who have been confined at length in bed. Perform a full aura charging procedure on your patient.
5. Auric energy impurities near the head and neck are commonly found, on stroke patients. Use the aura clearing technique all around the head and neck, as needed.

During regular treatment of the stroke patient, you should pay particular attention to the 5th and 6th chakras, which may require unblocking, charging, rebalancing or radiatory healing. The 4th chakra may require this attention as well. The stroke patient benefits from a greater sense of the whole self, rather than just treatment of specific areas, and so to give complete healing treatments, with the goal of restoring balance and harmony to the overall being, is especially beneficial.

Cardiac Infections (Pericarditis, Myocarditis, Endocarditis): Place your hands over the heart, and visualize, sense and become the light washing through the heart and whatever of its linings may be infected, like a river, cleansing and purifying the heart of the infecting microorganism. If the heart chakra is overactive, rebalance downwards.

Cardiac Inflammations: Often prolonged energy channeling into the heart chakra will be adequate to soothe the inflamed tissue. In those cases where this is not sufficient, treat the heart chakra last, as usual for heart patients, and then treat as follows:

Exercise 4-F: Cardiac Inflammation

1. With your eyes open and your patient lying down on your treatment table, place your hands on your patient's shoulders, in the shoulder position, with one hand on each shoulder.
2. Visualize, sense and become the Trine, composed of the light, while channeling the energy into the shoulders, and direct your attention to your patient's heart.
3. Visualize, sense and become the light coming from your hands, flowing into your patient's shoulders and then flowing down into your patient's heart, while continuing to visualize the Trine. Seek to impart a quality of *coolness*, like ice, to the light you are channeling to the heart in this way. This flow of energy should be applied gently and steadily, and will have a soothing effect on the heart. Hold this position for several moments.

4. Then request that your patient sit up, and treat the front and back of the heart chakra at the same time, your right palm on the front component and your left palm on the rear component for several minutes more.

With cardiac inflammation, an overactive heart chakra may be present. Rebalance downwards.

Cancer

Nearly all of the various organs and tissues of the body are potentially susceptible to cancer, but cancer has the same fundamental energetic nature wherever it occurs. Cancer is an energetic invader: it is an insidious disease that preys upon energetic weakness, gaining its entry at points of weakness, disharmony or imbalance in the chakras and aura layers and then expanding itself to other parts of the energy field. Cancer then "filters down" and seeks to invade the physical body at its weakest points—where it is given the greatest opportunity—and then spread itself in the physical body, as well. At each susceptible location in the body, cancer can be fought two ways: either before it begins, by sensing weak areas and strengthening them so as not to give cancer entrance, or after its onset, to restrict its growth. The various forms of cancer require aggressive treatment to control, and cancer is one of the greatest challenges you the healer will ever face in your treatment of seriously ill patients. Treatment of these malignancies requires skill, knowledge, power of will, perseverance, diligence and faith. Many cancer patients will require treatment frequently, even on a daily basis.

The first step in treating your cancer patient is to become fully aware of the extent of the disease: to identify all locations in both the energy field and physical body that have cancer. Often you will be given some of this information by your patient, who will know of locations in the physical body that harbor cancer, but you must not be limited by the medical information relayed to you. You should therefore perform intuitive readings to fully assess the condition of your patient's energy field *and* to obtain intuitive information on locations of cancerous areas in your patient's physical body. You will then treat all affected areas in both your patient's energy field and physical body. Proceed as follows:

Exercise 4-G: Cancer

1. With your eyes open and your patient lying down on your treatment table, first perform intuitive readings to assess the state of your patient's chakras.

Use the technique you learned in Exercise 2-C: Intuitive Reading: Sensing Simple Energetic Defects of the Aura and Chakras to look for blocked chakras (and also leaks and tears, auric energy impurities and energy depletion, all of which are common phenomena in the cancer patient). Perform the technique you learned in Exercise 3-E: Intuitive Reading: Sensing the Condition of the Chakra System to detect undercharged and unbalanced chakras. While giving your patient a brief standard treatment, using energy channeling, use your empathic sense during the normal sequence of treatment hand positions to look for chakras with structural energetic defects (as you learned to do in Exercise 3-F: Sensing Chakras With Structural Energetic Defects). As you perform this complete assessment of the condition of your patient's chakras, look for chakras that exhibit multiple energetic defects. *Related chakras*—chakras near to, and probable primary causes of, the cancer—are usually seriously ill chakras exhibiting multiple defects. Pass your hands over all such seriously ill chakras, to gain additional information, and integrate all these sources. Make careful mental note of all seriously ill chakras—usually there will be one or two, but sometimes there are more.

2. Perform an intuitive reading to view all seven layers of your patient's aura, using the technique you learned in Exercise 3-C: Intuitive Reading: Viewing All Seven Layers of Aura, to sense (and if possible view) all layers of aura, taking special care to notice areas exhibiting serious energetic impurities and energy disturbances. Viewing the aura will give you locations of current malignancies, which will usually appear as dark, unhealthy energies concentrated in the aura over the locations of the body where cancer may exist. Cancer has an ugly appearance in the aura—a dark, growing malignant appearance that may appear in various unhealthy colors depending on its stage of development. Focus in, as necessary, for further information—focus in on the chest and shoulder area of a breast cancer victim to determine the extent and location of possible growth beyond the breast to lymph nodes, for example. Look closely over areas near seriously ill chakras, as well, chakras that exhibit multiple energetic defects. Be sure to look for serious energetic defects in the higher aura—on the 4th through 7th layers—that may be harder to notice but that are related and that will also require treatment. Make careful mental note of all areas with these serious energetic defects.

3. After examining the energy field of your patient, perform an intuitive reading (using a body outline) to gain information on the current locations and possible metastasis of the cancer in your patient's physical body. Close your eyes and localize your awareness on a body outline of your patient, during the active phase, asking for this information, and then release into

receptive phase to obtain the intuitive information you need. The cancer will probably appear to you in one of two ways: as a *dark black energy, liquid or mold that seeks to spread*, or as a *growing active energy like fire or electricity*. Either way, you will "see" the cancer in certain locations, on the body outline, and may also see the directions—the patterns—in which it may seek to spread. These are the areas that you will treat using light visualization and the placement of health. You must always do this intuitive reading, even if you or your patient believes the cancer is only limited to certain areas; it may be spreading or your patient may not have had complete information on cancer locations in his or her body, and you must know and treat the full extent of the disease. Make careful mental note of all the information you receive.

4. Now integrate the information you have received: carefully note all this information, seeking to know the cancer as it appears in your patient's energy field and physical body. *Know and understand the complete state of your patient's cancer, in your mind and whole being.* Create a *comprehensive persistence of visualization* in yourself: visualize, sense and become all areas of your patient's energy field and physical body that are involved in the cancer healed, with all manifestations of the cancer gone.

5. Now begin to treat the cancer in your patient's energy field. Sealing of leaks and tears will be needed often, especially for patients who are receiving radiation. Aura charging should almost always be included for your cancer patient, especially if he or she has been receiving radiation or chemotherapy. It will also be common to remove auric energy impurities over cancerous areas, which you should do with the aura clearing technique.

   You must comprehensively treat related chakras and affected aura layers. Related chakras will almost always require charging, along with nearby chakras (which sometimes become affected). Related chakras will usually require rebalancing as well—they will be overactive in the early stages of the disease, as it spreads, and then underactive later, as areas succumb to the disease. Related chakras will almost always require radiatory healing, which is vitally important in treating cancer. You may need to add the unblocking chakras technique, for especially damaged chakras, in addition to radiatory healing. Treating the aura layers is vitally important. Very frequently the aura layers above cancerous tissues will show substantial darkening from energetic impurities, over the locations of the body where cancer exists. When performing the chakra charging or radiatory healing techniques on related chakras, you should be sure to also aggressively treat these affected aura layers. You may sometimes need to treat an aura layer for a substantially longer period of time than normal, as your hands move in semicircular movements dispersing energies laterally into the layer.

Seventh layer focal healing is required fairly often, to treat the highest cause(s) of the disease. Frisson healing may be required, although you usually will not detect this (using the diagnostic criteria given with that technique) until after a series of treatments. Carefully address all substantial energetic defects, in your patient's energy field.

6. Treat the cancer in your patient's physical body, using light visualization and the placement of health. **Refer to the specific treatment procedures listed below**, for details regarding hand placement and the light visualization(s) to employ. For cancers in specific organs and tissues, you will place your hands on the body as near to the cancerous area as possible. When treating areas that cannot be treated directly, due to modesty considerations (e.g. the colon, the prostate or women's breasts), you will place your hands as near as possible to the area, with one hand on one side and the other hand on the opposite side of the affected region. Specific hand positions are suggested for each location. While treating each cancerous area, seek in your whole being to contain the cancer. If the cancer appeared as a dark energy, liquid or mold, treat it by visualizing, sensing and becoming the brilliant light surrounding the darkened areas, burning away, drying and shrinking the cancer, placing health at the same time you do this. If you saw the cancer as a flame or electrical energy, visualize, sense and become the brilliant light as having a quenching, dampening or restraining effect on the growing, active areas of cancer, similarly placing health at the same time. When treating cancer with the light, you must strive to also convey a quality of *calm, stillness and clarity* with the light (clarity does not refer to a visual clearness, but a quality of clarity). You will often find yourself channeling a great deal of energy to areas of your patient's body affected by cancer, sometimes for extended periods of time. For each cancerous area, visualize full restriction and extinguishment of the cancer, with the light, until it is gone.

It is effective to vary the position of your hands, as you channel energy to affected areas, as well. When treating a certain area containing cancer, place your hands on the body in specific position, with your hands on opposite sides of the cancerous area. Treat the area for a while, using this first hand position, according to the instructions above. Then, move your hands to another, different position, yet again with your hands on opposite sides of the cancerous growth. Repeat this for a total of three to four different positions, close to the cancer, shifting your hands but keeping them roughly opposite each other. This may require 10 to 15 minutes of total time for each affected area. The treatment of cancer, using light visualization and the placement of health, is a dynamic, rather than static, process. It is of utmost importance to remember, also, that your hands (and their varying positions) are not the essence of cancer treatment. You are always treating the whole being of your patient with your whole being—your hands are merely instruments.

7. After completing treatment of the cancer, it is good to treat the 7th chakra one more time, and then perform grounding (even if you have done it previously).

It is important to know that, although the fight with cancer is serious, it is better to always maintain a confident rather than a grave or concerned attitude with your patient—the disease feeds on fear. An atmosphere of faith and positivity will add to your treatments. As mentioned, cancer must also be treated on a frequent, regular basis. It is good to treat your patient using distance healing if frequent physical treatment is not possible. When engaging in distance healing of cancer patients, use the brilliant light in the same way as described in detail for physical treatment, yet of course without the use of your hands. Be sure to always include charging and radiatory healing for related chakras.

Lung Cancer: Give your patient a standard treatment (including the special considerations given above for all cancer patients), but with these modifications: treat one lung at a time by placing your hands on either side of it, on the front of the body, varying the hand position three to four times over the affected lung as you visualize, sense and become the light surrounding the diseased areas in it, and place health. You may wish to include the hand position described under Exercise 4-H: Diseases of the Lungs, as one of the hand positions (this includes a hand on the back of your patient). You will need to take care and place your hands away from the breasts, in female patients. If the cancer is localized to one area, treat that area, if it has spread over one or both lungs, treat accordingly. Be sure to include the trachea and bronchi in your treatment, if affected. It is likely that the 4th and 5th chakras will be related chakras requiring substantial attention with unblocking, charging, rebalancing and especially radiatory healing, in addition to whatever other chakras require treatment.

Cancer of the Kidney and Digestive Organs (inc. Stomach, Small Intestine, Pancreas, Liver, Gall Bladder and Bile Ducts, Peritoneum): Give your patient a standard treatment (including the special considerations given above for all cancer patients), but with these modifications: place both hands, gently overlapping or side-by-side, over the affected organ or area. Vary the position of your hands during treatment, for three to four times in the immediate area over the organ, as you visualize, sense and become the light surrounding the diseased organ or area, placing health. It is likely that the 3rd chakra will be a related chakra requiring substantial attention with unblocking, charging, rebalancing and especially radiatory healing, in addition to whatever other chakras require treatment.

Non-Localized Cancers (e.g. Leukemias, Multiple Myeloma, Lymphomas): Give your patient a standard treatment (including the special considerations given above for all cancer patients), but with these modifications: place your hands randomly all over the body in various positions, using your intuitive sense to guide you. Treat the tissues by visualizing, sensing and becoming the light and placing health, as appropriate to the particular disease, restoring them to health. For leukemia this will be blood cells (and possibly bone marrow) all over the body. For multiple myeloma this will again be blood cells all over the body. There may also be areas, with some of these diseases, that are more affected (e.g. certain lymph nodes and organs, in lymphoma)—sense these intuitively and treat these directly. You may also see, with these syndromes, a discoloration of several or all of the chakras that will be particularly noticeable. Charge accordingly.

Colon or Rectal Cancer: Give your patient a standard treatment (including the special considerations given above for all cancer patients), but with these modifications: for the comfort of your patient, place the hands not directly on the affected area, but with one hand above, just above the pubic bone, and the other hand below, on the upper leg as near the pubic area as your patient is comfortable with. Visualize, sense and become the light surrounding the diseased areas, and place health for a few moments, and then move the hand on the upper leg to the other upper leg, and do the same for an additional time. Vary the hand positions again, as described. It is likely that the 2nd chakra will be a related chakra requiring substantial attention with unblocking, charging, rebalancing and especially radiatory healing, in addition to whatever other chakras require treatment.

Breast Cancer: Give your patient a standard treatment (including the special considerations given above for all cancer patients), but with these modifications: for the comfort of your patient, place the hands not directly on the affected area, but with one hand above, just above the breast, and the other hand below, just below the breast, with the hands as close as your patient is comfortable with. Visualize, sense and become the light surrounding the affected areas of the breast, and place health, with your hands in this position. Then shift your hands to other positions, perhaps with one hand near the heart and the other on the opposite side of the breast near the side of the body, for a total of three or four positions. It is likely that the 4th chakra will be a related chakra requiring substantial attention with unblocking, charging, rebalancing and especially radiatory healing, in addition to whatever other chakras require treatment.

Prostate Cancer: Give your patient a standard treatment (including the special considerations given above for all cancer patients), but with these modifications: for the comfort of your patient, place the hands not directly on the affected area, but with one hand just above the pubic bone, and the other hand below, on the upper leg as near the pubic area as your patient is comfortable with. Visualize, sense and become the light surrounding the prostate, and place health, for a few moments, and then move the hand on the upper leg to the other upper leg, and then do the same for an additional time. Shift the hand positions in this way for a total of three to four positions. It is likely that the 1st and/or 2nd chakras will be related chakras requiring substantial attention with unblocking, charging, rebalancing and especially radiatory healing, in addition to whatever other chakras require treatment.

Cancers of the Throat Area (Inc. Cancers of Thyroid, Pharynx, Larynx, Esophagus): Give your patient a standard treatment (including the special considerations given above for all cancer patients), but with these modifications: use both hands, around the affected area of the throat, in various positions, as described, either with hands on opposite sides of the throat or together, for three to four positions, as you visualize, sense and become the light surrounding the diseased area, and place health. It is likely that the 5th chakra will be a related chakra requiring substantial attention with unblocking, charging, rebalancing and especially radiatory healing, in addition to whatever other chakras require treatment.

Cancers of the Female Reproductive Organs (Carcinomas of Ovaries, Cervix, Uterus): Give your patient a standard treatment (including the special considerations given above for all cancer patients), but with these modifications: place your hands on the front of the lower abdomen, gently overlapping, under the 2nd chakra and between the pelvic bones, near the pubic bone, as you visualize, sense and become the light surrounding the diseased area, and place health. Shift the placement somewhat, in this region, three to four positions, as described. You may wish to treat each ovary individually, in this same manner. It is likely that the 2nd chakra will be a related chakra requiring substantial attention with unblocking, charging, rebalancing and especially radiatory healing, in addition to whatever other chakras require treatment.

Brain Tumors: Give your patient a standard treatment (including the special considerations given above for all cancer patients) but with these modifications: place both of your hands, gently overlapping, over the affected area of the brain. Vary the position, during treatment, for three to four times in the immediate area of the tumor, as you visualize, sense and become the light surrounding the tumor(s) in the brain, and place health. It is likely that the 7th chakra will be a related chakra requiring substantial attention with unblocking, charging, rebalancing and especially radiatory healing, in addition to whatever other chakras require treatment.

Skin Cancer (Melanoma): Give your patient a standard treatment (including the special considerations given above for all cancer patients), but with these modifications: place your hands directly over the affected region, visualizing, sensing and becoming the light surrounding the diseased areas of skin, and placing health. It there are multiple sites, one hand can be placed over one area and the other hand over a different growth, if the cancer has spread to several areas on the body. Your hands need not be together.

Diseases of the Lungs and Respiratory System

Diseases or weaknesses of the lungs are treated by first giving your patient a complete healing treatment and then performing the procedure below, modified to specifically address your patient's disease, using the modifications given after it:

Exercise 4-H: Diseases of the Lungs

1. With your eyes open, ask your patient to sit up, if possible, and place your right hand on the front upper left side of your patient's chest, below the shoulder and directly above the left nipple. Your right palm should be between the nipple and the shoulder, and two to three inches above the nipple.
2. Place your left palm on a position on your patient's back directly opposite your right palm (such that the left lung is "sandwiched" between your hands).
3. Now visualize, sense and become the light surrounding the diseased areas, using light visualization and the placement of health. **Refer to the specific treatment procedures listed below**, for details regarding the visualization(s) to employ.

4. Once this is finished, treat the right side of your patient's chest in a similar manner, placing your right palm on the front upper right side of your patient's chest, at the same location as before (two to three inches above the nipple), and your palm on your patient's back, directly opposite. These are the ideal hand positions for treating each lung and its side of the chest cavity, and serve not only to treat disease but also to generally energize and strengthen the respiratory system.

5. After treating both sides in this way, treat your patient's heart chakra by placing your right hand over the front component and your left hand over the rear component of the chakra, "sandwiching" the chakra between your hands, and visualize, sense and become the light surrounding the chakra as you place health in it, for several moments.

Some critically ill patients will not be able to sit up, and this lung treatment may be conducted with your patient lying down, by placing your right palm in the position described, and placing your left hand under your patient's body directly opposite it, as you treat each side. Place both of your hands, gently overlapping, over the front of the heart chakra to treat it, at the end.

With all diseases of the lungs, the 4th chakra is likely to require additional attention, in the form of unblocking, charging, rebalancing and/or radiatory healing. The 5th chakra may also require this additional attention.

Chronic Lower Respiratory Diseases (COPD, Emphysema, Bronchitis, Asthma): Give your patient a standard treatment (including the special procedure given above for all lung disease patients), but with these modifications: visualize, sense and become the light between your hands surrounding each lung and the entire side of the chest cavity, placing health in the entire area. Localize the treatment, then, by visualizing, sensing and becoming the light around the affected structures, while placing health. You may use an intuitive reading of the bronchial tree to locate specific areas requiring your treatment. Visualize the bronchi and/or alveolar sacs as open, healthy and clear. For bronchitis, asthma and COPD you should treat inflammation by imparting a quality of *coolness*, like ice, with the light. Perform this entire procedure on both sides. The 4th chakra may be underactive, unless, of course, infection or inflammation is also present. Rebalance as needed. Treat your patient one to two times per week.

Pneumonia (all types): Give your patient a standard treatment (including the special procedure given above for all lung disease patients), but with these modifications: visualize, sense and become the light washing through each lung, purifying and clearing away the infecting agent, purifying and imparting strength to its function, as you place health in it. Perform this procedure on both sides. For pleurisy, impart a *coolness*, like ice, when treating the pleura with light. Aura charging is indicated. The 4th chakra will often be overactive, and rebalancing is appropriate. Treat your patient two to three times per week, with your patient sitting, if possible. If your patient has a high fever, shorter treatments, of half duration at all other treatment positions, is necessary.

Pulmonary Infarction/Pulmonary Embolism: Give your patient a standard treatment (including the special procedure given above for all lung disease patients), but with these modifications: visualize, sense and become the light surrounding each lung, placing health in the entire area. Localize the treatment then by visualizing, sensing and becoming the light surrounding the blocked area, and see the blockage shrinking away, and the blood flow being restored, as you place health. Use an intuitive reading of the lung(s), if you wish, to help determine the location of the blockage. Treat both lungs, employing the localized treatment as necessary, wherever blockages exist.

Diseases of the Internal Organs

Serious diseases of the internal organs, such as the liver, kidneys, pancreas, etc. are treated with light visualization, first by treating any infection or inflammation that may be present, then *charging the organ with light* to stimulate health in it, and finally proceeding to the anatomical structures inside the organ to treat the specific disease conditions present with the specific light visualization required. Perform the procedures below, modified to specifically address your patient's disease, using the modifications given after them:

Exercise 4-I: Diseases of the Internal Organs

1. With your eyes open and your patient lying down on your treatment table, first treat infection (if present). If the organ is infected, first place both of your hands side by side, on the front of your patient's abdomen and directly over the affected organ. Now visualize, sense and become the light washing through the organ beneath your hands, like a river, purifying it and removing the microorganisms infecting it. Do this for several minutes. If the organ harbors inflammation, visualize, sense and become the light washing

through the organ while imparting a quality of *coolness*, like ice, with the light.

2. Now charge the organ with the light: ask your patient to sit up, if possible, and place one of your hands on the front of your patient's abdomen, with your palm directly over the organ, and your other hand on the back of your patient's abdomen with its palm directly behind the organ (you thus have the organ "sandwiched" between your hands). Now visualize, sense and become the organ filled with the light—you are not just visualizing the light surrounding the organ, but filling it entirely, as a solid application of the light. The light is a *bright, glowing solid ball of light* held between the palms of your hands, filling the organ. The bright glowing ball of light charges the organ, re-vitalizing it and stimulating the life spark in it once again. Place health in the entire organ as you do this.

3. After charging the entire organ, localize your treatment to the specific diseased structures within it, using the light visualization and the placement of health. **Refer to the specific treatment procedures listed below**, for details regarding the visualization(s) to employ.

With diseases of the internal organs there will often be a related chakra that exhibits multiple defects and requires unblocking, charging, rebalancing and/or radiatory healing. Radiatory healing will often be required. It will also be common to see an overactive related chakra in infections and inflammations of these organs, while an underactive chakra usually is seen at the later stages of organ degeneration. Rebalance accordingly. These patients should be treated one to two times per week (liver illnesses a minimum of two times per week), if possible.

Kidney Failure (aka Renal Failure, Nephritises, Nephrosis, Nephrotic/Nephritic Syndromes, Renal Hypertension): Give your patient a standard treatment (including the special procedure given above for all organ disease patients), but with these modifications: treat each kidney separately (using the light washing and organ charging techniques given above). Then, with each kidney, you may proceed in your light visualization down to the level of the disease, visualizing, sensing and becoming the light surrounding the affected tissues (e.g. glomeruli, nephrons, interstitial spaces) while placing health. You may use an intuitive reading of the kidneys to clarify and add to whatever information you already have, regarding the disease present. Visualize the form and function of the structures as returning to health, placing health in the damaged tissues. Structural changes of various kinds may also be present in the varying types of kidney disease. Treat accordingly.

Renal infarction is treated with the basic procedure above, but also visualizing, sensing and becoming the light surrounding the blocked area, seeing the block clearing while placing health. Arteriolar damage from renal hypertension (nephroangiosclerosis) is treated with the appropriate visualization of these structures. Should the kidney disease involve kidney stones, the blockage is visualized removed and cleared, in the same way, and the area is also treated for inflammation in these specific areas, with the cooling light.

The 2nd chakra will probably require extra attention in the form of unblocking, charging, rebalancing and/or radiatory healing. In a kidney infection, it will probably be overactive, while later stages of kidney degeneration and failure may display an underactive chakra. In some cases, the 3rd chakra may be involved, also.

Diabetes Mellitus: Give your patient a standard treatment (including the special procedure given above for all organ disease patients), but with these modifications: treat the pancreas (using the light washing and organ charging techniques given above). Then, visualize, sense and become the light promoting insulin secretion (for Type 1 diabetes), along with visualizations addressing tissue changes and nerve damage (should these be dramatically present), while placing health. Diabetics will likely require additional attention to the 2nd chakra, in the form of unblocking, charging, rebalancing and/or radiatory healing, and the 3rd chakra may require attention as well. The 3rd chakra will probably require rebalancing upward, as discussed under Diseases of the Endocrine System. Serious diabetes should be treated two times per week, if possible.

Liver Diseases (Hepatitis, Cirrhosis, Fibrosis, General Infections/Inflammations): Give your patient a standard treatment (including the special procedure given above for all organ disease patients), but with these modifications: treat the liver (using the light washing techniques given above), for infection and inflammation present. This is important: for hepatitis or other liver diseases infection and inflammation are often substantially present—be sure to first thoroughly cleanse the liver. Perform organ charging on the liver. Then, in patients with degeneration of the liver tissues (from various causes), visualize, sense and become the light surrounding the tissues of the liver, restoring them back to health, while placing health in them. For cirrhosis or fibrosis, which are common consequences of infection, inflammation or other damaging causes, you may visualize the liver tissues restored to their proper architecture, as you do this. Treatment of the 2nd and/or 3rd chakras with unblocking, charging, rebalancing, and radiatory healing may be needed.

Cystic Fibrosis: Give your patient a standard treatment (including the special procedure given above for all organ disease patients), but with these modifications: treat the pancreas (using the light washing and organ charging techniques given above). Tend to respiratory infections and obstructive complications as given in Diseases of the Lung, as these are often present. As you do this, it is very important to visualize, sense and become the light surrounding blockages in the airway and bronchi, seeing the blockages clearing in all affected locations, as you place health in them. The 2nd and 3rd chakras will likely require extra attention, especially in the form of radiatory healing.

Congestive Heart Failure: Congestive Heart Failure should be treated as under Diseases of the Heart and Circulatory System, but you may also incorporate the organ charging procedure above, in addition, to strengthen the heart. Should the heart or its membranes be infected or inflamed, treat them as described under Diseases of the Heart and Circulatory System.

Infections and Inflammations of Other Internal Structures: Place your hands over the infected or inflamed area, washing and purifying the structure clean of the invading organism, if infected, and imparting a quality of *coolness*, like ice, to inflammations. It is likely that these infections and inflammations will also require that you treat certain related chakras with unblocking, charging, rebalancing and/or radiatory healing, as shown:

Appendicitis	2nd chakra.
Peritonitis	2nd chakra.
Pancreatitis	2nd chakra and possibly 3rd chakra.
Gastroenteritis	2nd chakra.
Colitis	2nd chakra.
Cholecystitis	3rd chakra.
Choleangitis	3rd chakra.
Pelvic Inflammatory Disease	1st chakra.

Often when an infection or inflammation is present, you will find an overactive chakra, requiring that its activity be rebalanced downwards.

Diseases of the Brain and Nervous System

Diseases of the brain and central nervous system (neurological diseases) generally center on disturbances, failure, or improper conduction of the electrical nerve impulses. They take two general forms: misdirection in the paths of the impulses or blocks in the paths. The goal is to restore correct electrical conduction to the entire system, and incorporate specific light visualizations to treat areas affected by the particular disease. Sensing and treating these diseases therefore requires that you focus upon the brain and nerves, and upon the electrical neural impulses that drive the body.

Usually your patient will have come to you with prior knowledge of the disease present and this will assist you in knowing which specific light visualizations are required as you perform the general procedure detailed below. First give your patient a complete healing treatment but always treat *from the lower chakras upwards*. Then, perform this procedure modified to specifically address your patient's disease, using the modifications given after it:

Exercise 4-J: Diseases of the Brain and Nervous System

1. With your eyes open or closed, and your patient lying down on your treatment table, place your hands on your patient's 7th chakra in the same position you use during the normal sequence of treatment hand positions (with the hands on the top sides of your patient's head), and visualize the Star throughout the entire procedure that follows.

2. In your mind's eye, begin to follow, now, the paths of your patient's nervous system, beginning at the head, in the brain, and proceeding slowly down the neck and arms to the hands, and then down the spinal cord and chest to the lower torso and legs to the feet, the pathways extending from the brain and through the cranial nerves or spinal cord and spinal nerves, and on to their final terminus in muscles or sensory receptors. Along the entire way, follow, with your senses, the electrical paths through the body, visualizing a fine yet brilliant light while doing so, a light that follows the paths.

3. Visualize, sense and become the fine light healing the "wrong connections" or breaks in conduction. Visualize, sense and become the light and the electrical energy of the nerve impulses re-directed and conducting on the proper paths, with no blocks. Where it has become blocked or diverted, visualize the light surrounding and healing the neural paths, as you place health in them. **Refer to the specific treatment procedures listed below**, for details regarding the visualization(s) to employ. This will require a good

knowledge of the anatomy of the nervous system, and powerful visualization ability.

4. You may employ an intuitive reading of the nervous system (using either a whole-body outline, or an outline of specific areas, such as the brain) to gain additional knowledge of affected parts of the brain and nervous system, and treat accordingly.

A good knowledge of the disease will be required—the nervous system and its diseases are complex, and there are many variations, locations and types of damage. The procedures given below are examples and an introduction, and other procedures are possible for specific diseases/locations. For any disorder of the brain, including many psychological disorders, an intuitive reading of the brain to determine areas that are damaged, impaired, atrophied, prone to seizure, or under- or overactive is very useful. Treat these areas as required.

The 7th chakra will often, but not always, require extra attention in the form of unblocking, charging, rebalancing and/or radiatory healing. It will be often be that the 7th chakra is overactive, and will require rebalancing downwards. Check for and treat leaks and auric energy impurities that may be around the head area, when treating disorders of the brain. With many neurological diseases, it is likely that other parts of the body will require extra attention, as well. All neurological patients will require treatment one to two times per week, depending on severity of affliction.

Impairment of Memory or Depressed Consciousness (inc. Alzheimer's, Aphasia, Amnesias, Dementia, Coma): Give your patient a standard treatment (including the special procedure given above for all neurological patients), but with these modifications: focus especially on the brain. Use the light to treat any specific lobes or areas that your intuitive reading indicates as having impairment or depressed functioning. Place your hands on either side of the affected area, opposite the area if possible, and visualize, sense and become a brilliant light charging and stimulating the entire brain back to health and activity, while placing health. Then, do the same while visualizing the light surrounding whatever specific areas require it.

With many of these diseases, especially Alzheimer's and the other amnesias, substantial attention to the 3rd chakra, in the form of unblocking, charging, rebalancing and/or radiatory healing will also benefit your patient, helping to restore a sense of self.

Parkinsonism: Give your patient a standard treatment (including the special procedure given above for all neurological patients), but with these modifications: specifically treat the area around the mid-brain involved in the disease—visualize, sense and become the light surrounding the affected pigmented basal ganglia (substantia nigra, locus caeruleus) and their nerve connections, placing health. See the area composed of healthy, regenerated tissue. Use the light to repair the connections. The Parkinson's patient will also benefit from extra attention to the 5th chakra, in the form of unblocking, charging, rebalancing and/or radiatory healing.

Epilepsy and Seizures: Give your patient a standard treatment (including the special procedure given above for all neurological patients) but with these modifications: pay special attention to the brain. Perform an intuitive reading to determine the location of specific areas of the brain in which the convulsions originate or are stimulated, and whether the genesis of the convulsion is global or specific in nature. Often it will be specific. Visualize, sense and become the brilliant light repairing the faulty connections in the area, or in the whole brain, and imposing a corrective order to the areas affected. Place health in the brain by conveying a quality of *orderliness* to the functioning of the brain as a whole, and also to any specific areas, bringing them to more orderliness in their function and limiting the disorder conveyed from them to other areas. Often certain lobes of the brain will be particularly involved.

Cerebral Palsies: Give your patient a standard treatment (including the special procedure given above for all neurological patients), but with these modifications: pay particular attention to areas of the brain that may have been damaged (seen through intuitive reading of the brain) and also to the upper motor pathways to the limb muscles, mouth, etc. as needed, especially in spastic patients. Visualize, sense and become the light surrounding these tissues, placing health.

Myasthenia Gravis: Give your patient a standard treatment (including the special procedure given above for all neurological patients), but with these modifications: pay particular attention to the neuromuscular junctions between the cranial nerves and affected muscles. Visualize, sense and become the light surrounding these junctions, while placing health and see the junctions restored to proper activity, with strong impulse conduction to the muscles.

Huntington's Chorea: Give your patient a standard treatment (including the special procedure given above for all neurological patients), but with these modifications: pay particular attention to affected areas of the brain (corpus striatum, caudate nucleus, and frontal lobe, as required). Place your hands on the head, with these areas between the palms, if possible, and visualize, sense and become a brilliant light in these areas stimulating them back to health, as you seek to place health in these atrophied areas.

Multiple Sclerosis: Give your patient a standard treatment (including the special procedure given above for all neurological patients), but with these modifications: pay particular attention to the myelin sheaths in tracts of the brain and spinal cord. Visualize, sense and become the brilliant light healing and nurturing areas that may exhibit incidence of demyelinated spots, and place health, with a feeling of structural integrity, to the myelin sheath covering axons in the brain and spinal cord. See the myelin sheath whole and remyelinated. Specific areas of the body may be also be affected—treat these areas with extra energy and the chakras near these areas with unblocking, charging, rebalancing and/or radiatory healing, as needed.

Meningitis/Encephalitis: Treatment using the specific procedure given above is not necessary, unless other brain or nervous system disease is present, but place your hands on the 7th chakra, as usual, and use the light to wash away infecting agents, if an infection is present, visualizing, sensing and becoming the light washing throughout the brain and its meninges, purifying them and removing microorganisms, as you place health. Inflammation is likely to be present, and treat it by visualizing the light while imparting a quality of coolness, like ice, to soothe the inflammation.

Infectious Diseases

In most developed countries, many serious infectious diseases have been adequately controlled through vaccination and public health operations, yet in many areas of the world these diseases remain a health threat for many. Healing treatments will comfort and assist victims of these diseases, but such treatment must always be in addition to conventional medical treatment using antibiotics, etc. Energy healing treatments, by themselves, will not be adequate to contain these diseases.

Examine your patient's energy field carefully, and treat defects of the chakras and aura as you normally would, and this will assist your patient in restoring health. These diseases are caused by a great variety of infectious agents, and you may see subtle differences in your patient's aura with the different types of microorganisms. You may find that you will intuit much just by examining your patient's demeanor and physical appearance, as you also examine his or her energy field. Proceed as follows:

Exercise 4-K: Infectious Diseases

1. Give your patient a standard treatment, but at each chakra during the normal sequence of treatment hand positions you should visualize, sense and become the brilliant light entering your patient's body and washing through the entire body. See the light not as radiating from around your hands, but as washing through the entire body and its tissues, purifying them and washing away the infecting agent, as you place health to the entire body.
2. Should a particular organ be infected, concentrate your treatment on that organ, visualizing, sensing and becoming the light washing through it to cleanse it of infection, as you place health.
3. The patient under siege by one of these microorganisms will be weakened, and virtually all patients will require aura charging.
4. Certain chakras will often be particularly vulnerable and show multiple energetic defects. **Refer to the table below**, for chakras which will likely require extra treatment, including unblocking, charging, rebalancing and/or radiatory healing.

Herpes	Chakra nearest affected area.
Mononucleosis	4th chakra. Arms also.
Candida	4th chakra, 3rd chakra, and 2nd chakra.
Tuberculosis	Treat as under Diseases of the Lung.
RSV	Treat as under Diseases of the Lung.
DHFS	Treat 5th chakra, then treat 3rd chakra.
Rheumatic fever	Standard Treatment.
Cholera	6th chakra, then 3rd chakra, then 2nd chakra.
Whooping Cough	5th chakra, and 4th chakra.
Dysentery	3rd chakra, and 2nd chakra.
Typhoid	7th chakra, and 6th chakra.
Diphtheria	Back of 4th chakra, and back of 3rd chakra.
Tetanus	Standard treatment.
Malaria	6th chakra, and 3rd chakra.
Syphilis	2nd chakra.
Gonorrhea	2nd chakra.

Fever, when present, requires that the treatment be of shorter duration, half the usual time at each position.

Diseases of the Endocrine System

The endocrine system plays a complex role in health and disease, in the human body. Many diseases have complications involving hormone secretion, which can be too high, too low or poorly regulated. It is true that over- or underactivity of the chakras correlates with over- or underactivity of the associated glands, and when you rebalance a chakra you are often working to correct such a condition. To do this will be a common part of treating many diseases not specific to the endocrine system, but to understand this effect (and the part it can play in diseases specific to the endocrine system) is also beneficial.

Most people experience a normal fluctuation in the activity of the various endocrine glands, to higher and lower than normal levels of activity, with life changes and challenges. Rebalancing your patient's chakra system assists in building the health of your patient and restoring balance again. For some people, however, these chakras (and related glands) may be chronically overactive or underactive, and these conditions will lead to undesirable effects in the physiology. This is treated with frequent rebalancing of the affected chakra, as shown below, as part of a treatment regimen for a healing process that often includes other important concerns.

Pituitary Disorders: The 6th chakra's activity level affects both lobes. For hypofunction of the anterior pituitary, or depression of the posterior pituitary, rebalance the 6th chakra upwards. For hypersecretion of anterior pituitary hormones, rebalance the 6th chakra downwards.

Thyroid and Parathyroid Disorders: The 5th chakra's activity level affects both glands. For hypothyroidism or hypoparathyroidism, rebalance the 5th chakra upwards. For hyperthyroidism or hyperparathyroidism, rebalance the 5th chakra downwards in activity.

Pancreatic Disorders: The 3rd chakra's activity level influences both the endocrine and exocrine functions of the pancreas. For type 1 diabetes, rebalance the 3rd chakra upwards.

Disorders of Testes or Ovaries: The 2nd chakra's activity level affects these glands. For male hypogonadism, rebalance the 2nd chakra upwards.

242

Adrenal Disorders: For adrenocortical hypofunction (Addison's Disease), rebalance the 1st chakra upwards. For adrenocortical hyperfunction (adrenal virilism, Cushing's syndrome, hyperaldosteronism) rebalance the 1st chakra downwards.

Miscellaneous Disorders and Situations

Acquired Immounodeficiency Syndrome (inc. ARC, HIV+): AIDS manifests in the body as great weakness and unhappiness of the body, a fading of the energetic health and structural integrity of the body, plus a fading of energetic strength in the chakra system and all layers of aura, like a flame expiring. Use the following guidelines:

Exercise 4-L: AIDS

1. There will usually be a number of leaks and tears in locations all over the body, and these should be sealed.
2. While channeling energy into the chakras, during the normal sequence of treatment hand positions, always impart a quality of *stillness* to the energy. Visualize, sense and become the light and this quality of stillness, while also placing health. Certain chakras will also exhibit an irregular or diseased energy to them and will require extra energy.
3. Perform aura charging for your patient, which will almost always be required.
4. Restoring the strong, pure color hues of the chakras is very important—some or all of the chakras will be faded and weak in color, requiring intensive chakra charging.
5. Substantial rebalancing work will almost always be needed. You will find chakras that exhibit overactivity in the earlier part of the disease, and then underactivity later in the disease, as the patient succumbs. Radiatory healing of affected chakras is additionally very important, as well.
6. Your patient will often possess a weakness of the lungs and chest, and treatment of the lungs, as detailed under Diseases of the Lungs, should almost always be included.

AIDS patients will often exhibit many complications of varying severity (e.g. Kaposi's sarcoma, peripheral neuropathies, pneumonia and other infections, and many others) and these should also be addressed in treatment. If you are familiar with the function of the immune system you may see it strengthened through proper visualizations, visualizing certain lymphocyte counts increasing, for example.

The AIDS patient should be treated two to three times per week, and may require even more attention if the disease progresses into more frequent and severe complications and your patient grows weaker.

Arthritis: Place your hands over the areas affected, and visualize, sense and become the light surrounding the areas and also conveying a quality of warmth to the areas, as you place health in them.

Broken Bones: Place your hands over the break, visualizing, sensing and becoming the light healing the break and placing health in it.

Burns: Place your hands not on your patient's skin, but three or four inches above. Visualize, sense and become the light surrounding the burned area, imparting a quality of coolness, like ice, as with inflammations. See the skin regenerating.

Care for the Dying: For patients who cannot be cured, it is desirable to provide treatment in any case. Simple energy channeling can be an important palliative measure and will provide comfort to your dying patient.

There is more, however. You should give special attention to the condition of the chakra system through diligent chakra charging, rebalancing and radiatory healing. You should also diligently perform seventh layer focal healing and frisson healing, if needed. This healing work makes no ultimate difference to the body, but heals the spirit, and thus spiritually prepares your patient for death and eases the transition. This is a vitally important time not just for your patient, but for you the healer as well, because to prepare your patient to move onward in this way is one of the greatest services you will ever perform.

It is desirable to assist the dying patient twice a week, if possible. Your patient may exhibit anxiety, strain or excitement. Seek to provide rest and comfort.

Disorders of the Ear: Your hands may be placed over the ears, one or both. Treat infections and inflammations as usual, visualizing, sensing and becoming the light, washing out infecting microorganisms or imparting a coolness with the light to soothe inflammation.

For hearing problems, place your hands on the 7th chakra, and visualize the hearing becoming more sensitive—an improvement of the hearing. If you are aware of the precise nature of ear damage, employ a specific light visualization, as required, while placing health. If neural involvement exists, treat the nerve using the appropriate technique as described in Diseases of the Brain and Nervous System.

Disorders of the Eye: Place one palm over each eye to treat, if necessary. Treat infections and inflammations as usual, visualizing, sensing and becoming the light, washing out infecting microorganisms or imparting a coolness with the light to soothe inflammation. These may occur in very specific tissue areas of the eye—visualize accordingly. For cataracts, visualize clarity in the lens, while using the light and placing health on affected areas. For early glaucoma, visualize soothing the eyes and resting them, using the light and placing health. For advanced glaucoma, do the same, although you may not be able to contain it.

Organ Transplant Patients: Treat the transplanted organ by charging the organ, as described in the general procedure under Diseases of the Internal Organs. This will assist in imparting life to the organ. This should be done within 24 hours of transplant surgery, if possible.

Patients Recovering From Surgery: Treat the organs and areas involved, by visualizing, sensing and becoming the light surrounding the organs or tissues involved, while placing health in them. Treat the disease that was present, using the specific methods you would normally use, as detailed in this chapter. Patients who have recently had surgery will often have auric energy impurities present over the areas involved in the operation—use aura clearing as needed. A general treatment is restorative.

For mothers recuperating from childbirth, be sure to also pay particular attention to the internal reproductive organs, especially the uterus, by placing both hands, gently overlapping, under the 2nd chakra and between the pelvic bones. Visualize, sense and become the light surrounding the uterus, and all around, seeing it heal and placing health. Special treatment of the newborn baby is not required.

Psychological Disorders: Psychological disorders will sometimes accompany nervous system diseases, and these should be treated as specified in Diseases of the Brain and Nervous System, yet there are many conditions of the personality that have no organic basis. There is a relationship between psychological states and the chakra system and aura layers, but it is very complex, and specification of treatments for particular psychological disorders is not practical, given individual variations.

It is true, however, that these mental states have correspondences to the energetic phenomena in the chakras and aura layers, and it is surprising how effective chakra charging, chakra system rebalancing and radiatory healing can be in assisting patients with various psychological disorders. Seventh layer focal healing and frisson healing may also bring great changes, which can be slower in developing yet very dramatic. You may well be able to see manifestations of these mental states, and the effect of your treatment, in your patient's chakras and aura layers. Your treatment will often provide emotional and mental clearing and lend a greater clarity to the overall being.

For persons suffering from psychological disorders, a thorough general treatment is advised every week, at least, and somewhat more often for those who need it. Patients suffering from depression, for example, will benefit from a regular schedule of treatments given every five days. For patients in spiritual crisis, treatments should be given often, as well. Treatment using these techniques does not, by itself, advance the individual spiritually, but the clarity and removal of confusion allows the individual to work on him- or herself, and move towards resolving the problems. Do not doubt the good you can do these patients.

Caution should be used when treating patients with serious mental illness. Always first treat for a shorter time, perhaps one-third of the usual amount of time, and carefully note the effects. Proceed cautiously.

Septicemia: Give your patient a complete healing treatment, but then treat systemic infection and systemic inflammation: place your hands in varying positions all over the body (use your intuition to guide your hand placement). In each hand placement position, first visualize, sense and become the light washing through the entire body, cleansing it of infecting microorganisms (likely present). Then visualize, sense and become the light washing through the entire body and imparting a quality of coolness, like ice, while placing health. Treat patients with this potentially serious condition every one to two days.

Systemic or Generalized Connective Tissue Diseases (Systemic Lupus, Scleroderma, Polymyositis): Place your hands over the affected areas all over the body. It is not necessary to keep your hands together: one may be placed over one affected area or part of the body, and the other over another part of the body, and the positions varied as you intuitively feel is best. Inflammation should be treated by visualizing, sensing and becoming the light imparting a quality of coolness. Tissue changes, present in many of these type diseases, should be treated by incorporating an appropriate visualization.

Notes

Notes

Notes

5

Chios® Meditation

Welcome to the study of Chios® Meditation. Your decision to learn meditation is a wise one. Chios® Meditation is an excellent all-around meditation method and may provide many lifelong benefits to you. It is an important practice for the energy healer as well and leads to many of the abilities necessary in healing.

Meditation is the practice of pure awareness. Underneath the many experiences, thoughts and actions which comprise our day-to-day life lies a state of pure awareness—a field of pure consciousness—which is the source of all that we are and all that we experience. In our true nature, we *are* this pure consciousness. Inherent in this field of pure consciousness is unlimited knowledge and power, and it is the source of many higher abilities we always potentially have available within us yet which often lie unnoticed and undeveloped. Through the practice of meditation it is possible to come into greater connection to this state of pure consciousness. Thereby, we do not merely come into greater awareness and knowledge of the true nature of ourselves and everything we experience, but we also access these powers and abilities that ordinarily lie hidden. As we practice the art of energy healing, we are also able to use the knowledge and power of pure consciousness to become much more effective in our healing work.

The goal of meditation is to cultivate this state of greater awareness and greater connection to this field of pure consciousness, for which meditation is perhaps the fundamental spiritual practice. The practice of meditation does not "take anything away" from our everyday life, but rather, enables us to become aware and act in a more truly complete manner—a manner in full connection with our true selves and the greater reality in which we live. Regular practice of Chios® Meditation will provide all these benefits. It is important that you study the specific technique used in this meditation method carefully, however, to ensure that, right from the beginning, you are performing it correctly. You will then develop and enjoy the greater awareness and the abilities that lie within you waiting to be discovered.

The Process of Meditation

In everyday life, as you live in your "normal" state of consciousness, your awareness is usually focused upon the particular thoughts, emotions, perceptions and experiences you have on the surface level of your awareness, whether they are the experiences, perceptions and actions of your outer life, or the thoughts and feelings that occupy your inner world. As you engage in all these particular activities of life, you do so with the assistance of your thinking mind, the active portion of your mind that works on this surface level of reality. Your awareness is usually identified with—caught up in and attached to—these particular activities in which your thinking mind is engaged. And yet, you are more—you are ultimately pure consciousness. When you remain identified with, and therefore limited to, these surface activities of your mind, however—these surface appearances of your deeper being—you are far less able to access the greater awareness, knowledge and power available at the more fundamental level of pure consciousness.

In the practice of meditation you seek to still your thinking mind, thereby freeing your awareness from the surface level of reality. By doing this, you come into greater connection to the state of pure consciousness, where you have unconditioned awareness. This is awareness itself, without being shaped into the specific forms of awareness that your thoughts, emotions, perceptions and actions define. Your awareness expands beyond these particular forms into a state where there are no thoughts or particular states of mind, yet with potentially unlimited awareness, knowledge and power. (See Figure 51). Meditation is the process by which you seek to re-condition your awareness so that you release your attachment to the surface level of reality and instead allow it to gravitate towards this state of pure awareness, pure consciousness. As you develop this reconditioning of awareness, you become able to rest within the state of pure consciousness—you become one with it—and the knowledge and power inherent in it become available to you. Special abilities you would not otherwise have, should your awareness remain attached to the surface level of your mind, are the result.

To gain these potential benefits of meditation, by virtue of this reconditioning of the awareness, you should engage in regular practice—usually on a daily basis. Meditation does not provide all its benefits all at once, but over time, as the practice itself re-conditions your awareness more towards the state of pure consciousness. In each daily meditation session,

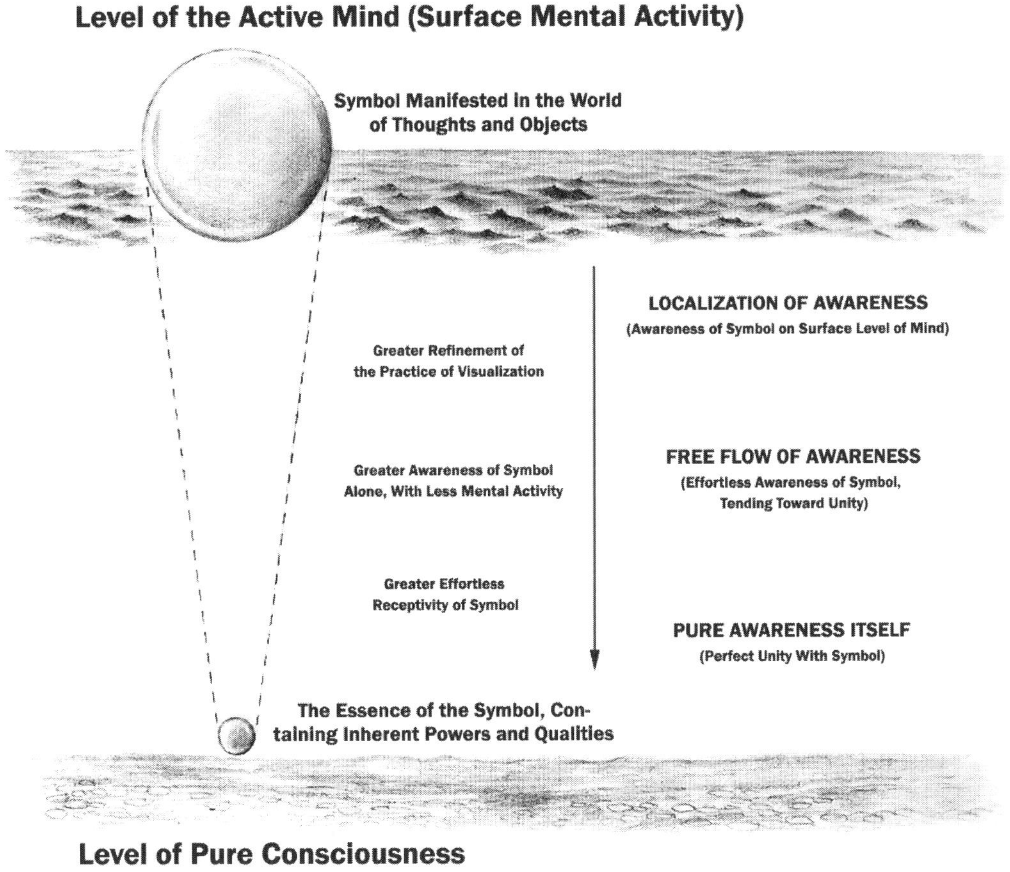

Level of the Active Mind (Surface Mental Activity)

Symbol Manifested in the World
of Thoughts and Objects

LOCALIZATION OF AWARENESS
(Awareness of Symbol on Surface Level of Mind)

Greater Refinement of
the Practice of Visualization

FREE FLOW OF AWARENESS
(Effortless Awareness of Symbol,
Tending Toward Unity)

Greater Awareness of Symbol
Alone, With Less Mental Activity

Greater Effortless
Receptivity of Symbol

PURE AWARENESS ITSELF
(Perfect Unity With Symbol)

The Essence of the Symbol, Containing Inherent Powers and Qualities

Level of Pure Consciousness

Figure 51 – The Process of Meditation

you will encourage your awareness, through the use of a certain technique, to free itself from the surface level of your thinking mind and instead come into greater contact with the field of pure consciousness. You will therefore practice achieving a state of pure awareness on a daily basis.

As you progress in your meditation practice, your tendency to come into greater contact with this state of pure awareness will be present not only during your meditation sessions, but will tend to "carry over" to the rest of your life as well. Your entire life experience— thoughts, feelings, actions and perceptions—will acquire a new, more fundamental ground in this state of pure consciousness. You develop the ability to contact and act from this deeper awareness throughout the day, instead of being constantly bound by, and identified with, the surface level of your mind. This ability may also be called upon during times when such awareness and abilities are specifically needed, too—during the practice of energy healing, for example. When you employ any particular energy healing technique you are merely seeking to channel the knowledge and power of pure consciousness in a specific way for healing work. When you acquire greater connection to this state of pure consciousness, your use of all your healing techniques becomes greatly enlivened and much more effective. You are able to access more of the knowledge of the state of pure consciousness, to sense the condition of the energy field of your patient. You become a stronger, purer channel for the healing power inherent in pure consciousness, to bring it to your patient in the way needed to heal. Because you are in closer connection with the state of pure consciousness that is also the ultimate source of health and wellness, the regular practice of meditation also tends to refine and enhance the functioning of your body, mind and spirit—to bring greater peace, effectiveness and harmony to all levels of your being. You are additionally able to convey these same benefits to your healing patients—to more effectively place health in those with serious physical illnesses, for example.

It is your release of identification with, and subsequent gradual quiescence of, the "busy" surface activity of your mind—and your concurrent ability to come into greater connection with the field of pure consciousness that lies underneath it and is its source—that provides you all these benefits. There are many forms of meditation, but to quiet the surface level of the mind and contact this state of pure awareness is the goal of meditation in all its forms. The many different kinds of meditation employ various techniques to work towards this desirable goal, but the overall process remains the same.

Meditation Using a Symbol

Meditation, in one form, is practiced with the use of a *symbol*. In this form of meditation you encourage your awareness to remain focused upon just the symbol, instead of becoming identified with, caught up in and attached to the series of thoughts and emotions that would otherwise occupy it. The symbol provides a prop, a single object which you sense in an effortless way as you gently encourage your awareness to remain on it alone. Sensing the symbol alone assists in reducing the activity of your thinking mind, because your mind no longer feeds off its own activity, from one thought or emotion to the next. Stabilizing your awareness upon just the meditation symbol allows the activity of the surface level of your mind, your thinking mind, to "wind down," to decrease in activity, slowly but surely.

As you meditate, you will usually still have thoughts and emotions arise, at least in the beginning, but you will simply recognize them to be distractions, and just allow them to drop away as you bring your awareness back effortlessly to the symbol alone. As you continue to meditate on the symbol, the activity of your mind winds down more and more, and you settle to progressively deeper and deeper levels of awareness. Whenever thoughts and emotions continue to arise in your mind as it "winds down," you again do not identify with them, and so, gradually they become fewer and fewer.

Your awareness may drift from the symbol many times while you are meditating, especially at first, but by simply and effortlessly coming back to the symbol your practice is slowly but surely refined. Eventually you will become adept at keeping the symbol alone in the awareness, and achieve a quiet mind. This may be a surprise, at first—to be awake and conscious, yet with no thoughts. You may begin to have such experiences of pure awareness, perhaps for just an instant at first. You will have completely released your identification with the surface level of the mind, and have begun to establish yourself in the state of pure consciousness. At this level of pure consciousness, you, the object of meditation (the symbol), and the process of meditation become one.

The Chios® Meditation Technique

Chios® Meditation employs a specific symbol as well as a specific way to meditate using the symbol. The symbol used is called the Round Orange-Red Ball, and the correct manner of meditating on this symbol is referred to as Visualization.

The Round Orange-Red Ball

The symbol used in Chios® Meditation is the round orange-red ball. The round orange-red ball is not to be thought of as any particular object (in the external world), but an idealized object; that is, a single object in your awareness that is of this particular shape and color. It is an object with the shape of roundness, as one would sense the round surface shape of a ball, and the color of orange-redness, which is halfway between orange and red on the visual spectrum, combined into one single whole object of this shape and color. It is not entirely solid and is without the solidity of a completely solid object, and yet it is not hollow nor is the surface transparent either. Its round ball shape and its orange-red color are the focus of awareness.

The round orange-red ball is not a symbol that has been chosen at random. It is a powerful, effective and complete meditation symbol that will serve for a lifetime of practice. This particular symbol has, inherent within it, the ability to place you in conscious touch with the field of pure consciousness and in such a way as to release powerful abilities. It is an inner discovery and learning, a journey inward. It is an unbiased symbol as well and bears no connection to any particular religious or spiritual tradition or belief system. It is a powerful and versatile meditation symbol that also has some advanced uses, which you may encounter after learning the basic Chios® meditation technique.

You may wish to have some idea of the origin of this symbol. It is an ancient symbol—very old—which has been part of secret spiritual traditions and is only now (with Chios®) being made generally known. Part of its origin lies in a deep spiritual awareness of nature and the source of life. The round orange-red ball is a symbol that corresponds to our sun, not merely the physical sun but the spiritual sun. This spiritual sun represents the life force and all that is contained in it, in an active and intelligent form—the force that has been instrumental in bringing life to the earth and that surrounds and supports all life on our world, including all of us. The round orange-red ball corresponds to this higher spiritual reality that makes life on our planet possible. And yet, beyond this is a more universal correspondence: it is also the "sun behind the sun," the central spiritual sun that is the origin of life and intelligence in the universe. It's important to understand that this spiritual source of life also lies within each of us, and in humanity as a whole. The round orange-red ball speaks to a racial memory, a deep racial and historic understanding of the spiritual source of all life, but also to the ultimate spiritual source of life inside ourselves. It is part of humanity's evolution, and is a rich and powerful meditation symbol for many reasons. *Important*: do not let your knowledge of the origin of this symbol interfere with your practice of it, however. This information is given to enrich your appreciation of this meditation method. The symbol itself is all you need to practice this meditation powerfully and correctly. You do not need any mental understanding of it, and to place any emphasis on the meaning will actually detract from the meditative state. When meditating on the symbol, do not ascribe any meaning to it; simply let the symbol itself occupy your awareness.

Correct Practice of Visualization

The round orange-red ball symbol, by itself, is not sufficient to engage in effective and pure meditation practice. It is also necessary to meditate upon this symbol in the proper manner. This form of correct practice of Chios® Meditation—the proper manner in which the symbol of the round orange-red ball is held in your awareness—is termed visualization.

In Chios® Meditation, you practice visualization by *becoming one with the round orange-red ball*. You do not merely "think about" it or "pretend to see" it. You visualize, sense and become it. Merely "thinking about" or "pretending to see" the round orange-red ball only creates a surface-level mental state that does not quiet your thinking mind and allow for stabilization and descent of your awareness to deeper levels. It merely provides an additional surface phenomenon (like thought or perception) to the operation of your mind. And so, proper practice of visualization consists of establishing a unity, an identity with the round orange-red ball, and sensing it with your *whole being*, not just the mind or senses. You are not just "thinking about" the round orange-red ball, you are not just "pretending to see" the round orange-red ball, you *are* the round orange-red ball. The round orange-red ball is not an object separate and apart from yourself, it is *you*.

Becoming one with the round orange-red ball is necessary so that your meditation does not involve sensory perception or thought. Meditation is not a mental phenomenon, nor any phenomenon akin to sensory perception, it is pure awareness only. You must become one with the round orange-red ball, so that the subject/object distinction disappears. If you "think about" it or "pretend to see" it you create an intrinsic subject/object distinction, which is the modus operandi of the thinking mind as it operates in the ordinary surface level of reality. Becoming the round orange-red ball, instead, is the form of practice which serves to allow the thinking mind to wind down and provide the resulting expansion of awareness that is desirable.

And so visualization, as used in this meditation method, is not the same as pretending to see a visual image, as with the physical eyes. It is necessary to let go of the idea of "seeing" as something that is only done with the physical eyes. This is a great step forward. Visualization is done with the *mind's eye*. Visualizing—seeing with the mind's eye—is a more fundamental process than physical vision. When you are truly visualizing, you are sensing with your entire consciousness, not merely with the thinking mind or the physical sense of vision. When you visualize the round orange-red ball, you have a knowledge of it which is not dependent on the visual sense. This is learning to visualize in an altogether new manner. You will acquire a feeling for what this means after a little practice.

And so, if you find yourself "pretending to see" the round orange-red ball, you must release the visual part of your experience. Meditation is usually practiced with eyes closed, yet you could have your eyes open seeing the objects around you and still be visualizing the round orange-red ball. Some also think of this as "putting the symbol in the mind's eye," or "third eye," as visualization is practiced with the aid of the 6th (third eye) chakra. If you find yourself "thinking about" the round orange-red ball, you must likewise release yourself from your thinking mind as it attempts to grasp it merely through the thinking process. It is not necessary to "think about" the orange-red ball to sense it with the consciousness—all that is required is that you become the orange-red ball, with your entire awareness. This is a very simple thing.

Meditation Instructions

Now that we have introduced Chios® Mediation and carefully described its correct practice, it is time to learn this powerful meditation method. You should first select the ideal time of day that you will learn and practice this meditation. Morning is an ideal time to meditate, yet any convenient regular time of day will do. You should also select a place that you will learn and practice meditation, one that will be completely private, free from undue noise, and free from interruptions of any kind. You should plan on each meditation session having an approximate length of time, as follows:

First month of practice:	18 minutes per daily session
Thereafter:	24 minutes per daily session

And now, at a convenient time and in a comfortable and secure place, begin your practice of meditation, as follows:

Exercise 5-A: Chios® Meditation

1. Sit upright, with your spine relatively vertical, on a bed, on the floor, on a cushion, or in a chair, whichever is most comfortable to you. If crossing your legs results in discomfort or stoppage of energy flow in your legs, try uncrossing and extending them, or otherwise altering your position.

2. After becoming comfortable, close your eyes and relax for a brief moment, seeking to calm your body and mind. Now allow the symbol of the round orange-red ball to come into your awareness. Do not try to re-create the round orange-red ball as if it were in front of you or near your forehead—do not "pretend to see" the round orange-red ball. Visualization is not the same as pretending to see. *Feel* that you are the round orange-red ball. Do not "think about" the round orange-red ball. Visualization is not the same as thinking. Sense and *become* the round orange-red ball with your entire awareness. This is a very simple thing.

3. To get a better sense of the round orange-red ball, ask yourself: how does it feel to be that shape—to be the round surface of a ball? Then ask yourself: how does that color feel—how does it feel to be the color of orange-red?

After getting a sense of each of these, individually, sense the color and shape together. Become, with your awareness, just this object. Be the ball—visualize, sense and become it with your whole being. If you sense and become in this way, you will begin to achieve a perfect completeness with the round orange-red ball. *It will be as if it were there with you and in you, whole*.

4. Do not force it, simply allow yourself to become aware of the round orange-red ball and effortlessly maintain your awareness upon it. Thoughts of other things will probably arise in your mind, and when you realize that your awareness has perhaps strayed to some mundane matter instead of remaining on the round orange-red ball, simply notice that a thought or emotion has appeared, without placing any bias or judgment upon it. Do not pay any further attention to the thought or emotion, just allow it to drop away, and allow your sense of the round orange-red ball to re-emerge.

    It is important that you do not struggle to keep the mind on the round orange-red ball, but simply notice when a stray thought has appeared, drop the thought, and then allow your mind to come back gently and effortlessly to the round orange-red ball. Simply allow it to re-emerge effortlessly in your awareness. Always remember that the round orange-red ball is *you*—it is not something "out there." Have the entire sense of the round orange-red ball within your being. Be the round orange-red ball, and your practice will be perfect and effortless. Do not struggle in any way. Again, this is a very, very simple thing.

5. Continue to meditate, according to steps 1 to 4 above, for the allotted time. You may slightly open your eyes to periodically check a clock or watch, to gauge the time while learning. After you have meditated for the allotted time, stop the practice and rest, lying down or sitting, for three or four minutes before opening your eyes and rising into activity. It is important to have this transition time, and not "shock" your awareness by returning to daily activity suddenly, after meditating.

As you begin your practice of daily meditation, you should know that it is normal to have a period of days or weeks in which you will "get comfortable" with the practice, and perfect the technique of this method. It is very important not to struggle with the technique. This is a very simple technique and you should just practice it correctly, according to the above instructions, and just take things as they come. As with learning any new skill, it is possible that at first this form of meditation will be unfamiliar to you. You may have a little difficulty in practicing it correctly. You will notice, however, that with just a little practice it becomes easier and easier. After just a few weeks or a month, you will find it start to become second nature to you; you will notice that you start to naturally sink into a deep meditative state shortly after beginning your daily practice.

As you continue your meditation practice, you will eventually probably occasionally experience disturbances during your meditation sessions. It is likely that you will at some point have recurrent thoughts or emotions "come up," for example, that emanate from your inner core issues. These can be powerful negative emotions or disturbing negative thoughts. You may even have strong bodily sensations as these negative thoughts and emotions are released into your awareness. It may be difficult for you to consciously recognize these things as distractions and prevent yourself from becoming "wrapped up" in them, but you must. Don't allow yourself to become reactive, and lapse into feelings of judgment, blame or negative self-esteem. Instead just once again notice the thoughts and emotions as distractions and "let them go." Do not identify with them nor repress them, but again just come back to an effortless visualization of the round orange-red ball. If you do this, you will not become identified in these thoughts, emotions and issues, and they will eventually lose their influence upon you. This is instrumental not merely for correct practice of the meditation but also to allow it to properly contribute to your healing and personal growth process. Meditation is a cleansing of body, emotions, mind and spirit.

You may also occasionally experience spiritual disturbances, during your meditation sessions. You may experience leaving your body, for example. Leaving your body is a common side effect during meditation, yet is similarly not to be desired nor undesired. You should simply notice that this has happened and then allow a grounded, in-the-body experience of effortless visualization of the round orange-red ball to re-emerge. You may have visions of beings and spirits (who may even try to communicate with you), or other visions of an unusual nature and which may be very distracting or even a little disturbing. You should know that at least some of these types of spiritual experiences will probably occur, at some point. And yet, also know that these experiences do not matter, ultimately— they are not the result you seek—and they are therefore not to be desired nor undesired yet simply allowed to drop away like any other thought, emotion or phenomenon. The ultimate goal of your meditation is to go beyond all these surface disturbances. Merely "let them go," and continue the practice without concern—just come back to an effortless visualization of the round orange-red ball. Whenever any such experiences arise, it is desirable to return to a grounded and in-the-body state. This form of meditation is intended to be a grounded practice. As you become more familiar with meditation, you will naturally remain in the body, and it is desirable to do so.

As you advance in your practice and acquire the ability to quiet your mind and sink to deeper levels of awareness, your awareness of the symbol during meditation will become more subtle. There is not an overpowering awareness of, for example, the shape or color of the symbol. There is simply the very gentle, subtle awareness of the symbol, in its wholeness, from the finest level of awareness. As you work towards this finer level of meditation practice, you should just barely be able to tell that you are meditating on this particular symbol. As you practice, and begin to experience this finer awareness, you are penetrating nearer and nearer to the state of pure consciousness, and are progressing successfully towards the point where the highest benefits will accrue from your practice.

Suggestions for Successful Practice of Chios® Meditation

To reap the full benefits of Chios® Meditation, the following are highly recommended:

- Make it a daily practice that you follow regularly. If you wish to enjoy the maximum possible benefits from your practice of meditation, regular daily practice is very important. A regular time and place are helpful for many—choose a daily time and place that is right for you. Approach it fresh each time, however. Make it a part of your routine, yet do not practice it routinely.

- Be careful to learn, and continue, in correct practice. Improper practice of meditation will not provide the benefits that might otherwise accrue and may actually work against you. If you are not sure you are practicing Chios® Meditation correctly, stop and review the instructions, as necessary, or seek assistance.

- Have faith that you will experience benefits from your practice of meditation. Expect positive results, but have no specific expectations of what those results should be. Do not let doubt keep you from the benefits that the practice of meditation will provide.

- Free yourself from all preconceptions of what meditation is. Just do it. You have probably read books, or heard others speak of, the experiences that meditation may provide. Forget about the opinions or experiences of others: this is your meditation, this is you, and what *you* experience is what is important. Your personal experience is the only true "grist for the mill" of your spiritual growth, so do not let ideas of "what should happen," or "what meditation is supposed to be" color your inner learning or your inner experiences.

Potential Long-Term Benefits of Chios® Meditation

Chios® Meditation, when practiced correctly, may give the following benefits:

- A deeper sense of your true self beyond your ego. You will learn to identify with pure consciousness, instead of the thoughts, emotions, ideas, perceptions and preconceptions by which you previously defined "yourself." You are more than all these things, and as your awareness expands this will become a palpable reality. We can use words like "spiritual growth" to describe this process, but it is a reality you will experience that is beyond these, or any, words.
- Enhanced sensitivity to all things, from which communication may result, such as the reception of intuitive information, impressions or thought communication ("telepathy"). All these various forms of communication are related, for they all take place through the field of pure consciousness. Your thinking mind, in its activity, usually serves as an obstruction and a filtering process, preventing your awareness from effectively receiving such communication. As you acquire the ability to quiet your thinking mind and come into greater contact with the state of pure consciousness, you will enhance your receptivity to these various forms of communication.
- The ability to visualize in a receptive way—to "see" psychically—which has also been called "psychic sight," "high sense perception," "second sight," and other names. This ability comes from development of the 6th chakra, as a result of the proper practice of visualization, and visions, various forms of "remote viewing," precognition, and the ability to see the human aura are just some examples of the receptive aspect of the visualization ability that develops.
- The ability to visualize in an active way—to send and shape energy, color and light. This is particularly useful in energy healing work, where it greatly enlivens and empowers the healing techniques you will use that require that energy, color and light be channeled and directed to certain locations in your patient's energy field, and in certain particular ways.
- Various other "supernormal" abilities, which will vary from person to person.

These abilities are developed over a period of months and years. They may manifest not just while meditating, but in daily life as well, often spontaneously.

Notes

Notes

Notes

6

The Self-Knowledge of the Healer

As an energy healer, you are in a unique position: you are the channel between the patient being healed and the field of pure consciousness that provides the knowledge and power that makes healing take place. As you have probably begun to experience, you become more open and transparent while healing: your individual identity temporarily recedes as you instead become an open, pure channel for the energy, color and light, as you perform healing techniques, and also for whatever intuitive information flows through you, to guide the healing work. You become a tool, a vehicle for pure consciousness to work through, to heal your patient.

To properly and effectively fulfill this role as a channel and vehicle for pure consciousness, however, you must be able to fully shed your worldly identity while healing. You must have the ability to fully set aside your ego and instead come into the state of temporary self-realization the master healer employs to heal. This is important because your ego, should it remain a focus of awareness during healing, will interfere with the healing work taking place. While channeling energy, color and light to your patient, your ego will prevent you from becoming a pure and clear channel: it may actually diminish the healing power flowing through you and may even "put a spin on" the energy, color and light, distorting these healing energies and rendering them impure. Your patient will therefore not receive the most effective or pure healing otherwise available. While receiving the intuitive information you depend on to guide you, during healing work, your ego may pollute the information: it will again distort, "put a spin on," color and bias whatever information is being received, and therefore render incorrect and possibly harmful what pure information might otherwise be available to you.

Fortunately, the very act of healing tends to cause your awareness to gravitate somewhat toward the egoless state required. This effect is not an entirely conscious act. When you open yourself to the energies during healing work, you begin to naturally move away from

267

your worldly self and towards your true self. While it is true that you may seem to lose yourself while healing, it is actually the case that your true identity—your essence or true self—remains present throughout. And yet, to become a master healer, you must complete the process that this effect begins: you must learn to fully release your ego while healing. You begin this by working to consciously recognize and acknowledge your ego (with its core issues and tendencies), and to become able to discriminate between this ego (or worldly self) and your true identity (your true self). This is the beginning of *self-knowledge*. It is self-knowledge that allows you to truly release yourself from your worldly self and move into the state of temporary self-realization that allows you to heal well. The quality of the healing that you the healer will provide your patient is dependent on your self-knowledge. Self-knowledge is the *sine qua non* of the master healer.

Your healing work provides you a place to start and assists you in this process. As you preserve openness, sense and act with your whole being and remain aware of the unity between yourself and your patient, you benefit from the experience, beyond your worldly self, that energy healing provides. And yet, more is required. You must engage in additional learning experiences that foster both a recognition and knowledge of your own ego and also an experience of your true self, to acquire the self-knowledge you need. You must deliberately seek self-knowledge. You do this through personal growth work and meditation. To heal well, you must work and grow towards the eventual achievement of full release of your ego and a knowledge and purity of your true self. You will then achieve the perfect transparency that will allow you to become a pure, unbiased vehicle for pure consciousness—a master healer guided by the dream flow of the light.

There are many ways to work towards this self-knowledge, and although you should pursue many personal growth opportunities outside what is contained in Chios®, there are some techniques from the Chios® repertoire that are useful. This section begins with a few such tools to include in your personal growth work: 1) intuitive self-readings for the purpose of recognizing   your fundamental issues of personality; 2) chakra self-healing, to charge and balance your own chakra system, and learn more about your personal issues as they relate to your chakras, and 3) body energy exercises, to ground the sense of energy (and spirit) in the body. You will then benefit from other tools designed to foster your sense of the true Self, beyond your ego: 4) empathic perception; 5) thought communication, and 6) advanced meditation.

Intuitive Self-Reading

Your ability to obtain intuitive information may be used to explore your own personality issues, especially as they relate to healing practice. In the exercise that follows, you perform an intuitive reading on yourself, using the round orange-red ball, the symbol used in Chios® Meditation. To perform this exercise it is best if you have learned and had at least a little experience with Chios® Meditation. Proceed as follows:

Exercise 6-A: Intuitive Self-Reading

1. Sit comfortably, with your eyes closed, and visualize, sense and become the round orange-red ball, as you do when you practice Chios® meditation. Meditate for a few minutes, to rest and quiet your mind and body.
2. Now, *at the same time* you are visualizing the round orange-red ball, ask a question about yourself in your mind. The question might be, for example: what is my greatest strength as a healer? In this active phase, continue visualizing the round orange-red ball and, for a few seconds, focus on your question simultaneously.
3. Now release into the receptive phase. Completely release, let go and suspend all thinking. Completely let go of the round orange-red ball and your question, and allow whatever pictures, sounds or feelings come up to effortlessly, without your thinking or judgment interfering with them. What images, sounds, feelings or inner knowings just come to you? Remember to look for information coming to you that is not from your own ego—information with the different "flavor" that indicates genuine intuitive information.
4. Repeat with other questions, such as: What is my greatest weakness as a healer? How can I best improve my healing work? What is the main issue in my life right now? What is my best course of action with regard to this issue? What are the main unresolved aspects in my personality (my core issues)? What assumptions do I harbor about myself that are involved with these core issues? How can I best resolve these issues in myself, and advance my personal growth process? Explore yourself by formulating your own questions. Use any and all questions you need to explore yourself and your healing and personal growth needs.

The round orange-red ball substantially expands your intuitive power. If you give this process a try, you may be amazed at the appropriateness and usefulness of the information you are provided. This exercise is useful because you are providing guidance for yourself, from inside yourself, instead of seeking it from (perhaps less-than-pure) external sources.

Chakra Self-Healing

In Chios® Level III you practiced the ability to sense and become chakras, to gain a deep knowledge of their ultimate nature. You also learned to sense the condition of the chakra system, using an intuitive reading (through visualization of the body profile). You can use these two techniques to also gain self-knowledge of your own chakra system and the conditions within it. You can even ask for information on how these conditions in your chakras correlate with your personality (ego) issues, and use this for your personal growth. You can additionally charge and balance your own chakras, using the Chios® Chakra Charging and Chakra System Rebalancing techniques. Employ these steps:

Exercise 6-B: Chakra Self-Healing

1. Lie down comfortably and close your eyes.
2. Select one of your own chakras, at random, and visualize, sense and become it, just as you have learned to do with chakras in your patients, yet now for your own chakra. Do not think about your chakra or pretend to see it, just sense and become it. Release, let go and suspend all thinking. Allow a deep sense of the chakra itself to emerge in your whole being. Do you get a deep sense of the chakra's place in your overall being—of its place in your awareness and life? This will include the nature of the chakra itself, as a realm of being, but also the individual characteristics, influences and biases that are particular to your personality. Allow this to form without placing qualifications upon your understanding, however (without use of words and ideas). Simply allow an awareness of your own chakra to develop in you, at a deep level.
3. Repeat step 2, above, with your remaining chakras, at random, so you have sensed the nature of all seven of them (including your individual characteristics). Allow an awareness of your own chakra system to develop in you, at a deep level. This is like a form of meditation.
4. Now visualize the outline of your own body profile. Briefly and effortlessly localize your awareness on an outline of your own body, as seen from the side, and a rainbow shell of color above it, from your 1st chakra (where the rainbow is red), to the 7th chakra top (where the rainbow is violet), as you have learned to do for a patient's chakra system yet now for your own. See

this complete image in the active phase, knowing you will soon get information about which of your chakras are undercharged or unbalanced.

5. Now release into the receptive phase. Notice any changes in the overall shape of the rainbow shell or in the colors exhibited in the seven colored segments (your seven chakra fields). Which of your chakras are undercharged, perhaps with energetic impurities in them? Which chakras are unbalanced, with an activity level that is too high or low? You can repeat the active/receptive cycle again, performing several rounds, if that assists you in gaining a full image of your chakra system with all this information.

6. You can focus on undercharged chakras, to ask for specific information about the meaning of their weakness or the impurities within them. Focus on unbalanced chakras, to ask for specific information on the meaning of their over or under-activity. Do you get any information regarding your personality and its core issues, your life experience and your physical, emotional, mental and spiritual state of being? Seek this more specific information in a state of quietness, also; open yourself to your chakras and the information you receive. This is also like a form of meditation.

7. Perform, now, a "distance healing" on your own chakras, without using your hands, to charge and balance them. Charge whichever of your chakras require it, using a visualization of the appropriate Chios® symbol in color and also a cloud of that color around your own chakra. Rebalance your chakra system by raising or lowering the activity of chakras which require it using the symbol related to the chakra in the necessary color(s) and a cloud of that color around your own chakra. Be sure to perform the Chios® chakra charging and chakra system rebalancing techniques correctly as you employ them on your own chakras.

Charging and balancing your own chakras will help you in your life and growth, and will also give you greater effectiveness in your healing work. Unblocking and radiatory healing of your own chakras can be done using self-healing techniques but are most effective when done for you by another healer.

Body Energies Exercise

There is another way to begin to gain self-knowledge: through an experience of body energies. By learning to draw the energy through your own body, you become attuned to both your body and the energy. The grounded experience of the energy, as it exists and moves in your body, also provides a perspective for the energies and nature of your spirit.

271

The exercise below even adds to your general energy-directing abilities, which will contribute to your healing ability, your ability to effectively perform the Chios® healing attunements, and your ability treat diseases in your seriously ill patients. Proceed in this way:

Exercise 6-C: Body Energies Exercise

1. Stand by yourself and visualize the Chios® symbols to call in the energy as you would normally do when beginning a healing treatment.
2. Then, using your intention and will, visualize, sense and become the energy and direct it to specific areas in your own body. Draw the energy, for example, in a localized flow from the earth to one or both of your knees, maintaining the energy there, noting the difference in feel between where the energy is and where it is not present in your body.
3. Draw the energy up further, as it flows from the earth, to one or both of your hips, again maintaining it in that place and continuing to be aware of the difference in feeling between where the energy is and where it is not present.
4. Draw it up yet further, and into the area around one or both of your shoulders, in the same way. You can even direct it down one or both of your arms, or up to your head.
5. After you bring the energy up, in this way, you can move it back downwards—from your shoulders back down to your knees, for example, or to other areas.
6. Continue this exercise for between three and 15 minutes, using various randomly selected locations in your body as locations for the energy, using a localized flow to specific body points, and holding the energy there, being aware all the while of the difference between where the energy is and where it is not present.

While it is generally better to visualize just the energy while performing this exercise—that ensures the very grounded practice that is ideal—you can also try using light visualization, and sense for yourself the difference. This exercise will create in you a greater awareness of the nature of the energy, from its ground in the body to its spiritual essence, and will open you to know it and become transparent to it.

Experiencing the True Self Beyond the Ego

The first stage of your journey to self-knowledge is a journey inward. Through the practice of meditation you learn to come into greater connection with pure consciousness and your true self within. By also engaging in personal growth work, to learn to recognize and understand your own ego (with its issues and tendencies) and discriminate between your ego and your true self, you begin to release this ego. You become more and more identified with your true self, within, instead of your ego.

After this first stage of moving inward, however, you then proceed to a moving outward. After contacting and developing a primary connection to the true self within, it is time to develop a contact and primary connection to the true self without. The true Self—the field of pure consciousness—exists not just within us but in the entire creation. Everything that exists is merely a particular expression of the one universal consciousness—the Self—which is indescribable in its nature yet is the ultimate reality all that exists. The Self merely takes the *appearance* of separate objects, as we perceive them on the surface level of reality. As your awareness expands, however, you will find that this surface appearance recedes into the background as you instead begin to perceive everything as this one consciousness. Your sense of individuality changes, as well. While you may now conceive of yourself as a separate entity, with a boundary between yourself and all else, in reality this is not the case. As your awareness expands, you will find that you no longer perceive yourself as you did before. You will see a unity of self, inside and outside: you will see yourself in everything that exists, and you will see everything that exists, in yourself.

Self-knowledge is the expansion of awareness, beyond the limited emotions, thoughts and perceptions with which our individual egos become preoccupied, to encompass the true Self, both inside and outside. Everything is consciousness—everything is this Self—including you, all other life forms and the universe as a whole. Everything is connected as one single consciousness. This field of pure consciousness is experienced, more and more, as a state of pure awareness that transcends all particular objects and states of mind. The eventual goal of the expansion of awareness is the state of self-realization in which the objects in the universe still maintain an existence, but in which the balance has shifted such that we perceive the Self in all, first and foremost, from this state of universal awareness.

The advanced exercises in the remainder of this chapter are designed to assist you in moving toward this expanded awareness. Each of the exercises, although different from the others, is linked with the others and shares the common goal of expanding your awareness into the universal Self, using its own particular method. To work towards expanding awareness in more than one way enhances and balances the overall process. The exercises in the remainder of this chapter work together to create a perspective of this universal awareness, and in this sense are actually one.

Try to approach each exercise by letting go of all expectations; try not to "pre-think" or "pre-guess" what the outcome might be. Approach these exercises with complete innocence. If you find yourself "preparing" yourself, in any way, either one minute or one day prior to a time when you will be performing one, let go of your thought, set it aside, saying to yourself that the exercise will take care of itself when the time comes. It is important to "let go" and allow these exercises to foster an awareness different from your usual daily experience.

When performing the exercises, trust your impressions. During the exercises, impressions and experiences form at the deeper levels, at the roots of the mind—you may be experiencing more than your conscious mind is fully aware of. Your conscious mind is but a small window in the scope of your wider awareness, and true growth of awareness proceeds not only at the level of the conscious mind, but at each deeper level of awareness as well. Each level of awareness expands. Open yourself to a wider field of being—cast aside doubt and give yourself over to the universal.

A degree of faith is very beneficial in this process. Try not to allow doubt, self-consciousness or your thinking mind interfere with your learning and practice of these advanced exercises. After an exercise has been performed, allow yourself to integrate whatever you have experienced with your whole being, and do not feel a necessity to analyze or judge your experiences. Use your sense of expanded awareness to feel whatever effects and perceptions these exercises may produce in you. The effects may at first seem to be subtle, due to the fact that your conscious mind is not fully aware of the perceptions and the effects of the exercises you will perform, but they are there. Do not discount them.

Empathic Perception

All things in the manifested universe, including all living beings, are particular expressions of a single universal consciousness, the Self. It is possible to expand your awareness beyond the sense of being an individual and begin to experience the Self in other life forms. Becoming other life forms or objects, and experiencing the consciousness and the sensations of awareness that they experience, is *empathic perception*.

Empathic perception is made possible through the power of visualization: you visualize, sense and become other living things. It is, in a sense, to leave your body and experience the Self in other forms of existence, and to feel other forms of existence in yourself. It is both of these. All living things are connected, through their common ground in universal consciousness, and it is this ultimate unity of all living things that makes this transfer of awareness—this empathic perception—possible. Once learned and practiced, this ability will remain with you and is not forgotten.

The exercise (actually a series of exercises) below will aid you in developing this ability. You will visualize, sense and become a series of progressively higher life forms—a leaf, then an insect, then a small animal. As you do this try to set your "human" perceptions and beliefs aside and allow the alien nature of these different life forms emerge in your awareness. If you find yourself imposing your everyday human awareness on the experience, release the conditioned, thinking portion of your mind, or the portion of your awareness that seeks to color the experience, and experience these other life forms as they are. Have no expectation or preconception as to what you will experience, for it may be strange to you and outside what you have previously known. Proceed as below:

Exercise 6-D: Empathic Perception

You should begin the process of refining your empathic perception, or the ability to merge with other life forms, with the leaf meditation.

1. Find a quiet, undisturbed place. With your eyes open, take a small leaf, freshly plucked from a tree or shrub, and place it in the palm of your right hand (center it over your palm chakra).
2. Now, with your eyes open and gaze gently resting on the leaf, visualize, sense and become the leaf. Allow whatever thoughts or impressions arise in your mind to come, but keep your awareness gently on the leaf. Do this for a total of one to three minutes the first few times, and then three to four minutes thereafter.
3. Repeat steps 1 and 2 above, once per day, for four to six days. Each time, allow yourself to "feel yourself as the leaf" when doing this exercise, and keep a simple diary of your experiences. This is a physical exercise as well as an intuitive one: keep your eyes open, gaining knowledge of the leaf and feeling yourself as it, and at the same time be open, transparent, to impression.

It may be a little uncomfortable at first to do this exercise, but with practice it will become easier to "let go" of your normal human identity and allow yourself to experience other life forms. The leaf is a fine starting point to begin honing your empathic ability—it is a universal symbol and possesses life while remaining still. The leaf meditation is also quite soothing. Practice with the leaf until you feel that you have had a good sense of becoming and experiencing it.

Your next step, after the leaf exercise, is to progress to small creatures, beginning with insects:

4. Choose an insect, a fly, spider, moth, butterfly, etc. that is relatively small and still enough to be easily observed for a few moments. You can contain it under a glass, temporarily, while performing this exercise.

5. Without touching or disturbing the insect, and with your eyes open and gazing gently upon the insect, visualize, sense and become the insect. Allow whatever thoughts and impressions arise in your mind to come, but keep your attention on the insect, visualizing and becoming it as described. Do this for three to four minutes.

6. Repeat steps 4 and 5 above, once each day, for four to six days. You may have to be on guard, especially at first, in order to avoid anthropomorphism (or coloring your experience of the insect consciousness with your human perspective), perhaps even more so than with the leaf. After performing this exercise a few times, insects that are not still may be used, although it is best to use still ones at first. Enter your experiences in your diary.

After insects, proceed onward to small animals:

7. Choose a small animal, a cat, dog, frog, mouse, bird (if still enough), etc.

8. With your eyes open and gazing gently upon the animal, visualize, sense and become the animal. Allow whatever thoughts and impressions arise in your mind to come, but keep your attention on the animal, visualizing and becoming it as described. Do this for up to five minutes or slightly less time, if you feel it is appropriate, but not for a longer period of time.

9. Repeat steps 7 and 8 above, once each day for four to six days. After performing this exercise a few times, you can use different animals. It is important to understand when attempting empathic perception with animals that animals have thoughts, contrary to what some human beings believe. These thoughts will become apparent to you—primitive thoughts, or, in higher animals, more sophisticated ones.

After completing this series of exercises, becoming somewhat empathic, and able to sense the thoughts of animals, proceed to the following exercises for developing thought communication.

Thought Communication

Thought communication, the transmission of impression from a sender to a receiver, is a property inherent in the very nature of universal consciousness—the universal Self. To think and share thoughts without the use of speech is a natural human ability. Present-day human beings "filter out" and reject awareness which is not part of the "individual" identity, however, and this is the reason thought communication is not more commonly experienced. Thought communication can be acquired through practice, however, by retraining your awareness to allow the impressions to transfer, as you *learn to forget to not allow*. It is not learning a new skill, but accustoming the mind to discover this ability by learning not to block out the impressions.

The pure consciousness of which the Self is composed may be likened to a sea, a sea where impressions are carried by a flowing in and flowing out, carried upon colorless, formless, moving waves. This conduction of impression occurs beyond space and time—it is characterized by a *release from time*. The impressions are carried, not upon thought waves, but upon *waves of release, waves without light, color or form, that wash clear for impression*. The idea is to create an opening to impression through a release, a release from time, from the moment, from time and space, and from individuality.

This is not easy, as your human mind seeks to impose order on the impressions being received, to establish known elements, patterns or shapes. Your mind expends effort to "pigeonhole" the impressions, and hence the difficulty. It is often the case that impressions are easily received, yet it is this filtering function of the mind that makes recognition difficult. At each moment your awareness receives countless impressions and filters them into conscious awareness, eliminating many. You, like each of us, seek to recognize the impressions you have decided to receive.

When learning thought communication, it is beneficial to first open yourself to receive, rather than transmit. The following exercises will assist you in developing this ability:

Exercise 6-E: Thought Communication

1. Begin this exercise earlier in the day—in the morning. Ask for the assistance of another person.
2. Have your assistant sit with you cross-legged on the floor, such that you face each other but with your knees close but not touching. You and your assistant should both close your eyes.

3. Ask your assistant to now think of a thing—it may be a thought, an object or an act—but not to tell you what it is.

4. Now hold your hands out in front of you, cupped as if holding a ball from the side, and visualize, sense and become the round orange-red ball, held in the cup of your hands. Have your assistant do the same. The round orange-red ball you are both visualizing is perhaps one foot in diameter, as you both hold it up, jointly between you, in this way (see Figure 52).

5. Now have your assistant think of the thing he or she chose; have your assistant hold it in his or her mind. Encourage your assistant to be relaxed and comfortable, and concentrate or think on that one thing alone, as you both remain sitting, eyes closed, together visualizing and holding the round orange-red ball. Do this for one to two minutes, opening your mind to whatever impressions come.

6. After doing this, thank your assistant and go about your daily business.

7. Later during the day, between six and 12 hours later (but not overnight or 24 hours), sit with your assistant in the very same position, both of you with your eyes closed and hands cupped and jointly holding the round orange-red ball, just as you did before, as you both visualize, sense and become it. Now have your assistant think once again of the thing he or she chose earlier in the day. Ask your assistant to once again be relaxed and comfortable, and concentrate or think on that one thing alone, as you both remain sitting, eyes closed, together visualizing and holding the round orange-red ball. Do this, as before, for one to two minutes, opening yourself again to whatever impressions come.

8. After this second time, ask your assistant to write down a list of five things, one of which will be the correct subject of his or her thoughts. Read the list, and mark that item which you feel was in your assistant's thoughts, but keep your choice private (do not inform your assistant of your choice).

9. Perform steps 1 to 8 above, once a day, for three consecutive days, and then compare your choices with your assistant's correct answers. It is beneficial to keep a simple diary and record each impression you became aware of during the exercises.

After you have gained some success with the exercise above, you may modify it as follows:

1. Perform steps 1 to 6 above, exactly as before.

7. Later during that day, between 6 and 12 hours later (but not overnight or 24 hours), sit on the floor in solitude (*without your assistant present*), and hold your hands out in front of you, cupped as if holding a ball from the side, just

as before, and again visualize, sense and become the round orange-red ball held in the cup of your hands. Open yourself to whatever impressions come, allowing additional impressions to now form beyond what you may have received from your assistant as you sat with them earlier in the day.

8. Later still, at the end of the day, do not sit with your assistant again, but merely ask your assistant to again write down a list of five things, one of which was the correct subject of his or her thoughts, when first performing the technique with you at the beginning of the day. Read the list, and mark that item which you feel was in your assistant's thoughts, but keep your choice private (do not inform your assistant of your choice).

9. Perform steps 1 to 8 above, once a day, for three consecutive days, and then compare your choices with your assistant's correct answers. It is beneficial to keep a simple diary and record each impression you became aware of during the exercises.

Figure 52 – Thought Communication

Advanced Meditation

This final Chios® exercise requires that you have already learned Chios® Meditation and practiced it regularly for several months, at least. If you have not learned Chios® Meditation and had this prior experience with it, it is best to wait. You will achieve much better results than if you attempt this advanced meditation exercise too soon.

In your practice of Chios® Meditation you have probably had some experiences of pure awareness, however short. You have probably developed some inner sense of pure consciousness—a pure awareness beyond your habitual identifications with the thoughts, feelings and perceptions of the surface level of your mind. Meditation is, in the beginning, a journey inward, and provides this inward awareness of self.

At the beginning of a daily meditation session, your awareness often begins to draw and progress inward. After practicing meditation for some weeks or months, however, you may have also noticed, during your meditations, other moments where your awareness was focused outward: moments where although you were sitting with eyes closed meditating, you were aware of your existence in the outer universe, perhaps with a sense of the sky or heavens above, of being in the universe.

You may not have noticed it with your conscious mind, as yet, but there is a point where your inward awareness reverses itself, instantly, and moves outward, a moment of broadening or expansion. This point is often reached more than once in each day's meditation session. It is an instantaneous reversal in the focus of awareness, and there is often a subtle sense of elation or euphoria at this point where your inward awareness expands. This point is not a point in time or space, but it is a state of being. It is subtle, yet discernible with practice. This precise point of reversal of awareness is called *the point of pure being*.

The idea of this point, as a reversal of awareness, can be described with a visual illustration. The point, and the process of reversal of awareness, is like a double funnel—as if your awareness proceeded through a double funnel. As you meditate, your awareness draws inward, funnels inward to a point (inward awareness), passes through a "hole," a pinpoint or very small hole in the universe, and then instantly funnels outward again (outward awareness) into the universe. There is the experience, at this point, of a difference, however: it is a non-experience of either inward or outward awareness alone. It is an experience of the essence of reality; it is an experience of both inner and outer awareness and also of not either of these by themselves. It is an experience of an existence between two existences (see Figure 53).

280

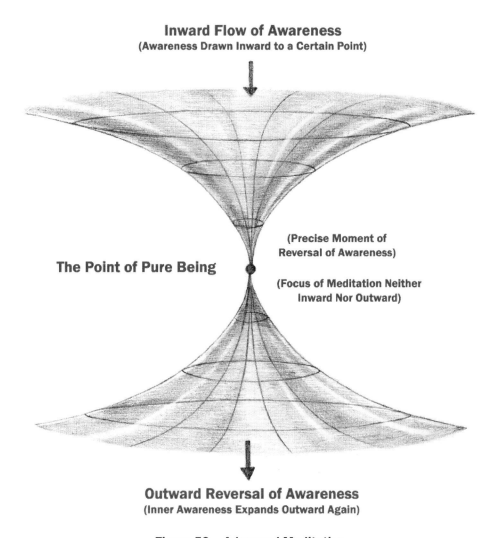

Inward Flow of Awareness
(Awareness Drawn Inward to a Certain Point)

(Precise Moment of
Reversal of Awareness)

(Focus of Meditation Neither
Inward Nor Outward)

The Point of Pure Being

Outward Reversal of Awareness
(Inner Awareness Expands Outward Again)

Figure 53 – Advanced Meditation

This point is not an actual location—and the visual illustration given is only to assist in your understanding and awareness of this point—but at this point of pure being where the focus of meditation is neither inward nor outward, your being rests in a condition that transcends both the inner and the outer worlds, the duality of the inner and outward awareness. At this point there is a totality of being; it is a point where the being is pure. At the precise moment of achievement of this point, there is a unity with all creation, a coming to rest in pure consciousness itself. At this point *you rest in the field of pure consciousness*.

There is an important analogy to this point. A black hole in space is the direct analog of this meditative transition, and its singularity is a physical counterpart to the state of pure being—it is the physical object in the universe that recapitulates this metaphysical idea. As in the singularity of a black hole in space, the usual rules of time and space do not apply at the point of pure being. This point, and whatever happens within it, is beyond the concept of time. At this point, the human spirit, which is inherently unlimited in its nature, can potentially experience all possibilities, without limitation. There is great power in this point.

Ask yourself: What would happen if I went into a black hole? What would become of space, and all the objects I perceive in the world and the entire visible universe as they appear to me? What would become of time? What would become of me, as I conceive of myself? What would remain? What conclusion might I have to make about the ultimate nature of reality and myself, as a result of this experience? These questions may give you some inkling of the state of consciousness that this advanced meditation exercise seeks to instill in you. It is the experience of pure consciousness itself, without limitation—it is the experience of becoming the Self, and all that exists—the achievement of ultimate Self-knowledge.

Begin to gain an awareness of this point by incorporating the following exercise into your daily meditation practice:

Exercise 6-F: Advanced Meditation

1. During your daily practice of Chios® Meditation, begin to become aware of the point of pure being. Begin to notice the focus of your meditation at various random times, during each day's meditation session. Every few moments as you are meditating, take notice of your focus of awareness by asking yourself: is my focus of awareness inward or outward?

2. If you had previously noted an inward focus, yet you now notice an outward focus, search your being, for just a brief moment, to see if you have any awareness of the point where your awareness shifted from the inward to outward focus. This point would have occurred since you last "checked" the inward/outward focus, and it will be a very subtle awareness that will persist and that you will become aware of, like a memory that will flash effortlessly into your awareness. Note this easily, and then go on with the meditation.

3. Perform steps 1 and 2 during each day's practice of meditation, seeking to gain awareness of the point. It is likely you already have some awareness of this point at a deeper level of your awareness.

After you have reached some conscious awareness of the point, you can begin to practice the second stage of this exercise. Noticing the point is the first step, but you may then proceed as follows:

4. After you have acquired some conscious awareness of the point of pure being, seek to become aware of this shift from inward to outward awareness, when it happens, and gain the ability to *slow the transition of your awareness through this point*—to maintain your awareness at the point of pure being, such that, just for a brief moment, you rest in the state of pure being itself.

5. Allow your perception of this point to become more complete—focus on, sense and become this point with your entire awareness, such that you begin to possess a knowledge of it, in your whole being. Know yourself as the point and possess the point in your awareness. If you do, you will find that a persistence of it will begin to prevail during your meditation session—and beyond.

6. Allow your deeper awareness of the point to carry over outside your meditation session, as well. With practice, you can eventually allow the awareness you experience at the point of pure being to re-emerge at various times during your daily life. When you feel this, look at the various objects you see during the day—people, places and things—with the state of awareness that you experienced within the point of pure being. Can you see anything of the state of pure being you experience in this point—the field of pure consciousness—in the world and its objects?

Notes

Notes

Appendix #1 - Preparation for Chios® Attunements

A potentially very beneficial part of learning Chios® energy healing is receiving the series of three Chios® attunement procedures. The Chios® attunements (the first, second and third) are ideally given to you by your Chios® Master Teacher at the beginning of your study of each of the corresponding Chios® healing levels—the first attunement before you begin your study of Chios® Level I, etc.

Chios® attunements are available either in-person or as distance attunements. It is the series of attunements that enables you to quickly and effectively "open up" progressively greater degrees of energy, color and light channeling ability, so that you may effectively practice the many Chios® healing techniques you will learn. Although it is quite possible to learn to channel energy, color and light without the benefit of the attunements, it requires substantially more time and practice to acquire the same degree of ability without being attuned. The attunements often convey other abilities vital to energy healing work, as well: a greater ability to sense and see the energy, color and light, the ability to see and read phenomena in the aura and chakras, and other spiritual and healing abilities. The Chios® attunements can be very effective at bringing out these healing abilities, but only if you are properly prepared to receive them. If you are not prepared for them, it is possible that they will not "take" as well, and will not be as effective at opening you to the energy, color and light in the way they normally would. That is why you should read these suggestions carefully and make sure you are ready to receive each attunement, so that you receive the full benefits that the Chios® attunements have to offer.

One important consideration that your Chios® Master Teacher will observe when giving you the series of Chios® attunements (whether in-person or by distance) is the waiting time that should be observed prior to your second and third attunements. This waiting time is necessary to ensure that your attunements "take" successfully. There is no need for a waiting time to receive your first attunement. After you have received your first attunement, however, the recommended minimum waiting time is three days prior to receiving your second attunement. After your second attunement, the recommended minimum waiting time is two weeks (14 days) prior to you receiving your third (Master) attunement, which is the strongest attunement in the series. The reason for these waiting times is that each attunement procedure performed on you "unsettles" your energy field to some extent, by virtue of the action of the attunement and the energy flow that it creates in your energy field. This tendency to create an unsettled condition increases with each attunement. The first attunement is a very mild one, and so only usually has the potential to unsettle you only a mild amount—this is why the waiting time for the second attunement is only three days. The second attunement is substantially stronger, however, and so likewise has a substantially greater potential to unsettle your energy field—this is the reason for the longer 14 day waiting time before your third and final attunement. Because your energy field must have a chance to settle before your next attunement, it is important for you and your teacher to observe these waiting times so your second and third attunements (which are very important) will have maximum effect.

As the time approaches for you to receive a Chios® attunement, there are also specific preparatory steps you should take to ensure you receive the full benefits. These are important, so please observe them! Before each attunement in the series, prepare by *cultivating a state of purity in body and mind, for one to two days before each attunement.* During this preparation time you should eat a light, pure, preferably vegetarian diet (fresh fruits and vegetables, whole grains and pure water are especially good), limit dairy products, and eliminate meat and unhealthy, highly processed or impure foods. Please also be sure to avoid alcohol and all drugs (except those medically required). It is equally important to maintain a purity of mind by avoiding negative emotions, interpersonal conflicts, and stress, during this preparation time before each attunement. To get enough rest and sleep, the day or two before, is also vital. All these things will help to ensure your body and mind are in a rested, pure and receptive state, which will greatly assist you in receiving each attunement and receiving its benefits. It is possible that, even if you observe all these preparatory steps, that you may not be in this rested, pure and receptive state on the day of your attunement. This is a natural possibility, as many factors of daily living may come up and intervene, despite your best intentions. This is not cause for concern, however. If you find, on the day your attunement is scheduled, that you are not in a relaxed, rested, pure and receptive state—for whatever reason—simply explain this to your teacher and reschedule your attunement for another day.

Another aspect of preparation is to arrange to be in a place where you will not be disturbed while the attunement is performed. If your teacher is coming to your home to give you an in-person attunement, or is performing your attunement by distance, this may involve explaining to family, friends or roommates that you will need privacy and quiet and must not be disturbed. If you are traveling to another location for your attunement, your teacher will ensure these quiet, private conditions are maintained. Attunements should always be received in a quiet, private room or other appropriate place, where there will be no possibility of interruption. Turning off telephone ringers, cell phones and any other electronic devices that might interfere is another important part of creating this private, quiet environment for your attunement.

If you are receiving a distance attunement, your Chios® Master Teacher will probably take additional preparatory steps for your attunements. Your teacher will probably ask you for a photo so he or she can more easily "tune into" you by distance, and may also want to talk with you briefly by phone, before each attunement, for the same purpose. Your teacher will confirm your readiness, and will let you know how much total time your attunement will require, as well.

When it is time for the attunement itself, it is important to have your body in the proper position. If you are receiving an in-person attunement from your teacher, you should stand comfortably facing your teacher, with your body relaxed but with your back straight and your feet about shoulder-width apart, and with eyes closed. If you are receiving a distance attunement, it is fine to sit alone in a comfortable chair, with eyes closed, but your back should likewise be vertical, or very nearly so. Having your spine vertical makes it much easier for the energy to come in and move up your spine and through your chakra system, during the attunement. You should be in a relaxed, open and receptive state of mind during the entire time the attunement is given, too, and should not be practicing any specific form of meditation or any other specific spiritual practice. The ideal mental state is one of a quieting of your thinking mind and release into a state of *simple, relaxed awareness*. Be sure not to worry or be concerned in any way regarding the attunement, or have any specific expectation about what you will experience. Just relax, set body and mind free, and be open and receptive—that is all you need to do! Approach each attunement with openness and innocence.

You might wonder what you will experience during the attunements. You do not need to be fully aware an attunement is happening, while it is in progress. Like attunements in other energy healing arts, Chios® attunements are felt by some people and not felt by others. Many years of research into these attunements confirms the fact that whether or not you feel any physical sensation during your attunement bears little relation to the attunement's actual effectiveness. The most important thing is to be comfortable, relaxed and willing to receive, at your attunement time, and to release yourself from all concerns and expectations. You can be assured that each attunement will be done carefully and completely. During the attunement, some people feel heat or a little "rush" of energy, others have spiritual experiences (of many different kinds), but it is not necessary to sense these things for the attunement to be effective. The main effects of the attunements become manifest in the days, weeks, months and years following, and not while they are taking place.

There are possible side-effects that may result from the attunements. Many (perhaps most) students experience none of these, but it is possible that in the days following your attunement you may experience mild mood swings, anxiety, "jitteriness," a sense of elation or other effects. These possible aftereffects become more likely as you advance to the (progressively stronger) second and third attunements. Because the third (Master) attunement is the strongest of all, and has the potential to unsettle your energy field for a substantial amount of time after it is given, such aftereffects may manifest at varying times for weeks and even months after you have completed your attunement series. They are completely normal, however, are not always present, and are seldom any cause for concern. Be sure to contact your Chios® Master Teacher if these side-effects (or any others) concern you, however, in the days following your attunement. The primary effects of the attunements—an increased ability to channel energy, color and light, a new sensitivity to the energy (with your hands), the development of the ability to see the energy, color and light (e.g. in the aura) and an acceleration of your ability to receive intuitive information—begins in the days and weeks after your attunement and continues for the rest of your life. To practice the exercises and techniques of Chios® healing will assist you in bringing out these abilities; it is receiving these attunements *plus* practicing the Chios® techniques that will bring out the full healing abilities from within you. Spontaneous spiritual experiences, in the days, weeks and months following, have also commonly been reported by many who have received these attunements. These are usually of a very positive, desirable nature, and many choose to keep them private.

You might want to know a little about how the Chios® attunements work. Your Chios® Master Teacher performs the attunement procedures on you using the *Key*—the fourth symbol in Chios® healing—in combination with specific visualizations that create beneficial energy flows in your energy field. Bringing the spiritual energy up your spine—and hence through all your chakras—is a foundational part of all the Chios® attunements, and there are other important procedures that are included. You will learn the method of performing these attunements, and be able to give attunements to others, if you choose to pursue certification as a Chios® Master Teacher. These attunements do not work solely on the physical, earth level, however. We are not just physical beings, but also exist at the higher, spiritual levels. The attunements also have a spiritual dimension, of which student (and even teacher) may not be fully aware. We are all, in our true essence, really beings of light—the light that creates and illuminates all—and these attunements enhance and deepen our relationship to the light. The first attunement opens you to the touch of the light—it brings a contact with the essence. The second attunement creates in you the ability to shape the light—to work with the light, as a manifestation of the essence. The third attunement further facilitates your ability to act as a direct channel to and from the essence—to very effectively receive and direct energy, color and light, as manifestations of the essence, and to attune others. Attunements give you the opportunity to develop and make use of this higher relationship to the light, in addition to the healing abilities they convey. Remember to fully and properly prepare for each attunement, so you may enjoy all these benefits!

Appendix #2-- Outline of Treatment Steps for Chios® Levels I, II and III

These outlines of recommended treatment steps for Chios® Levels I, II and III are included on the following pages as an aid to learning the Chios® techniques and giving complete healing treatments. You may wish to photocopy these pages for your personal use, as a quick reference during your learning and practice of each of the Chios® levels.

These outlines are *general guidelines only*, however, and should be rigidly adhered to only while learning. After acquiring competence in the basic techniques—as you proceed to Chios® Level II and especially to Chios® Level III—you should begin to *break free and include or omit techniques, re-order techniques or occasionally even modify techniques per the particular needs of your patient* and according to the intuitive information you receive. Each patient and each healing situation and healing treatment is unique.

Outline of Treatment Steps - Chios® Level I

1. Calling in the Energy
2. The Passing of Hands
3. The Normal Sequence of Treatment Hand Positions
   a. 7th chakra
   b. 6th chakra
   c. 5th chakra
   d. 4th chakra (front)
   e. 3rd chakra (front)
   f. 2nd chakra (front)
   g. Arms and Legs (optional)
   g. Supplementary or Diseased Areas (optional)
   h. 2nd chakra (rear)
   i. 3rd chakra (rear)
   j. 4th chakra (rear)
4. Ending Treatment

Outline of Treatment Steps - Chios® Level II

1. Calling in the Energy Using Symbols
2. Intuitive Reading: Sensing Simple Energetic Defects of the Aura and Chakras
3. Viewing the Aura
4. The Passing of Hands
5. Integrated Interpretation of Treatment Needs—Simple Energetic Defects
6. Sealing of Leaks and Tears in Aura
7. Aura Clearing
8. The Normal Sequence of Treatment Hand Positions
   a. Shoulder Position (optional)
   b. 7th chakra (using Star)
   c. Correction of Energy Flow (if needed)
   d. 6th chakra
   e. 5th chakra
   f. 4th chakra (front)
   g. 3rd chakra (front)
   h. 2nd chakra (front)
   i. Arms and Legs (optional)
   j. Supplementary or Diseased Areas (optional)
   k. Grounding (if needed)
   l. Aura Charging (if needed)
   m. 2nd chakra (rear)
   n. 3rd chakra (rear)
   o. 4th chakra (rear)
   p. Spine Cleaning (if needed)
9. Ending Treatment (using Circle)

Unblocking Chakras, as needed

Using Light (optional)

Intuitive Reading: Sensing the Chakra Colors (Back of Hand) (optional)

Outline of Treatment Steps - Chios® Level III

1. Calling in the Energy Using Symbols
2. Intuitive Reading: Sensing Simple Energetic Defects of the Aura and Chakras
3. Intuitive Reading: Viewing the Higher Layers of Aura
4. Viewing the Aura (Physical Eyes)
5. The Passing of Hands
6. Integrated Interpretation of Treatment Needs—Simple Energetic Defects
7. Sealing of Leaks and Tears in the Aura (Using Light)
8. Aura Clearing
9. The Normal Sequence of Treatment Hand Positions
    a. Shoulder Position (optional)
    b. 7th chakra (using Star)
    c. Correction of Energy Flow (if needed)
    d. 6th chakra
    e. 5th chakra
    f. 4th chakra (front)
    g. 3rd chakra (front)
    h. 2nd chakra (front)
    i. Arms and Legs (optional)
    j. Supplementary or Diseased Areas
    k. Grounding (if needed)
    l. Aura Charging (if needed)
    m. 2nd chakra (rear)
    n. 3rd chakra (rear)
    o. 4th chakra (rear)
    p. Spine Cleaning (Using Light, if needed)

    Unblocking Chakras, as needed

    Using Light

    Intuitive Reading: Sensing the Chakra Colors (Back of Hand)

    Empathic Sensing of Chakras with Structural Energetic Defects

10. Intuitive Reading: Sensing the Condition of the Chakra System
11. Integrated Interpretation of Treatment Needs—Chakra System & Higher Aura Layers
12. Chakra Charging (as needed)
13. Chakra System Rebalancing (as needed)
14. Radiatory Healing (as needed)
15. Seventh Layer Focal Healing (if needed)
16. Treatment Procedures for Serious Physical Illnesses (if needed)
17. Ending Treatment (using Circle)

Appendix #3—The Development of Chios®

I have been asked literally hundreds of times for information on how Chios® Energy Healing was created. I have hesitated telling the full story, because it contains esoteric elements (e.g. spirit guides, channeling, past lives) that have not yet been validated by science and are not accepted by everyone. And yet, I must say that over twenty years of intensive personal experience with these phenomena have convinced me that they are real, and I am sure that in the future they will be studied and fully validated areas of human knowledge. Because so many have asked, and because I see no harm in the truth and would prefer to be completely forthright about the origins of this work, here is the story of Chios®—just as it happened:

In the ancient world—during the first few centuries after Christ—there had already become established a civilization known as Bactria, located in a fertile region of central Asia now encompassed by far-Northern Afghanistan, Tajikistan and Uzbekistan. As with many ancient societies, our history knows little of Bactria beyond the scant information discerned from the physical artifacts that archeologists have unearthed. It was a simple agriculturally-based society, but one that was a crossroads—in the ancient world—for not only trade (and sometimes invading tribes), but also for spiritual and cultural ideas.

Into this world was born a young man. As the youngest of three sons he did not receive quite the same social status and desirable work as his older brothers or his contemporaries, often only allowed to repair cart wheels and perform other simple tasks. Instead of focusing on career, he made use of his time in contemplation, and investigation of the spiritual philosophies of the day. He devoted himself to a quest less common (then as now): to understanding the purpose and meaning of life. His culture reflected much on the powers of nature, but the young man—like some others in this ancient world—saw these phenomena as manifestations of a deeper process. He became fascinated with a word in the now-dead language of Bactria: Chios. This word, also the name of a Greek island close to the shore of Asia Minor, had a rich and deep meaning. Chios was the life-welling in all things, the struggle and growth upwards of all life. Chios was the growth of a plant, upwards towards the light of the sun. It was the struggle and growth of the spiritual process, in human beings, towards enlightenment. The young man realized that the universe was entirely alive, that it was one great being with all things evolving and reaching towards this purpose, and he rejoiced in this knowledge.

One day a traveler from afar came to the village in which the young man lived. The traveler was an unusual man, with a twinkle in his eye connoting a deep wisdom and intelligence beyond that found in the village and ultimately perhaps even this world. The traveler befriended the young man, discussing spiritual concepts, but then began speaking about the universal energy that circulated in the atmosphere and around plants, animals and human beings. He explained the colors of the energy centers—the seven chakras from red to violet—and the colors and energies in the aura. He discussed with the young man various ways that the energy centers and aura could be healed, using energy, color and light. To add an energy center's color to it to charge, strengthen and purify it...to add a higher or lower color to an energy center, to balance its activity level with the others...to meditate upon and become an energy center, to heal its energy flow...to heal the effects of traumas from past lives by treating the 7th (golden eggshell) layer of the aura...the young man was astounded at the power and purity of what the traveler taught. And then, after this brief yet very in-depth and profound teaching, the traveler departed and the young man was alone again. He reveled in his new knowledge—and used it for the remainder of his life in this ancient civilization— but then passed from this life in ancient Bactria. The healing knowledge would lie dormant for nearly two millennia, while the spirit of the young man travelled through other lives, in other places, learning other lessons...

My present life began with my birth into 20th century America, and into a life that provided difficult circumstances and traumatic experiences from early childhood. I would understand later that my struggles—like those of so many healers and others drawn deeply into the spiritual process—provided the destined lessons and catalyst for spiritual growth. I developed an interest in spirituality from an early age, and by age 12 had read very widely on the subject and acknowledged an inner desire to understand the real nature and meaning of life. I also followed an inner drive to communicate with whomever and whatever was out there, beyond my small corner of the world: by age 13 I had obtained an advanced amateur radio license and talked regularly with people all over the world, using my 50 foot high antenna overlooking the Pacific Ocean. Within two more years—long before the movie *Contact*—I had built a radio telescope in my backyard, to listen to and record signals from much farther away. I wanted to hear from *way out there*, and I had some questions about life, the universe and everything...

The remainder of my adolescence, and my early twenties, were full of the successes, failures and sometimes difficult adjustments typical of those years. By my mid-twenties, however, an unseen power acting through people I met had drawn me into unanticipated and often unusual spiritual experiences and teachings. I developed an interest in meditation, spiritual yoga, lucid dreaming and out-of-body experiences that has continued ever since. By my early 30's I had also developed a strong interest in hypnosis and hypnotherapy, including the use of hypnotic regression to explore past lives. I became particularly interested in the abilities of the very best hypnotic subjects: those capable of somnambulistic trance and exhibiting paranormal abilities therein, including channeling spirits and spirit guides. Shortly thereafter one such gifted channel provided the contact that would lead to the creation of Chios®.

I was contacted by a spirit guide who claimed to be a spokesperson for a network of guides that had waited for my contact, claimed to have important information for me and wished to work with me in learning energy healing. These guides knew my thoughts, and facts about me no living person knew (including the channel). This, plus careful evaluation of the purity of the information, lent great credibility to their communications. I accepted their offer, and began to conduct taped channeling sessions where I would discuss many aspects of energy healing and meditation, with the guides, and afterwards carefully transcribe the results. They offered voluminous and highly detailed information on the practice of energy healing techniques, and encouraged me to experiment with and refine the techniques we discussed. I placed ads offering healing treatments in several California new age publications, to obtain patients upon whom to practice. The guides told me I had been a healer before, in a past life, and that fit well with my experience: I was surprised at how easily the healing knowledge came back to me.

So began the conversation and path of study which would lead to the creation of Chios®. I kept careful records of the information and techniques the guides provided, practiced energy healing on several hundred patients and began assembling the results into a unified, cohesive energy healing art. I was never a passive recipient, during this long educational process, but was at every step encouraged to question, test, refine and re-refine the knowledge and techniques. I do not have words to truly convey how every day of this work became a fascinating, joyful and extraordinary adventure. I became particularly confident of the method I employed: conscientious use of an external very gifted, clear channel to obtain genuine, accurate information from an authentic spiritual source beyond myself (as opposed to merely my own, possibly flawed or distorted sense of inner guidance, knowledge borne only from my personal experience and interpretation, or even "knowledge" merely the product of my imagination), and then rigorous evaluation and testing of the information and techniques provided. There was often the temptation to introduce complexities or incorporate belief systems (old or new) into the practice, but over the long-term I realized that simple, close to the essence and fundamental techniques were both the heart of, and the most powerful form of, this kind of healing. That is what makes it so consciousness-expanding to practice and so powerful in application. The Chios® Level III (Master) techniques, including Chakra Charging, Chakra System Rebalancing, Radiatory Healing and Seventh-Layer Healing are examples of the breakthrough techniques developed during this time. Treatment techniques for patients with serious illnesses was an important priority, as the work expanded, as was the creation of an integral system of meditation and simple personal growth exercises, for the healer. After sculpting away excess to reveal essence, the mature healing art which finally emerged I named Chios®, from the Bactrian word of such rich meaning.

After developing Chios®, I was encouraged to make it available the world. The guides explained that this contact and information was intentionally brought to me so that I could give shape to this knowledge and provide it to all. They indicated that the knowledge contained in Chios® is important, for the genuine advancement of energy healing and the future of evolving humanity. Shortly thereafter, I completed a series of instructional manuals on the techniques. The Chios® manuals (like this book) were not directly channeled material but were my own writing—the product of my own extensive healing practice, writing, editing and refinement of the knowledge and techniques taught to me by the guides. The popular Chios® healing website—based upon the series of instructional manuals—was born shortly thereafter, for the purpose of making much of the Chios® information unrestricted and freely available to all, throughout the world, so it may be easily accessed and used by everyone. This book is the final evolution of the Chios® knowledge: compiled and refined with the benefit of many thousands of hours of healing work and twenty years of experience, it is rigorously true to the teachings of the guides, yet put into a very comprehensive, fully explained and easy-to-learn form.

To assist with the spread of Chios® throughout the world, and the training of Chios® healers, the Chios® attunements (which open up the healing student's energy, color and light channeling abilities) were provided verbatim by the guides; on a predetermined date and time (at the exact time of a new moon precisely coincident with an autumnal equinox), the guides came into the channeler's body and gave me the Master attunement that made me the first Master Teacher of Chios®. The guides also provided the precise instructions on how to give the Chios® healing attunements to others. The same Master Attunement and those same attunement instructions are now given to all new Chios® Master Teachers.

The Chios® contact had other fascinating aspects. The guides shared information on the future—of the great changes that will come about in every aspect of human society, toward the "New Time" when humanity will walk a different way upon the earth. Improvements in technology will play a part, but the greatest change will be the dawning of higher consciousness and higher abilities in human beings, and the use of these for many things we do not envision in our present day. Much interesting anecdotal information was also shared—the story of the creation of Reiki by a woman in Tibet several thousand years ago, for example. She was impressed with the Reiki symbols in her dreams, and then guided in their use by her own spirit guides. Reiki was "rediscovered" in our own era by Dr. Mikao Usui, born in mid-19th century Japan...

After the completion of Chios®, my interests in this particular vein of spiritual inquiry continued to such explorations as contact with parallel realities, with spirits in various stages of healing and rebirth in the afterlife, with beings from other worlds and with the future earth. This has been an extraordinary and mind-opening path of knowledge, and yet I still consider the development of Chios® to be the greatest spiritual adventure of my life. To this day—even after twenty years—I practice the Chios® healing and meditation techniques with undiminished wonder and awe at their purity and power. The development of Chios® enabled me to go far beyond what I previously considered to be myself, and into a greater spiritual reality—an entry into universality. It gave me a perspective I never dreamed of, yet has become an integral part of me. What I have done, in response, is to remain true to the knowledge. I have kept the techniques of Chios® perfectly accurate and true-to-the-essence, preserved their purity and made them freely available to everyone throughout the world who wishes to seek and find them—without polluting this knowledge with marketing tactics for personal gain or to seek personal popularity.

I hope Chios® will become part of the great change imminent on our earth. The ills in our present day world are many, and growing. Humanity, and most human institutions, have not yet chosen the path of truth and healing. Much of what is in the world today must pass away for the health and survival of the planet and humankind. And yet, a dawning light bodes clearly on the horizon; the seeds of the goodness, wisdom and balance which will prevail and which will heal and save humanity and the earth are even now being sown. Bringing Chios® to the light of this world is my contribution to that effort. Chios® is pure, authentic unadulterated energy healing, true to spirit. It is here for you, without dross, when you are ready for it. I hope that by learning and practicing Chios® you will receive the same wonderful benefits that I have enjoyed.

Stephen H. Barrett
Creator of Chios®

Index

Made in the USA
San Bernardino, CA
08 March 2014